RAT PALMS

RAT PALMS

DAVID HOMEL

HarperPerennial
HarperCollins*Publishers*Ltd

The author wishes to thank the Canada Council for its generous support during the writing of this book.

RAT PALMS. Copyright © 1992 by David Homel. All rights reserved. No part of this book may be used or reproduced in any manner whatsoever without prior written permission except in the case of brief quotations embodied in reviews. For information address HarperCollins Publishers Ltd, Suite 2900, 55 Avenue Road, Toronto, Canada M5R 3L2.

A hardcover edition of this book was published by HarperCollins Publishers Ltd: 1992

First HarperPerennial Edition: 1993

Canadian Cataloguing in Publication Data

Homel, David
   Rat palms

ISBN 0-00-647405-5

I. Title.

PS8565.054R3 1992   C813'.54   C92-093025-5
PR9199.3.H65R3 1992

93 94 95 96 97 98 99 ❖ RRD 10 9 8 7 6 5 4 3 2 1

IN MEMORIAM
Ray Chamberlain

For Marie-Louise

This is the legend of the rat palm: the palm trees that grace the streets of Los Angeles, all planted by man's beautifying hand, none native, are home to thousands of rats' nests. At times a rat, or two, will fall from the top of a bushy-headed palm into a passing convertible car, altering the consciousness of the driver.

The rat palm is also another name for the scrubby palmetto that grows along the Atlantic coast of Georgia and South Carolina.

I
HURT'S LANDING

1

My mother is drunk on words again. She leads me onto the widow's walk of our house on Hurt's Landing, on the Isle of Hope. Together, we stand and gaze out at the wide curve the Lazaretto River makes as it turns past the Landing and breaks off into the Cabbage Marshes.

"All this is yours," my mother tells me.

She tells me that every time we stand out here and watch the swamp. Then she sets her drinking glass down on the peeling wooden railing of the walk, and pauses to let her words hang in the humid air. She carries that glass wherever she goes but never — or almost never — drinks from it. The bourbon inside can evaporate before she gets around to taking a taste. She carries that glass around as if she was in a dark cave and it was some kind of torch.

"All this is yours," she repeats. "Your inheritance, son, what the Marster family has put here over the generations, ever since they've been here. And what does not belong to you by family bond is no less yours, by fact of history."

By fact of tale telling and gossip, too, I want to add. But I say nothing, and instead, look out to see what it is exactly that I do own. Our dock with its salt-stained footings, and the oysters clinging to it, exposed at low tide. The fool mullet leaping silver out of the green-black Lazaretto River. A couple of Negroes in a bass boat going fast between the floating crab traps in front of the No Wake sign, wearing their baseball caps with the bills pointed back.

"You do have the teaching strain, Mother," I tease her.

She laughs, then coughs her dry, restrained smoker's cough.

"Someone is bound to educate you, now that you've been expelled from that fine school we sent you to. I don't suppose they'll reimburse us for the tuition now, either. The Benedictine fathers don't run that Academy of theirs like an insurance company. They won't refund the unused portion."

That is what's behind these sessions in Marster lore and history on the widow's walk: I proved unable to endure the Academy. With only a month left before graduation, a single month after four whole years of Benedictine admonishments, one Sunday morning I took it into my head to attend church services from underneath the chapel that stands on pilings, as everything does out here. A single month before my clearance to go to Penn to embark on the study of ethics, morals and logic, which was as close as I could get to studying sin and still remain secular.

I went to ground, I admit. It was the only way I could stand Father Dooley's rantings and the threats that were sure to follow. And I had planned it, too. I took a quick look around the grounds in front of the Pax chapel, then went crablike under the building. There was the world I wanted. I toyed with the skeleton of a rabbit that some cat must have dragged under there to devour, as I listened to Father Damian Dooley raging about the sorry state of our immortal souls, that heavy, loathsome, invisible package we all carry around inside us like a piece of shrapnel. There, I managed to achieve a little of the cool contemplation amateur philosophers are supposed to enjoy. Every time Father Dooley stamped his foot, a fine dust of termite-eaten oak rained down upon me like manna. "You are nothing! You are fit to be cast down! Look into your souls, consider your fate.

Do you honestly think your souls are worthy of the blessing of the Christ Jesus? You believe your souls are things of splendor, whereas they defy contemplation!"

His voice thudded through the oaken floorboards as I crouched in the feculent air. This is how I preferred to consider the fate of my soul: in my own little self-created, comfortable, moist-smelling hell. Was I worthy of blessing? Would I be cast down? And were I to be cast down, as everything in my soul and around me seemed to indicate, would I have the strength to do it myself, first, and get it over with?

Father Dooley was winding toward the inevitable end, wherein forgiveness is dangled before us like a Punch-and-Judy puppet. My plan was to scurry out of my hiding place just before his sermon closed and linger by the front door of the chapel, looking as though I had been there all the while, with maybe a cobweb more than the other worshipers, but their souls would have been too battered to take notice. I did execute my plan, but found myself face to face with that glowering old German disciplinarian Alphonsus Byhauer, who had just come up the plank walk to the Pax chapel.

"You rodent!" he addressed me. "You crawling thing! You carrion eater!"

He was staring at my hand. I looked down to see what he was looking at. I still had that pair of rabbit rib bones, and I looked further down and saw the stains on the knees of my gray woolen uniform pants and the mud cakes on the bottom of my shined shoes. Then I went and laughed.

Byhauer grabbed me. He smelled like old robes and farts. He ground his blue-black stubble into my cheek.

"You *make* me have to do this!" he growled, and kept on grinding away. It was like having a rough-grained metal file dragged over your face.

"You puke, you little puke. You buzzard! You *make* me curse!"

And I swear, there were tears in the man's eyes.

Retribution was swift. As I stood in his office the next day, I could tell that Father Dooley wanted to display clemency, despite the threats his sermon contained the morning before. But before clemency could be displayed, contrition had to be exhibited. We stood before his desk, Evangeline and I, in his stuffy, priest-smelling study. I chose not to exhibit anything.

"I know there is something you are not telling, son," he said in his weighty, sad, ageless Father's voice, as if he had personally witnessed the Crucifixion. "And I can't make you say it, or feel it. You know you'll be a loss to the baseball team, especially with the state finals coming up. We had such hopes . . .

"You know you are our most prodigious student. Even if your mastery of the vernacular will sooner or later betray you, I predict. The sin is called pride, I believe, a certain vainglory in words. Though I have to admit it is an interesting variation on that too-common sin . . . In any case, I am going to have to send you home to think about this for a time."

He paused for a moment in hopes I would say what I did not want to say. I found that touching, in a way.

What could I say? That I would not wash and polish Mr. Byhauer's sedan, or do any of the other things he suggested I do? Or that I could not shrug off his sermons the way everyone else in the chapel did? My punishment for an incorruptible, literal soul was to end up on the widow's walk with my mother, watching the tides.

"While you are at home," Dooley said, wearing his thoughtful face, "I do not intend you to be idle; that would be no punishment at all. If you still wish to regain entrance to the Academy, as I am sure you do, you will submit to me a written report on your period of reflection. When you hand in this report to me, it will signify that you wish to rejoin us."

Dooley was an odd priest — or was his type the rule? One day telling us our souls were as loathsome spiders, then the next day in his kindest, most wounded voice, enjoining me to look into my soul and reflect. Just how do you reflect upon loathsome things?

This, I understood, was to be my assignment. Shit! If I had had the choice, I would have stayed after school and beat the erasers.

On the drive back from the Benedictines, my mother wept decorously.

"I wish your father were here. He'd know what to do with you."

That was the standard thing for her to say, and we both knew it. My father would not have known what to do with me, either.

Now, my mother, whom I have learned to call Evangeline in my private thoughts — but how I took to that habit is another story — is gazing down from the widow's walk. The tide is beginning to wash in and replenish the Lazaretto. I know where her eyes are: she is looking at the rectangular foundation where the general store once stood, several Marster generations ago, when the Isle of Hope was just starting to fill up with people fleeing the yellow fever in town. The Marsters were store owners back then, gentlemen retailers, if there is such a thing. It is astonishing to possess so much and remember things I have never lived through, I think as I watch the river swelling. Everywhere the weight and comfort of the past hangs over me like the oaks with their Jeremiah beards of moss.

"You are a half-Marster, of course," my mother is saying. She has gone back to her poetic tone and stopped fretting about whether the Benedictine fathers are going to reimburse us for the unused portion. "But you still have full rights in the possession of these things. People may talk against the Jews in this town, they may mock that funny little synagogue of theirs that looks like nothing if it don't look like a Catholic church, but they made the mother's side the basis of their laws. I have to credit them for that much."

Then she delivers the wedge.

"Your father is from the North. I don't believe he understands these things. The North," she sums up, "was invented yesterday."

I don't answer. I don't approve of all this signifying, as the Negroes in Sandfly Crossing say. After all, I am half-Northerner, too.

My mother can go on like this for hours during the idle Isle of Hope afternoons. The tide has time to rise and fall as she tells how the Marsters anticipated the population's fear of the fever and came racing out to the island to set up their stores on lots they bought for a song. She polishes and caresses every word before she lets it go, and when she does, it is with great regret, as if the beauty and sweet nostalgic sheen could protect her from the pain in her stories, the way an oyster will build a pearl around a hurt.

The Marster education has become more rigorous since my father went North to play in the Big Leagues, after years of toiling in the minors, hurling for the Savannah Indians of the Sally League, as the sports pages call it. Zeke Justice, my father, is a major leaguer now. I remember the afternoon he got the news that he would be following the team North, for I secretly suspect it has something to do with why I am no longer a member of the Benedictine Military Academy.

We were parading in Colonial Park, soldiers for the Lord in gray wool and glinting brass, as the professor of military science and tactics and the disciplinarian looked on. I hated the exercises we held in town where all, black and white alike, could and would gape at us. We paraded down Oglethorpe Street in the warm April air, under the row of royal palms that had been planted there to commemorate our victory in the European and Pacific theaters.

A shame that this route took us past Bo-Peep's establishment, and the John Wesley Hotel where Mr. Peep had his rooms. As we paraded past the establishment for sporting men, the heavy, windowless door opened slowly and my father stepped out, blinking like a newt in the bright sun, and as stewed as a newt, too. I saw him there, a tall, rangy man getting his bearings in the middle of the day, and for the first time I also saw he had something fragile in him. He was good-looking, of course, the way everybody said he was, despite his stunned eyes. Handsome and fragile, together in the same man.

He stood frozen to the spot as we hup-hupped past, watching us incredulously as if we were some kind of vision that had just escaped from a bottle of hooch. Then he spotted me, and that snapped him out of it.

"Son! Private first class! Toadfish!" he hollered as I tried to soldier past him. He grabbed me out of line and someone stepped on my heels from behind and swore. "I got the call! I'm going up North! The Bigs! Finally, somebody started paying attention!"

I dropped out of formation and tried to act invisible. Impossible with the Benedictines. If they can read into your thoughts and be there when you sneak out from a delinquent position underneath a chapel, they can certainly see you when you step out of parade. Byhauer was standing with his hands on his hips, hatred for my father on his square, cobalt-blue face.

I tried to pull away from my father.

"I know, I know, I understand," he was saying, but he did not understand. He had a headlock on me and he was hugging and kissing me and doing his Northern imitation of a rebel holler.

"I'm on parade," I pleaded with him. "I've got to go." Then I slipped free and double-timed it to catch up with the formation.

Byhauer fell in behind us. I heard his boots caving in the sun-softened asphalt.

"I pity you, boy," he hissed at me from behind.

A picture postcard came from my father, from a city up North. Cleveland, or Boston, I believe. I took it out to the dock to read. The picture side showed a baseball park. "Eating steaks for breakfast, leaving two-dollar tips. The big time. All is well. Don't forget to practice your hand."

He hadn't, that was for sure. His writing was all loops and fancy flourishes, the way some nun lady had taught him to do a long time ago.

There was a tug on my line and I reeled it in. Another goddamned toadfish, puffing itself up to call attention to its loathsomeness, a bottom feeder that only the Negroes would eat, or so my mother told me the first and only time I proudly brought one home. It was the ugliest thing in the river, with a wide mouth like a frog's, and subject to all kinds of superstitions. It would bite you, it would sting you, it would give you warts. "Nigger gristle," Evangeline called it when my father was not around to forbid the natural Isle of Hope use of that word. I seemed to have a talent for pulling those things in. Which is how I got that mortifying nickname my father used in the first place. *Toadfish.*

I pulled the hook out rough and threw the injured thing back into the Lazaretto.

My mother floated down to the dock as the ripples from the toadfish splash were wearing away. She had a way of moving soundlessly, as if she were a ghost, even over the booming planks of the dock. She was on top of me before I could hide the postcard.

"What might that be?"

"Picture postcard," I told her.

"From your father?"

"Yes, ma'am."

"That's funny. Funny he sent it."

Her voice had a habit of rising at the end, as if everything was a perpetual question.

"What's funny about a postcard?"

"Nothing. But I understand he'll be back here soon, maybe as soon as tomorrow."

I got a sick feeling. There was a call on my line but I didn't bother answering it.

"How can that be?"

Evangeline made a wispy little move with her hand.

"You know I don't understand how the game works."

You do so. You married him because he was a ball player, I felt like telling her, but I kept that to myself. Kept my eyes down. My father calls it the Marster scuff, when you look at the ground in that way that's supposed to display respect, and scuff your feet. My father hates it, and he's right. It doesn't display respect, only resistance.

"By the way," Evangeline said before she moved off the dock, a place where she did not feel overly comfortable, even though it belonged to the things that belonged to her, "be watching for your grandfather. He'll be coming by to pick you up. He's decided he wants to pass some time with you."

"Did I have any say in that?"

"The same as I did, son," she answered, then turned on her heel and walked off the dock.

My father's stint in the Bigs had hardly lasted two weeks. Disappointed times had to be coming to Hurt's Landing.

Not too much later I heard a car horn on the Lazaretto Road. Slowly, I ascended the slope toward the road and saw the car waiting there, with Grandfather Jefferson Marster inside. Ungreeted, as usual, with my mother safely hidden in the house. Apparently, his belonging to the great chain of Marsters did not mean that he and his own daughter actually had to speak to one another. Some old wound, or series thereof, had made normal human word exchange impossible between the two of them. The last time I saw them together had been years ago, he with a piece of paper in his hand that I later understood was the title to the house we lived in, she exhibiting her own version of the Marster scuff, but a thousand times more opaque than mine, perfected through practice, no doubt. I hadn't pushed to know the nature of their dispute; the piece of yellowing paper was merely a prop, a pretext. I hadn't pushed because I didn't need to. Sooner or later, the story would come to me, naturally, as if by its own volition.

As a character in my mother's Marster stories, Grandfather Jefferson appeared as a grand old man, worthy of reverence, as if one of those gull-stained bronze statues in a downtown square had suddenly sprung to life and begun walking in our midst, spouting widsom.

A museum piece of a kind. But the real Jefferson Marster looked more like a down-on-his-luck version of the Kentucky colonel they have selling fried chicken around here. He had a brick-red, overly florid face and white hair stained yellow with cigar smoke, and a suit the same pale nicotine color.

I climbed into the car and closed the heavy door behind me. Then took to examining the creme-colored upholstery of the automobile. It was a two-toned Buick Special, red and creme, with the three round air holes along each fender.

"How's your mama keeping?" he asked, as he did every time.

"Fine, sir."

"Where do you feel like going today?"

I did the Marster scuff, figuring he had his mind made up anyway.

He put the car in gear. "I believe I'll take you to the Telfair Museum. I don't suppose your folks have ever taken you there."

"No, sir."

"They're not museum-going people," he added.

"No, sir."

We drove past the better houses on the Isle of Hope, then got onto Laroche Avenue, going toward town. Away from the water, the temperature rose, and there was not much traffic at midday. Everyone was busy doing something, but that something did not include driving up and down the road to the Isle of Hope, engaged in a period of forced reflection imposed by Benedictine masters. To tell the truth, I hadn't had the opportunity to embark on much reflection yet. All my time had been eaten up by Marster stories.

Some men on this island let you know they're in the room by talking loud. Jefferson Marster did it with his cigar, which was slowly staining a yellow streak through the middle of his hair, like a skunk's. He looked so content and lordly with that thing stuck in the middle of his face that you just had to figure he ran the show and knew what he was talking about. His cigar put him into such a contented state that, between his contentment and my doing the Marster scuff, we stayed silent all the way through town to the Telfair Museum of Fine Arts, where he had to extinguish it to get in through the doors.

The Telfair was a temple dedicated to beauty that had been carved out of some old Methodist's mansion. Curious, because any Methodist I'd ever encountered was not overly enthusiastic about beauty, except in song, perhaps, and even then, music was always secondary to praise. Walking up to the museum, I smelled Lazaretto water and toadfish on my hands, and wished I was somewhere else. I could not imagine Grandfather Marster had come here to enjoy himself, either. It was a form of civic and family duty. He nodded at the ossified guard who tended the door, and at the ladies who cackled at the approach of visitors, a rare thing, apparently. He placed a sizable donation in the wicker basket, then refused the offer of color pamphlets on the place.

"I know what they say. I made it possible for them to be printed," he told the terrorized member of the women's corps.

"If we could speak to you, Mr. Marster," one of them entreated him. "Considering your habitual generosity . . ."

"Later," he said. "I'm with this boy here."

Light flowed in through the great semicircle of glass above the door. We crossed the entry hall, our solemn, ceremonious footsteps echoing after us. In the first gallery, the walls were lined with dark brown paintings, all jumbled together, and even I could tell just how ugly they were. Welcome to another chapter of the Marster history book! Secretly, I dared the old Marster to make me feel any sense of belonging to these portraits of pockmarked gentlemen in powdery wigs who all vaguely resembled George Washington, all posing before their grandfather clocks. Some of them, I supposed, I was even related to. But I'd rather contemplate the face of a blue crab than any of these corpses.

The second gallery was something of an improvement. Two naked alabaster ladies with dolphins springing at their feet stood at its entrance. *Pudentia*, read the legend on one of them. The statues had no eyeballs in their eyes, like Little Orphan Annie in the comics, and their heads were wrapped in caps of snakes.

Jefferson Marster stepped up behind me.

"That is *ideal* beauty," he alerted me. "You think you are looking at a naked lady, young man, but what you're really looking at is an ideal."

I lowered my eyes to her womanly parts, which were as pale and chalky looking as the rest of her. She had no hair between her legs, which may have been the reason she was ideal. A pair of dark fingermarks ran down each of her breasts, as if she had been recently deposited in this location by a sloppy museum worker. Traces of the real.

"What does *Pudentia* mean, anyway?"

"It's Latin," Grandfather Marster schooled me. "Comes from the word for 'shame.'"

Shame and ideal beauty turned around in my head as we moved onto the side exhibits, where eighteenth- and nineteenth-century parlors were reconstructed. I truly hated old furniture and the stifling atmosphere it created. I had enough of it in the rooms of my own house; I didn't need a museum to instruct me as to its malevolent effects.

And because I hated being here, entrusted to Jefferson Marster as if I were a load of compromising merchandise, and made to confront the shame of admiring naked ladies, I decided to strike back. Not openly, of course, but in the sly, slow, surreptitious Lazaretto toadfish way. As we stood contemplating the furniture designed to punish the sitter's body, I remarked to Jefferson Marster, "When you talk about my mother, you always call her by her Christian name. Nobody else does that around here. How come you do?"

"Evangeline, you mean? That's because it's her name, son. It's a woman's name. And your mother is, after all, a woman. A pert and vivacious woman at that."

"Vivacious?" I inquired.

"Some would say beautiful, son, but that is not for a father to say of his own flesh. Especially in the case of a daughter."

I thought about that awhile. As I did, he began steering me out of the old furniture gallery.

"You two don't see much of each other."

"We don't have to," he assured me. "We're family. It never goes away."

He stopped in the wide entrance hall to admire the ceiling, which he must have done a hundred times previous. "You are full of questions, which isn't a bad thing in itself. But would you have any more appropriate to this place?"

"Sure," I said, cheerfully. "Tell me how the Lazaretto River got its name."

"That, at least, I can tell you. During the War between the States, there was a lazar house built at the mouth of the river, where it meets the ship channel, to house our men. The name comes from it."

"What's a lazar house?"

"A place to isolate those afflicted by the disease of Lazarus."

I scrambled through my half-remembered Bible stories. If I recalled correctly, this Lazarus had risen from the grave after four days. They pushed away the boulder and out he popped, triumphant, to walk again, though he was loathsome and covered in bandages. His was the disease of resurrection. That appealed to me.

We paraded past the front desk, with the ladies of the museum fluttering behind us like moths. "Mr. Marster," one of them called, trailing after us. He stopped to grace her with his attention, and she began beseeching him to once again contribute his not inconsiderable generosity to the worthy cause of preserving the past through the Telfair Museum. It was a spectacle I did not want to witness.

"If you don't mind," I told him, "I'll wait outside."

While we'd been inside worshiping ideal beauty, the heat had had time to droop itself over everything, as palpable as resignation. In town, without the breeze off the Lazaretto, the air stood still as gravestones. I went and sat on a bench in front of the statue of Mr. Telfair the Methodist in the little square. The knife-sharpening man was pushing his cart along the sidewalk, his collar up despite the heat, partially covering the pink blotches on his dark skin. *Ding-dong-ding*, his three-toned bell sounded. He watched the sidewalk carefully for cracks and bumps that might trouble his cart, and had there been any customers, he wouldn't have seen them, and I doubted that it mattered. His job was to push his cart, and simply be there, as useless to the city as a second conscience.

Mr. Telfair's statue was surrounded by a picket of iron which, I thought, was unnecessarily pointed, as if the curator of statues was afraid vandals would break in and steal the past under cover of the heat. I don't know how it is that the good Lord conspires to do such damage, but as I sat trying to conjure the blind, baleful, pigeon-stained eye of Mr. Telfair, who should come wheeling by but Pharris Buckley? Like the knife sharpener, Pharris Buckley was paying inordinate attention to the surface on which he walked, but for different reasons. He had never mastered the genteel art of sipping. Once he had been an Indians ball player. I knew his story and the differences of opinion that surrounded it, and I preferred the version that was gentler to him. His bad eyesight kept him from going very far in the game, and without a reason not to, he took up drinking, and was inclined to purposely misplace his glasses while in a compromised state, since he was as vain as he was nearsighted.

He crossed in front of me, registered my presence and laboriously brought me into focus. When he recognized me, he was so happy at having accomplished the feat that he burst into enthusiastic conversation.

"Young Timmy Toadfish, what are you doing so far from the Isle of Hope?"

"Statue watching, sir. How about yourself?"

"Oh, you know me. Keeping an eye on the gutter water so it flows down the sewer hole. Hate to think what would happen if I took my eyes off it. There's not too much to do for a talking man like myself since your daddy left town. Shit, back when we was playing ball together, people used to say he was a bad influence on me, on account of drinking, like it was his fault, as if he'd personally invented the stuff, as if they never heard of moonshine out by Claxton. Well, since your daddy's been gone I believe I've fallen deeper into my sin, on account of there being no one to talk to."

I was debating whether to tell him that my father was coming back when Jefferson Marster came striding down the museum steps and into the Telfair square. He did not look very pleased to see Pharris Buckley. Buckley did not see my grandfather at all.

"Now, who is this sandlot star?" Jefferson Marster asked loudly.

I jumped up from the bench.

"Grandfather, this is Pharris Buckley. He's an old friend of my —"

"I know damn well who he is, and he'd know who I am, too, if he could just remember where he put his glasses. Another one of your daddy's ilk."

"Zeke Justice don't have no ilk," Pharris Buckley replied, squinting into my grandfather's face. "He's one of a kind, just like every human soul. That's what I studied — what about you?"

Jefferson Marster sniffed, as if detecting a bad smell, then attacked Pharris Buckley on his weak flank. Mind you, my grandfather had his choice in the weakness department when it came to poor Pharris.

"You're not losing the battle with the bottle, are you there, Buckley? With that mole eyesight of yours, a gutter's liable to jump up and brain you."

Pharris Buckley laughed, untroubled. "I would check my own backyard if I were you. You make your living selling the stuff. You can't afford to be chasing away your best customers. You may regret it someday."

And with that, Pharris gave me a myopic wink and flipped a mock salute at my grandfather, then crossed the square. To where, I didn't know, but certainly not to the establishment called Pinky Marster's.

"Dealing with a man like that makes me feel soiled," my grandfather said.

"When you wrestle in the dust, you're bound to get your clothes dirty," I said with mock cheerfulness.

He didn't answer. Just as well. He was too busy watching Pharris Buckley make his way across the far side of the square and up toward Broughton Street. But even while he watched him, it was clear he was seeing someone else entirely.

"You want an RC Cola?"

I didn't, but I said yes.

We moved through the heat up to the Rexall and sat down at the counter. They had a battery of fans blowing every which way, scattering the paper napkins, each fan canceling out the other fan's breeze. The counter waitress in her black half-moon apron looked surprised to see my grandfather. Surprised, and a little displeased, because around here, a change in a person's habits is always a suspicious sign. But when she saw me, she understood.

"Good day to you, Mr. Marster. Taking the young man out for a Royal Crown?" she asked. The plastic pin-on name tag she wore read Nell.

"I'll have one, too," he said.

The waitress set the colas on the counter, then eyed my civilian clothes.

"I thought you were busy going to that fine military school," she angled.

"He was expelled from the Benedictine Academy," my grandfather announced.

Then he sucked up the entire RC Cola until the ice jingled at the bottom of the glass. I didn't know we were supposed to reveal our little family shames down at the Rexall lunch counter. The bad seed continues to bloom, he seemed to be telling anyone who would listen. But that particular drama didn't matter to Nell.

"What did you do?" she asked me. "Shoot a spitball at your teacher?"

"He was guilty of moral turpitude," Jefferson Marster told her.

"It's true, I confess. My sentence was a period of reflection."

RAT PALMS

You could see that Nell was trying to keep a straight face. She didn't quite succeed. "You two do have a way with words!" She ran her rag under my grandfather's empty glass. "A poor waitress like me can't figure out a thing."

"That's priest talk. They do it on purpose," I explained to her. "They make it real complicated so the Devil can't find his way around inside. Just like some country folk used to build round barns so old Satan wouldn't have anywhere to hide."

"There's always plenty of room for the Devil to hide," my grandfather said sententiously.

Nell waved her counter rag in the air, showering us with droplets of RC Cola and dishwater. "It ain't Sunday," she told us. "Don't talk to me about the Devil. All I know is, it's a shame you got thrown out of that school of yours."

"A shame?" My grandfather cocked his head quizzically. "If it is, it's but a small shame. I have seen some better examples of shame in this town."

Nell narrowed her eyes and asked herself what kind of man Jefferson Marster was turning into, then spotted a providential customer at the far end of the counter. Shame and the Devil, it was clear to see, did not usually drop in to the Rexall lunch counter for an RC Cola. At least not in the middle of the day. Besides, they weren't as big tippers as old Jefferson.

"A period of reflection?" my grandfather repeated as we walked to the car. "Sounds unnatural. Just how do you intend to spend this time?"

"Catching toadfish and throwing them back, I suppose. Thinking about ideal beauty."

"You mean naked ladies," he corrected me.

"Naked ladies and toadfish. They kind of go together in a strange way, don't you think?"

We circled the squares of Savannah in censorious silence, in the creme-colored comfort of the old Marster's Buick. Avidly, I took in the objects of the living world on the other side of the windshield glass. In that world, a few blocks further on, I spotted Pharris Buckley moving along the sidewalk in total innocence, his hands in his pockets and slightly slumped forward, as if he were in a perpetual state of falling down. Jefferson Marster slowed the car, and I knew he had seen him, too.

Then just as Buckley was about to cross Jones Street, I felt the Buick surge forward as my grandfather hit the gas. He swung the wheel to the right as Buckley took his first step off the curb. He felt our car before it hit him, and had enough time to turn out of the way before the front fender caught him hip high and threw him to the pavement.

Then Jefferson Marster chose to sound his horn.

"Watch where you're going, boy!" he shouted out the window at Pharris.

"Watch out yourself," I told the old Marster.

I turned around. Through the back window I saw Pharris Buckley bound to his feet and set out running after us. He took three or four strides, then pulled up, clutching his hip. He sank to one knee in the middle of Jones Street, cursing the car, and I was certain he knew whom it belonged to.

"Blind and drunk, what a combination," my grandfather muttered, then wheeled onto Drayton Street, his tires squealing in the soft asphalt.

"No sense fleeing the scene of the crime. I'm sure he knows who you are."

Jefferson Marster took his eyes off the road and gave me a long look.

"I don't care," he told me.

"What do you have against that man anyway?"

"Him? Nothing special. No more than I have against any of that ball-playing trash."

"Like my father, for example?"

"Let me put it this way." My grandfather was practically shouting, as if a mile, and not a yard, separated us. His face was so red I thought blood would spurt from every pore.

"Let me put it this way. What would you do if your only living daughter had run off and gotten herself covered by some Northern sandlot baseball star who frequents the Negroes and philosophizes in my own establishment?"

He turned and glowered at me, as if he really expected I could answer such a question, ignoring the trees that flashed by on Victory Drive, inches from his fender. Then he replaced his cigar in his mouth, the smoke of which seemed to allow him to recover himself. Too bad I didn't possess such an instrument.

Victory led to Laroche, and Laroche led onto the Isle of Hope. It was high tide there, and my beloved river, my refuge, was full to its soft banks. My grandfather stopped in front of the house and I put one foot onto the road.

"Thank you for the instruction," I told him. "It's good to know where I stand in the great Marster chain: as the weak link. Now, I don't suppose you'll be coming in for something cool to drink?"

The old Marster drove away with what I thought was undue pressure on the gas pedal, even under the circumstances. The man was a menace.

It turned out that engaging in reflection was no easy task with so much activity around. Ours was a two-story house, plenty large enough for the three of us, with a porch on the ground floor and the widow's walk upstairs, and a yard in back, and a view of the river named after a disease. But the place could hardly accommodate Evangeline and me as we waited for my father to return from his defeat in the Bigs.

My temporary salvation was the dock. I retreated there just as soon as Jefferson Marster set me loose, and I spent the next day there, too. But this dock is not far enough, I thought as I watched the bass boats and bateaux skipping by, taking the big bend toward where the Lazaretto begins to break up into marsh. For lasting salvation, you needed a boat and an outboard to fight off the tides. I did not have either.

The beginning of reflection, I reflected, is having a place to reflect in. I had agreed to write Father Dooley's report because it served my purpose: to reflect, you have to get away. First the dock, then places further still, once I had the means. From those places I was not yet acquainted with, I would study the waves of war between the Justices and the Marsters, and among the Marsters themselves, and reflect upon what had gotten me banished from the Academy in the first place. The attraction of the earth's good, feculent breath, the peace and meditation of life among the sideways crab creatures who used the fact that the chapel was on pilings to go to ground under the house of God.

I began to see into the authentic blasphemy of my actions. I had displayed something akin to an interest in God's underthings, the unclean elements that made our good Isle of Hope manners so important. Not only had I mocked God, I had snuck around to the other side of the stage to investigate the trappings and hoists of faith. That's why I was out. Had I consorted with the Devil, that would have been less grievous; at least I would have been within the terms of the church. But instead, I had burrowed under the place of worship and literally inspected the rotting, mildewed timbers that underpinned the teachings of the Fathers.

Add to that impenitence. For even as I sat on the dock, watching the water turkeys dive for fish, I had that pair of rabbit rib bones in my pocket, and I was giving them a good working over.

After all, is not the dictum of the Benedictines to study the ways of this world? And wasn't I willing to think about anything, as long as it was not Jefferson Marster?

The wind conspired to warn me of my mother's approach by carrying a whiff of her perfume on it. I looked up the dock. She had a Sunday dress on.

"Not even fishing?"

"Reflecting, ma'am."

"Don't mock me," she ordered. "Aren't you going to compliment me on my dress?"

"I was just getting around to it."

"Touché, boy. We're going to meet your father at the train. I want you to come to the station with me. I am going to attempt to keep him from slipping away to one of his sporting houses the minute he sets foot on our soil. It will not be pleasant having a disappointed man around the house."

2

We stood in the middle of the big, booming station, Evangeline and I, under the clock beneath which the passengers file past on their way into the heat outside. She was holding on to my hand very tightly. I let her do it, though the age for such attentions between mother and son was long since past.

She lit up a Viceroy. We must have been quite a sight, her in her motoring scarf, as if she had just driven across the Sahara Desert, and not up from the island to pick up her ball-playing husband. As she hung on to me with unmaternal desperation, I reflected on the shame of my father being shipped down to the minors. It had been a short flirtation with the Bigs. Zeke Justice, perennial twenty-game winner for the Savannah Indians, Sally League star on a team that had sent all kinds of greats to the majors, from Enos Slaughter to Juan Pizarro. Their luck had not rubbed off on him. When my father's friends heard the news of his return they would be disappointed for him, but deep down they would be just as happy, though they would not say so, the way bottle men are happy when one of their water-drinking comrades gets reacquainted with the sauce.

I pictured the scene Evangeline wanted to head off. My father escorted to Johnny Harris's to reclaim his former booth, the mayor happening by and slyly reminding him to stay out of scrapes, forgiving him ahead of time for the mischief that was bound to occur. The word would go around that Zeke Justice was back in town, too bad he got sent down, but he's back with us now.

Sometimes I felt half of Savannah and the islands knew my father better than I did.

My mother dropped her Viceroy and ground out the butt as ladylike as anyone could.

"You looking forward to seeing him?" I asked her.

"What do you mean, *him*? He's your father!"

I went back to the long slow business of waiting. Before long the PA system crackled and announced that the Panama Limited was pulling in. Then something happened that I will never forget. An old Negro man shuffled out to the middle of the station where we stood, Evangeline and I, like a pair of statues. I knew the man — his name was Paul Gant. I'd seen him caulking Jefferson Marster's bateaux out on the island. He was one of those black men whose age I could never guess in a thousand years, because he did not age the way white people did.

Paul Gant positioned himself next to us, took a breath and opened his mouth wide. Then he proceeded to outsing the Savannah Union Station PA system.

New Yoke.
Filly Dilly.
Ball Tee More.
Wash a Ton.
Rich Man.

It wasn't just his pronunciation that stopped me there in the station as it filled up with passengers from the Panama Limited. Anyone can change around the name of a town to make fun; I'd heard all kinds of talk of that sort out on the Landing. It was the way Paul Gant's voice filled the space all the way up to the gray-green girders at the top of Union Station. The air rushed out of the way of the train caller's song, and it didn't matter that the train caller's job had disappeared a long time ago, after some bait eater had invented the PA system, and that Paul Gant was just a crazy old nigger who hadn't heard the news. The air was afraid of what his voice did to it on its way to the top. It got out of the way, and excuse me, Mr. Gant.

I followed his voice up to the station dome. For a minute I was moved and crazy enough to wish I was black so I could sing the way he did, the way they do at the True Vineyard Deliverance Center over in Sandfly Crossing on a Sunday afternoon.

Such thoughts were surely not what the Benedictines had in mind when they sentenced me to a time of reflection. They had only themselves to blame. They had unloosed the world upon me. Take note, Father Dooley, when it comes time to punish your next offender.

My mother pulled on my hand like a bell cord.

"What are you looking at, boy? Your daddy's not going to come down from those rafters! He's not Jesus Christ. He's a flesh-and-blood man, don't I know it, and the Lord forgive him for that."

Paul Gant finished up his calling and shuffled off to some recess in the station where they let the Negroes wait for whatever they are waiting for, a miracle or a pair of shoes to shine. But his voice was still up there in the Union Station dome, and I was, too.

Then my father appeared, a slow walker, a hindrance in the stream of passengers hurrying out of the station and into the sunlight. He was dragging his major-league equipment bag on the floor. Evangeline let loose of my hand.

"Nice of you to come down," he told her. He kissed her on the cheek, and as an afterthought, I could see, on the mouth.

Then he stepped around her and faced me.

"Toadfish," he said, "they hit my curveball."

"That's okay, Dad." It's an odd undertaking, trying to comfort your own father. "You'll be back North in no time. You just need a few quality outings."

He threw his head back and laughed, and his laughter went up to the dome where Paul Gant's song was. He punched me in the biceps, gently for once.

"That's my boy, talking like the sports pages. I can see you've been studying the game!"

There was a smell of bourbon and leather and cigar smoke around him like a comforting cloud. The smell of men, and the little sins permitted them.

"Did you get that picture postcard I sent you?"

"Yes, sir."

"Don't you sir me. It makes me feel old."

He laughed again. My mother had me expecting funeral dirges at the station, but there was nothing of the sort. My father picked his equipment bag off the floor and swung it over his shoulder. We started for the main exit with Evangeline tagging behind.

"You really liked my postcard?"

"The writing was real pretty."

"A man ain't nothing if he doesn't have a fine hand. And a good arm — which doesn't seem to be my case these days. But shit, I didn't do so badly."

"Zeke, don't you be using that locker-room language," my mother warned.

We got into the automobile and he took the keys off my mother. He did not seem like a man who had just been sent down to the minor leagues.

Evangeline succeeded in keeping my father out of the sporting establishments for the whole rest of the afternoon and part of the evening. Then something happened that made it not entirely his fault for going out. At least that's the way I saw it. Then again, my mother is always accusing me of taking his side.

He and I were sitting on the front porch in the twilight.

I was watching the light turn dark green under the live oaks, and the color run out of the river as the sun set behind the house. There was nobody much on the water, and the marshes across the way on Burntpot Island were noisy with birds, feeding and settling down for the night. My father was telling me about the size of the steaks and the tips they left the waitresses, and how much he missed it down here. Nothing about the games he pitched in, nothing about how his curveball flattened out and got massacred, no defense of his record, nothing of the disappointment my mother had promised me, and the rage that would have to follow. Maybe he was not disappointed. Maybe he was glad to be back. Looking across the river and the marsh in the heat-moistened twilight, I could understand why anyone would be happy to be back at Hurt's Landing.

It was that kind of soft, endless twilight that lends itself to such hopeful speculation.

From inside the house, part of the peaceful drone of the evening, the big stand-up cabinet radio was tuned in to WTOC, the voice of the Savannah Indians. The drone seemed to firm up and get familiar to our ears, and we both caught it at the same time: a baseball game was being called. Only tonight, there was no Indians game. My father glanced at me, alarmed, then ran inside and turned up the set so we could hear it out on the porch. The peace of the evening was gone.

"We're broadcasting from Savannah's famed William Grayson Stadium on Victory Drive," the radio was saying. "The cradle of the great, where so many Big League stars stepped out onto the field for the first time. Stars like Mick Eden of the New York Yankees, and Bob Eliot, the home-run champion of the Boston Red Sox, and others too many and numerous to mention. Ladies and gentlemen, this park simply oozes with history."

"Oozes?" I asked my father.

He shushed me. Windy Herring was doing the play-by-play on the radio. He sounded as if he was having a good time all by himself, without a real game to mess up his fun.

"Tonight, Indians ace right-hander Zeke Justice will take the mound against Charleston, Savannah's Sally League arch-rivals."

"There's no game tonight, is there?" my father wondered. "Anyway, how can I be there if I'm here?"

That did not seem so farfetched to me. My father was often in many places at once, through his friends, his agents, his broadcasters and storytellers.

He stuck his head inside the house and tapped the radio cabinet a couple of times.

"Windy? Windy, are you in there? Speak to me! What's the matter with you? How can I be on that mound when there's no game, when I'm sitting here on the porch with my kid? Windy Herring, have you gone and had yourself a toot too many?"

He came back and sat on the porch rocker.

"Hey, maybe I really *am* there tonight. Maybe I'm not here at all. Maybe that old souse is right."

I started to laugh, then I saw he was serious. He really could think a thought like that. I got up from the porch rail and went to sit on the armrest of his chair.

"Of course you're here," I told him. "Where else would you be?" I knocked on the wooden chair. "It's as clear as that."

He did not answer. Then he threw his arms around me, but not the way he had done that afternoon on Oglethorpe Street, when we'd been horsing around. My parents were squeezing me black and blue in the space of one afternoon.

On the radio, Windy Herring launched into the play-by-play. Believe in it or not, a baseball game being called has a magic and we could not help but listen. My father mowed down the top of the Charleston batting order 1-2-3 in the first. Maybe they could hit his curve in the Bigs, but not down here. Whenever a hitter made contact, that was Windy slapping the mike with a lead pencil. The crowd was him hub-bubbing into a glass of water, or of something else. His ticker-tape imitation for the out-of-town scores coming over the wire was better than the real thing. In fact, it was the best, most ideal ball game that had ever been played. Windy was free of the managers' harebrained strategies. No runners ran through their signs. No infielders bobbled the ball. Windy Herring had the diamond all to himself, and he was staging the best-played game there ever could be. I couldn't blame my father for wanting to believe in it.

By the top of the sixth inning, we were coasting along with a comfortable lead. On the mound, Zeke Justice looked as though he was getting stronger as the game went on, which will happen sometimes when a pitcher really has his stuff. Then some WTOC boss must have tuned in. He must have heard the imitation crowd noises and Windy's jovial, self-satisfied laughter. He would have consulted his Indians schedule and discovered there was no game tonight. Then he ordered the plug pulled on our game. A musical interlude took its place. My father and I slumped back in our chairs.

"It was fun while it lasted," I said to him. "Even if it never did happen."

"It doesn't matter. We got five full innings in. I *won* that game. Let me tell you, it felt good — I needed that victory. It's bound to put me back on track."

I gave him a little sideways glance and tried to catch his eye, but he had snapped out of our evening. He was somewhere else now, somewhere I couldn't go. He really did believe in that game, and it gave me the chills.

He bounced out of the porch rocker and left it swinging, almost knocking me onto my behind in the process. My mother came out when she heard the car engine turn over.

"Zeke, where are you going? You told me . . ."

"I've got to go down and congratulate old Windy for winning me that game," he called through the open car window. "Anyway, for sure he's out of a job. A man in that position can always use some help. And I've got a little of my road money left over."

RAT PALMS

Evangeline and I watched his taillights flash once as he turned off the Lazaretto Road, toward Laroche and into town. We were on our own again. She switched off the musical interlude.

"Drink," she said slowly. "Look at what it does. It makes you belong to other people. Remember that, son."

Then she went into the house to attend to God knows what, but whatever it was, it put the place off-limits to me. I crossed the road and drifted down to our dock. Little circles in the still river showed where the night feeders were breaking the surface. The darkness was complete now.

I stood at the end of the dock. *Lazaretto, come forth*, I ordered the river. No reply, not even a toadfish. Nothing ever happened on this island. No wonder my father left every chance he could. I laughed at myself: defending him again.

I decided to use a little piece of this darkness for myself. From the end of the dock I cupped my hands around my mouth to make a trumpet. I did not have Paul Gant's voice, low with years and righteousness. That didn't matter. I'd use what I had. I commenced to sing the loudest, highest, screechiest note I had and held it as long as I could. Then I broke it off and listened to it shoot across the river and rock the bateaux tied up there and part the marsh grass where the egrets were trying to nest.

Not bad for the first time. I laughed, out of embarrassment and pleasure. I was going to be the first white Little Richard.

Now that I'd done what I had come to do, there was nothing left for me on the dock. I turned around and scuffed back toward the house, where the waiting-up lights were burning, yellow and mournful.

3

Zeke was spending more time with Windy Herring, now that Windy was out of a job, and more time down at Bo-Peep's establishment, than he was working on the curveball that had supposedly given him so much trouble up North. I studied the situation. From the outside, where I stood, there was not much I could do. It was like being out on the water in a leaky bass boat and watching a storm march across the sea into your path. He was set to pitch for the Indians that evening, but one look at him and you knew he wasn't ready. The fragility in him was undermining his sway and confidence and good looks. I wondered how he was going to make his shaky hands grip a baseball. The skin under his eyes was bruised-looking, and he was talking too much. He had an explanation for everything. And in his explanations, there were too many connections between unconnected things.

We sat on the porch watching the high storm clouds mushrooming up out of the afternoon heat. I could feel how wound up he was, like an oversprung watch, and I knew he was wishing he could pitch in a Windy Herring radio game where every allowance would be made. Where some understanding umpire would be calling balls and strikes. His bag with his uniform and equipment inside was slumped on the porch floor at the top of the step. He stared at it and I began to see it as he did: a crumpled, menacing thing, full of evil intentions, and enormously heavy.

"You know, Toadfish, I'm the Satchel Paige of the Sally League," he told me. "I'm throwing and throwing and I'm as good as I'm ever going to get, and they keep telling me to get better. I just keep throwing and throwing, and I'm throwing my life away. I'm not getting any younger to play this game."

I picked up one of the baseballs off the porch floor and started rubbing it up, the way I had seen him do. Pitchers do that when they want to stall for time.

"You'll be all right," I told him. My voice sounded dead to my ears.

"What else can a man's son be expected to say?"

"Men's sons have said a lot worse things," I defended myself.

"I suppose so," he admitted. "And some do around here, too."

He glared at the hazy sunlight cast back by the Lazaretto, and I could read the thought of escape on his face as if it were a sign. "Why don't we drive down to the beach?"

He stood up and went down the porch steps, stiff-kneed.

"What about your bag?" I reminded him.

He turned around and grabbed it irritably, then threw it in the back of the car. We got into the New Yorker and drove off, first over the Thunderbolt Bridge where the shrimpers tie up, then out the strip of blacktop toward the Tybee Island beach. They call that asphalt strip the Tommy Dorsey Road in honor of the band that used to play out on the Tybee Pier, back in the old days, before a hurricane came along and broke it up, and the Baptist preachers stepped in and wouldn't let the fun-loving people rebuild it.

Out on Tybee, everything was wide and open and torturous with glaring light. Butler Avenue, the big thoroughfare on the island, looked like the main street of a ghost town, with nothing but those scrawny rat palms trying to give shade. We parked on a lot cordoned off with man-made concrete boulders and stepped onto the desolation called the beach.

Tybee did not turn out to be a good idea. Neither of us knew what to do on the beach now that we were here. We went to take off our shoes, but the sand was burning hot and we hadn't thought of blankets or towels or any of that beach equipment. We sat in our stocking feet on the shore like a couple of fools, throwing rocks and shell bits into the calm surf that you could hardly make out through the blinding sunlight. Nobody's spirit was going to be uplifted on a beach, when every sane person is in the shade, and every normal one at work.

Through the heat waves rising off the sand we saw a man walking awkwardly down the beach, just as foolish looking as us, holding a box on his hip. The box did not look heavy, just bulky, and he was all alone to do the job.

It so happened my father knew the man. He was another member of the sandlot fraternity.

"Rags!" he cried. "Come on over and stand here, and make us some shade."

The man walked up to us and dropped the box, which turned out to be a Styrofoam cooler. He sat down on it.

"Well, Zeke Justice, what the hell you doing out in the sunshine? I thought you was allergic to daylight!"

The man had one of those Yamacraw Irish geechie accents that will turn the word *boat* into something with two syllables, if not more.

My father shrugged for an answer. "You hear how old Windy Herring won me a game last week?"

"Naw," said Rags. "You know we ain't got no radio out here on the beach. We living like a bunch of backwoods niggers here, except worse: we ain't got no trees, and we get sunburned."

My father told Rags about Windy Herring's baseball game.

"I pitched last night," Zeke said. "Now I got to pitch tonight, too."

"Better you loosen up for that game," Rags advised him mischievously.

"That very thought was wandering through my mind."

"Watch them wandering thoughts, or they'll get hit on a vagrancy charge. Tybee sheriff's awful mean."

Rags lifted his behind a foot or two off the cover and rummaged around underneath himself, as if he was cleaning up after a trip to the backhouse. He had a church key around his neck and he pried off the caps from a couple of malt liquors.

They drank. I watched the beer level going down through the brown bottle.

"I forgot to introduce you!" my father remembered all of a sudden. "Toadfish, son, this is Rags Scoggin. He played for the Indians, too. In fact, when I first came to this town to play ball, Rags was my battery mate. Zeke and Rags, one and two."

"A goddamned green Yankee he was, too, but anyone could see he was crazier than a shithouse rat with a muzzle on, even back then."

Rags laughed and shook my hand, and I said my real name. Not Toadfish — Timmy. Timmy Justice.

"I'm out of the game now," Rags confided in me.

I had no trouble believing that. The only way you would have known he'd been a catcher was all the trouble he had prevailing upon his knees to raise him off the cooler top. He pulled off his cap and wiped his forehead. His skin was ruddy and his hair was sparse, and he had burned patches all over his scalp.

A couple of Negro boys who, like me, belonged in school, came drifting down to the beach. They edged around us, and you could tell they had their eyes on the empties that were about to hit the sand, and how they were thinking about the deposit money they would have if they could get them back to the store.

Rags went to shoo them away.

"Let those boys have those bottles," my father said. "It's all they got. Anyway, are you going to carry them back?"

Rags elbowed me. "See, I told you he was a goddamned Yankee."

My father went quiet a minute, as if he was contemplating whether to tell Rags the news. Then he did.

"You know, I finally went North. A month ago."

"How come you're here, then?"

"They hit my fucking curveball!" Zeke shouted at him so suddenly the boys went skittering away without their bottles.

Rags practically fell off his cooler. "Easy, son." He readjusted himself and tucked at his balls. "Now, there, you just tell me what happened, in a regular tone of voice."

"I've been keeping this goddamned Sally League team at the top all the years I've been pitching here. And I keep getting passed by. I was here when Pizarro came up. He moves on. I stay put. I've seen them all go by. Okay, so I didn't strike out as many as he did. Then all of a sudden, when it's just about too late, they call me up. I'm up maybe three, four weeks, then it's back to this goddamned place again — no offense to you. Okay, so I got shellacked once or twice, but you need time to get used to the Bigs. No fucking curveball, they tell me. But if you ask me, it's something else. Something they're not telling me."

"If it's not your curveball, what do you think it is?" Rags asked.

"I don't know, that's what I'm telling you. But it's something! Now, do you think you could move your wide, slow catcher's ass off that thing and get me another cold one?"

"Got to get looser, huh?" Rags laughed heartily so my father wouldn't think he was criticizing him. "The way I see it, the problem is you keep forgetting it's a game. You take it too hard, it's not good for your pitching. I played with you, I was on your team, I know how it used to be. I had me some good years, I won us some games. But that's over. Now I'm shrimping for a living and watching my baseball from the stands, or on the television set."

My father shook his head.

"I just can't let up like you can. Anyway, you're from down here. When you left the game, you stepped out of the park and onto a shrimper. Don't forget I came down from up North to play. That's the only reason I'm here. I can't do anything else."

"Don't give me that shit, Yankee boy. You've turned into one of us. Or almost, anyway!"

Rags slapped my father on the shoulder. He was doing his best for him, and I loved him for it.

"Sure I felt bad when I got cut," he told my father. "But I got to see some towns and meet some women who didn't have any business consorting with a geech like me who grew up playing half rubber on the beach. Loosen up, there, Zeke!"

"I can't." My father pointed at the cooler. "There isn't any more loosening-up left."

"Then we'll take us an exhibition to Doc's!"

I figured Rags meant *expedition*, but whatever he meant, we got up off of our duffs and headed down the burning hot beach toward Sixteenth Street. They have some sandy-floor establishments there, and a T. S. Chu's department store, in case you need provisions for the beach.

When we came to where Sixteenth Street touches the beach, with the honky-tonks to the right and the stubby fishing pier to the left, my father stopped and made a show of patting down his pockets.

"Rags, I'm a little short. I gave the rest of my travel money to Windy, and I haven't gotten around to replacing it yet. Could you help a man out?"

"I will to the best of my ability," Rags said. "Which means leaning on Doc to let us chalk it up."

We moved up the shadeless street past the Novelty Bar, which was shuttered, and the empty lot where some carnival machinery was busy rusting in the salty air. This was supposed to be our little time together, father and son, but I was as inconsequential to him now as a toadfish. But I still couldn't summon up much bitterness against him. At least I was here, and grateful for that much, for the opportunity to study and keep watch over him, both at the same time, as from a widow's walk.

I had never been inside a true drinking establishment before. When I got into Doc's, I could see why people might find it so comforting.

The place was dark, and cool from the air conditioner in the window. There was something built right into the very room, call it comfort or complicity or forgiveness, I don't know. We were the only ones in the place, besides Doc.

"Pair of bourbon and water," my father said.

"Call or well?" Doc asked.

"Since we're chalking it up, might as well make it call. I call Mr. Beam."

Rags laughed. He surveyed the room with its three little television sets, all running and all tuned to different channels.

"Hey, Doc, which one you watching?"

"All of them. And this, too." He tapped a crossword puzzle he had on the bar with the eraser end of his pencil. "Keeps the gray matter active. Have to do something when you're locked up in a place like this with a bunch of monkeys all day."

"Doc is a genius of a kind," my father declared, nudging me. I almost toppled off my stool, unaccustomed as I was to that kind of perch.

Doc brought the drinks and set them on the bar. But he kept his hands wrapped around them.

"You know we can't have kids in here. So you keep your eyes on the boy."

"I know this is an honest place — that's why we're here. Don't worry about him. He's under my tutelage."

Doc squinted at the word; he wasn't that much of a genius after all. He did not know what a tutelage was, but he was not about to let on.

"And if he wants a drink, don't let him put it on our tab. He can pay for it out of his paper route money."

My father laughed, and they all decided to enjoy the joke at my expense. I felt pretty stupid sitting on a bar stool, so I slipped off it and went to busy myself with the shuffleboard game. You're supposed to slide a shiny silver disk down the alley and knock down the pins, like in a bowling lane. I did that a couple times. Then I saw that all I could win was the chance to knock down the exact same pins again, except for free this time. I sneezed into my palm a couple of times, then moved away from the air-conditioner box.

My father and Rags went on chatting with Doc. Their laughter was thick and greasy, like the brown paper that some barbecue has been in. Thick with forgiveness. They were laughing about debts that would never be paid back, and about poor Windy Herring's ball game, and how he and his wife were going to put bread on the table now.

"The town will provide," my father declared with a preacherly finger in the air.

Then Doc started in about a man who had been found with another man's wife by the second man, who had gotten him a hammer and hit the first man on the head with it. "It changed his life," Doc said.

After a while, I realized, to my relief, that they had forgotten all about me. I slipped out the door into the leaden heat and creamy asphalt of Sixteenth Street. Ain't wasn't nobody the wiser, as they say on Tybee Island.

I wandered down the street in the blade-thin shade along the storefronts until I found myself facing Mr. Chu's beach department store. T. S. Chu must have been the loneliest Chinaman on Tybee, seeing as he was the only one. What could have brought him to a place like this? Through the window, I looked over his trinkets. His shell mobiles turning in the wind. His overpriced crab lines, his sunglasses with bathing beauties on each temple. God, the beach was horrible on a weekday afternoon! I went into Chu's store to get some breeze from his overhead fans.

"Hello, young sir," he greeted me through his snuff-yellow buck teeth.

I was the only one in the place. I had to spend some money on something. I put a dime in his Lawman pinball machine, and commenced knocking down the blue plastic mustachioed sheriffs. It was about as much fun as shuffleboard.

I don't know how long it takes to drink what you're supposed to drink in an establishment like Doc's, but however long it takes, that time must have passed. I was leaning on the plate-glass window in front of Chu's. My father and Rags came rolling up Sixteenth Street. Their eyes were squinted down to little slits and they were punching each other in the shoulder, then looking up and waving their arms at the sky, as if they were angry at the sun for shining so bright and exposing their foolishness for all to see in the light of day.

"Toadfish!" my father burst out when he sighted me. "Where the hell have you been? We looked for you everywhere!"

"Aren't you set to pitch tonight?" I asked, getting in my splinter of revenge.

"Dammit, you're right!"

There was a kind of helpless gratitude in his voice, and I understood he was drunk. He sure could do it fast when he had to. When he needed to be loose enough to face the big comeback game.

He went through the motions of his windup, right there in the molten heat of Sixteenth Street. He looked pretty good to me, but then again, he didn't have to face any batters there on the asphalt.

"Late afternoon start," I reminded him, making like I was looking at a watch, which I did not own.

"That's what you need, Rags. A boy that'll take care of you! I guess I'd better get back to town. Shit, I could use a swim right now. Freshen up some. No time . . . That's the working life!"

He turned around in the street two or three times, locating the car, the sea, the general direction of the stadium among the surrounding objects. Then his voice got all pleading and pitiful.

"Shit, Rags, I wish you were catching me tonight. You'd set the target. You'd understand."

Rags shook his head. "Nothing to understand. Just put it in there."

My father did not like that answer. He flipped into a mean drunk as fast as you'd switch off a light.

"You drive," he mumbled at me.

He threw the keys at me but I wasn't ready. It was all I could do to lift my arms and cover up like a scared boxer.

"That's not how you catch," he howled. "That's not how you play the game."

Rags did a quick fade. He must have sensed rough road ahead. The Chrysler New Yorker was baking away in the parking lot, oven temperature even with the windows open. My father negotiated his way around the great white car that looked like a beached whale there in the lot. He was heading for the passenger side, just missing impaling himself on the rear fin, like a bug in a bug collection.

"You know I don't know how to drive this thing," I told him as he wrestled with the passenger-side door.

"Easy. Just point it. Remember, you're under my tutelage. Anyway, you're old enough to have a license. Why the hell don't you have one?"

Then he transported himself into the backseat and stretched out horizontal there, where he fell into a desperate, noisy, perhaps even feigned sleep.

It turned out my father was right. I just pointed the hood ornament at the center of my lane and depressed the gas pedal. I moved out of Tybee Island on Butler Street real slow to avoid attracting the sheriff's attention. I sat straight and high, my arms so stiff on the wheel they ached. I was transporting precious cargo, no one had to remind me of that. If the sheriff happened to stop me, I could always plead that it wasn't my fault, being underage at the wheel like this. But that plea would have violated the terms of my agreement with my father. *Take care of me*, it ran. Amazing to have to father your father, and amazing, too, how my father got people to do just that. I wasn't the only one.

But sooner or later, everyone overstays their welcome when it comes to that kind of exchange. People are going to feel disappointed if you've convinced them that you're running the show and that everything's under control, and then you end up broken down and blubbery and remorseful at their feet.

By the time I had crossed over the Tybee Bridge toward Grayson Stadium, with the Savannah River ship channel on my right, I was picking up good speed. It was smooth sailing. Nobody on the road. I stole a glance at Zeke Justice, minor league star, dead to the world in the backseat. *Sleep, Father. Your sleep is my license.*

Again, I heard Evangeline's grand, dolorous voice scolding me for perpetually siding with him. Not just siding, Mother, I corrected her — studying, too. And take note of this: not studying to imitate. Studying to outdo.

The rough level crossing and the long wait at the light at Presidents Street woke my father up.

"You're in town," I told him.

He bounded up from the backseat like he was on springs.

"I had a dream," he said.

I listened.

"I dreamed a horse. Distinct Intent, it was called. That's never happened to me before. Go on over to Oglethorpe Street."

I drove the Chrysler carefully through the squares of downtown Savannah, stopping at every Yield sign as if I was trying to impress a driving-school teacher.

"Faster," he urged.

When I got within a block of the address on Oglethorpe Street, I realized he wanted to go to Bo-Peep's. I stopped in front of the side door to the John Wesley Hotel and jammed the lever up into Park.

"Not here," he hissed. There was panic and exhilaration in his voice. "Park around the corner."

It seemed like a useless precaution to me, as if someone seeing his car around the corner from Peep's might think he had some other business in the neighborhood. But I did as I was told. He rang the downstairs bell and the door buzzed open. I had to take the stairs two at a time to keep up.

Bo-Peep's was the size of a small ballroom with a curving, J-shaped bar on one side, and a bank of phones on the other. In the middle were a half dozen pool tables, every one in mint condition. Inlaid in the floor tiles, on every fourth square, were the four signs of a deck of cards. A place where wagers are made this way is not permitted, I knew. But here it is, permitted all the same, since, after all, it *is* here, and in so gentlemanly a fashion.

Either my father's dream had been true prophesy, or he had been studying the racing form earlier that day, because there really was a horse named Distinct Intent. It was running in the Kentucky Derby, and the odds against it winning were sixteen to one. My father had no ready cash, but he made an arrangement with Mr. Peep and a man on one of the phones who was talking to the horse track. My father would borrow $200 for a few hours to place the bet.

"Two hundred and two dollars," he specified to Mr. Peep, who was unfurling his billfold like a flag.

Mr. Peep was a man with lacquered nails that ended in perfect little ovals. His eyebrows were bushy and soared upward like two birds' wings, and his heavy jowls sat smugly on a bull neck. He was a bad man; you could tell by the flawless state of his hands and the white suit he wore.

"Why the extra two?" he asked.

He counted his money. Our money. That would probably become his money again.

"I'm going to place a bet for my boy here. Two more bucks on Distinct Intent."

Mr. Peep shrugged. "Some people will do anything to twist Lady Luck's arm. Including using their children."

My father grabbed a handful of Mr. Peep's white suit coat and red tie and pink shirt and jerked him straight up.

"You greasy little sheeny! I had a dream that that horse is going to win! You don't even know what a dream is!"

A pair of Peep's men materialized, two muscled Greeks who looked like stevedores from the port.

"We break his head?" they offered.

My father dropped him. Peep smoothed out his clothes.

"Don't bother. He'll break it of his own free will. You're not welcome here any more, Mr. Justice," he said to my father. "But, of course, your money still is. Now place your bet and go out and play ball in the dirt."

"One day I'm going to take you out," my father swore. "And it'll be on my own terms. We'll see who bleeds the deepest. Oh, I've read my Shakespeare, I know you bleed like the rest of us."

"We have a literary man here! Now, that's a rarity! Mr. Justice, you won't be taking me anywhere, except to your private table at Johnny Harris's. You need me too much."

One of Peep's men put the two stubs from the two bets into my father's hand.

"I think I'll have a drink," my father said loudly.

"As you like." Mr. Peep shrugged. "Your money is always welcome."

Then he swept off in a cloud of cologne.

I followed my father to the bar, which was padded and covered with red vinyl, like a cheap hassock. You could bang your head against it all you wanted and still not feel a thing.

"We're in a bar," he stated the obvious. "You want to try your first drink?"

There was a row of bottles twenty feet long, all lined up like soldiers about to go into battle. I didn't know what the stuff inside them would do to me, or why I should want to try it.

"I think I'll pass," I told him.

"Just as well," he mumbled. "Don't start drinking, whatever you do. It's no kind of life."

Then he shot a glass of bourbon down his throat so fast there was no way he could have caught the taste of it.

4

I get a thrill every time I walk into Grayson Stadium. You go through the brick archway, under the metal grating painted shiny red, past the concession stand where I never bought a scorecard because I made my own. Then you walk up the short set of stairs and the green diamond appears, with the perfect white lines the groundskeeper lays down with his lime-spreading machine. The infield dirt swirls with rake lines, and it looks as clean as a doorstep after you've swept it. The division of red dirt and grass is a sharp as a razor cut, and the grass is so green you want to take off your clothes and roll around in it.

My father was going to climb the clay mound in the middle of that field and stand and paw the rubber, and try to pitch his way back to the Bigs, as stewed as a newt, with $202 riding on Distinct Intent, a sixteen-to-one long shot. Two of those dollars had my name on them.

It didn't look too good, actually.

I was filled with dark reflections, and they grew darker when I spotted Evangeline in the players' wives section where we usually sat, the best seats in the park. My mother had not taken in a game in years, ever since my father was courting her, she had told me one afternoon during a session of Marster family lore. Tonight, she had come to the park to attend to the damage. She had a sure instinct for catastrophe, like a seasoned ambulance driver.

She must have taken it upon herself to call a cab for the ride off the island, up Laroche and over to Victory Drive, something unheard of for a Marster woman in better times, to ride in a car in which anyone could, and probably did, ride. I watched her settle into her seat. Scarf on her head as if she was expecting stormy weather, eyes not on the field where the players were practicing, laconic and loose-limbed in the heat, but further away, above the surface of things. I stood a few rows behind her and looked where she looked. Her eyes flew over the left center field fence like a gopher ball, over the bull's-eye Baseball and Beechnut sign painted there, and into the tall, moss-burdened oaks that stood like a row of spectators who did not understand the game.

I went to take my place beside her.

"Oh, there you are, boy. I understand you and your father went for a drive. I understood that when I didn't see the car, and neither of you with it."

I scuffed. "Nerves," I said. "Daddy was nervous before the game."

She nodded. There was a silence filled with the happier sounds of the game funneling up from the field.

"You know something, boy," she began. "I have hardly been to a game since your father was courting me."

My mother believed all good stories bore repeating. More than that — they actually got better with the telling. If a story was good, you had an obligation to keep telling it, until you told it to death.

"Those were in better days, of course, need I say. I remember I used to like sitting with my sister Adelina, before she passed away. There we were in the first row, just above the dugout. I had me a bag of boiled peanuts, and when a foul ball came flying up toward where we were, I was so scared I dropped that bag. And do you know what, the peanuts landed slap on the head of the man whom I eventually married. He looked up at us, and I could tell in his eyes that he did not know which one of us to go for, my sister Adelina or me. I should have known then and there that he would be no good, not as a husband, at least. A man who has to think which woman to choose, and who isn't afraid to let his eyes show it. And I did know that, but when I could tell he was going to choose me, I forgot all about that little inner voice of mine, just the way all of us do."

She laughed. "All this talk the preachers have about developing your conscience! What good is it to have one that's developed, if you don't listen to it anyway?"

I looked out over the field. No Zeke Justice. We were playing Columbia that evening, and their pitcher was taking a few last easy warm-up pitches in front of his dugout. But the practice rubber on our side was empty, except for the outfielders hitting pop flies to each other and blowing big pink bubble-gum bubbles.

All the while, Evangeline was talking away to fill this soft, beautiful evening buzzing with the most extraordinary, finely crafted dread.

"Baseball was still a mere game back then, and it didn't matter if I didn't understand all the rules. I suppose you know that your father and I were married on the pitcher's mound. It was before a game, on an early evening, just like this one. A doubleheader, as I recall."

"You told me once. I always thought it was a great idea."

"Don't interrupt me."

Her usual admonishment. I had committed my typical indiscretion: getting enthusiastic about a detail of the story before she could steer us around to its sad, inevitable conclusion.

"The hem of my gown was all red with that greasy old clay dust. Everything seemed to take so long, and the home-plate umpire started calling 'Play ball.' When we finally did exchange the rings and vows I was so flustered I dropped my bouquet and ran right off the mound. There I was, scampering across that dusty old infield with my sister Adelina, may she rest in peace, who was my bridesmaid, and my father, your Grandpa Marster, and the pastor, and Zeke standing there on the mound in his uniform all freshly laundered and pressed for the occasion. We just barely did have time to get married before I bolted.

"Everyone filed off the field behind me, real dignified, except for Zeke, who was set to pitch. There was the bouquet, lying on the ground. He picked it up. He didn't know what to do with it. I don't think he even knew how to hold a bouquet of flowers — he was holding it upside down, by the stems, with the flowers pointing down. We were playing Jacksonville, and the first batter was already standing in the box. Then Zeke shrugged his shoulders, stuck the flowers in his shirt and patted his heart. I didn't know whether to laugh and applaud like everybody else in the Stadium was doing, even the pastor, or feel mortified by the public display."

I sat quietly, waiting for the sad part of the story. So far, it had been sad only for the flowers. They had had to spend an inning inside a baseball player's shirt on a hot Savannah evening.

"And the reception! I didn't know whether to be honored or humiliated. It was after the game, at Johnny Harris's, which was nothing more than a roadhouse back in those days, not a dining lounge the way it is today. A lawless sort of a place with slot machines in the lobby that assaulted your senses as soon as you walked in. The owner had made some sort of arrangement with the mayor to draw the city limits all around the establishment, without including it, so they could do anything they wanted to inside, and not be bothered by matters of public morality.

"Sweaty ball players, uncombed and unshaven, men who had never consorted with women before and had no knowledge of the subject, lining up to kiss the bride. Men I had never laid eyes on before, drinking champagne from the bottle like it was Coca-Cola. Everyone slapping Zeke on the back, and telling him he was Major League material. The waiters waiting on him for his autograph, since of course he had won the game that evening — I don't think the league would have permitted it to be any other way. Everybody loved him except for one coach, I was given to understand, because he had run through that coach's sign at third base during the game, and made it home to score a run anyway, with a big dirt-raising slide.

And at the end of the evening, when everyone, including myself, had drunk so much sparkling wine they could hardly stand straight, your father maneuvered me into one of those side booths they have at Johnny Harris's, pulled the curtain and told me that since we were married now, we could just as well make a little whoopee!"

Evangeline let out an indignant squeal.

"The idea of it! And him trying to act so sly and daring and manly, as if it had all been his idea, as if we hadn't been at it already — which is how you came along, I might add."

Then Windy Herring's voice began echoing around the park on the loudspeaker system. Herring, fired by WTOC and hired back by the Indians. Forgiveness is ever abounding for the likable sinner.

"Ladies and gentlemen, tonight please make welcome the Savannah starting pitcher, Zeke Justice, back with us once again!"

Windy made it sound as though Zeke Justice's being sent down to the minors was a promotion in disguise. Sent down, back home, where he was a somebody. The Savannah players burst onto the field and fanned out to their positions as we cheered our team. But for the longest time, my father did not stroll out onto the field in his usual way, up to the mound. Then just before it started dawning on people that something might be wrong, he walked out slowly with his head bowed, holding his glove in his left hand and the ball in his right. The cheering rose but he did not acknowledge it. He kept his head down, as if he was watching his feet to see where they might go next. He had an overcareful kind of step, and I think he saw right through Windy Herring's welcome home, even if everyone in the Stadium loved it.

I still have my homemade scorecard for that game, as far as I could chart it. It's on the rough side of a shirt cardboard, but I don't need to refer to it. I can tell you what it says: 5-3, 6, K. A good inning, up to crowd expectations. Columbia didn't hit the ball out of the infield.

But the whole time he was on the mound, my father was like a man caught by the sheriff behind the wheel with whiskey on his breath, and made to walk the center line. *Concentrate. Concentrate.* The center line was the pitching rubber. On our porch on Hurt's Landing I'd heard men boast about how much they had put away the night before, and how they didn't even remember how they'd gotten their cars back into the garage. "Automatic pilot," they would explain. I knew you could do some things that way, without knowing you were doing the right and routine thing. It was a skill the drinking man had to possess if he wanted to get around.

A pitcher's motion should be just that automatic. As automatic as a drinking man squeezing his car between two live oaks on either side of a country road. *Just point it,* I whispered to my father down there on the mound. *I did. You can, too, dammit.*

I didn't record it on my scorecard for that inning, because there are no symbols for that kind of thing, but I could feel him pacing and talking to himself on the mound. When the first hitter made contact — it was just an easy bouncing ball to second — my father jumped out of his skin, as if he'd seen his ghost. After the putout, the first baseman held on to the ball a second or two longer and cocked his head and motioned to Zeke to settle down. I thought of the day he had married Evangeline out there, how the crowd had cheered the sweaty bouquet and everyone enjoyed the show. This was going to be a spectacle of a different kind.

He struck out Columbia's number-three hitter to get out of the inning. But the way he got him was all wrong. He went to deliver a fastball on a two-strike pitch, but somewhere in his motion his strength left him. The ball came floating in out of a fastball windup as the most outrageous change of pace, and the Columbia hitter had time to swing and miss twice before the ball finally made its way into the catcher's mitt. The Grayson Stadium crowd cheered.

"Ain't nobody can throw a pitch like that!" a fan exclaimed a couple of rows back.

That fan was right.

I glanced at my mother. She was torturing a Viceroy.

"What do you think?" I asked her.

"Just thinking about those old oaks on the other side of the fence. Aren't they handsome?"

I wanted to strangle her. Was she really so blind to the spectacle of her husband falling apart on the mound before his adoring fans? She carried on with her sweet, vague stories, no more interested in the players on the field than if they'd been a cloud of shit flies.

"You know, I thought I would have to marry your father blessingless. Your grandfather Jefferson was so opposed to Zeke and me getting married at first. But I must say, when I watched him carrying on at Johnny Harris's the evening of the reception, and when I understood how familiar he was with the ways of that establishment, and that it had not been his first time through those doors or others like them, I knew he was a man like any other. When I watched him rolling from table to table and flirting with the women, I must admit I felt a secret satisfaction. I knew he couldn't honestly be opposed to anything I might do, and if he was, it was only because of my sex. Oh, I used to be an impetuous girl before your father came along. He wasn't the first. When I told your grandfather as much, he accused me of possessing unnatural knowledge — I'll never forget those words! Ha! If only I'd had more of it! And of a kind that would be farseeing, not just unnatural . . . But I'm getting ahead of myself. Happens every time I want to tell a story. So, when I took your father in tow to your grandpa Marster's dusty old study, Mr. Jefferson Marster opens up like the fire-and-brimstone preacher he should have been. Going on about how Zeke was a Catholic — something your grandfather always wished he was, by the way — and a Northerner, and a baseball player, and that he possessed an odd first name that would have been more appropriate on a Negro. Meanwhile, Zeke just stood there, rocking on his heels, with his mind manifestly somewhere else. Then your grandpa starts wailing away on the sport of baseball, in that derisive tone of his that I've discovered since is always a prelude to his blessing. Baseball is a sandlot sport that anyone can and will play, he tells your father. Why, look at that Brissie fellow your team had during the war: a one-legged pitcher, using the ways of a circus act to attract a crowd.

"Then there's a lull in the attack. I figure your father is going to haul off and sock him one in the face, which is what I wished I could do, and on my account, not just his. Then all of a sudden your father pops out with the strangest stuff. He starts in quoting all sorts of Roman emperors and dead poets in Latin, things a ballplayer is not supposed to know, but that this particular one knows, because of his Catholic schooling, which you have since forsaken, I might point out. You see, Zeke had a kind of animal instinct for such things, and he must have felt how mightily envious my father was of the splendid trappings of the Catholic religion. Grandpa Marster puts his cigar down in his oyster-shell ashtray. He gets to his feet. I'm wondering whether he and Zeke are finally going to come to blows, which means we'll be able to run off together, or cancel the wedding; at that time, either one would have been fine with me. But no. Your grandpa Marster brushes the ashes off his jacket and says, You surprise me, son, with your learning. But why should I be surprised, when you think of it? You're a ball player, but after all, what am I? A merchant — less than that: a retailer. A man who sells alcohol for a living. Then he raises his hands like he was blessing the Thunderbolt shrimp fleet at Easter time. And I understood that this was to be our blessing.

"For the better or for the worse, those old Latin poets did the trick. They sounded so noble to your poor grandfather Marster. He always loved those hard-to-say names, and anything with a little ceremony to it. As long as it lifted him up from his lowly station as a gentleman retailer of alcoholic beverages."

Evangeline adjusted herself on the uncomfortable wooden seat and eyed the beer trolley banging down the aisle, squirting draft out the spigot at every bump. But for now, her story was intoxication enough.

"But, of course, it couldn't have ended there. That would have been so easy for our complicated family. The two of them, my husband and my father, kept sniffing around each other's behinds like a pair of low-down mutts, pardon my French. They were just waiting for a bottle of whiskey and a proper stage with a sufficiently appreciative audience. And where do you think they found all that? At Johnny Harris's, of course, and the hell with the fact that it was, after all, my wedding reception. About halfway through the evening, with my father rolling from table to table visiting the female habituées of the place, Zeke grabs him by the shoulder, gives him a squeeze and says, 'Hey, Pops, why don't you introduce me to some of your show girls?' And if that isn't bad enough, he starts in mocking him as a merchant prince who spent all his time with his ledger books and never had the chance to improve himself. The show girls titter. Your grandfather winds up and lets fly with a great roundhouse right that he might as well have telegraphed the week before. Zeke doesn't duck. He just steps back a little, so when the punch comes in it doesn't do any damage. Zeke gives him a big grin and rubs the sting off his chin. The room is completely quiet, and at Johnny Harris's, that's saying a lot. Then Zeke tells him, loud enough for everyone to hear, 'Pops, if that's the best you can manage, you'd better stay out of the ring. You're liable to get hurt.'"

A cheer went up. I turned back to the field and saw our shortstop lunging across home in an awkward, head-first slide and a cloud of red dust. I never did get a chance to record how we scored that run. That wasn't where the real game was being played, anyway. I think we scratched out the run on two hits and a Columbia error. Not what you'd call a comfortable lead for my father as he scaled the mound for the next inning, scarcely fit for the job. But his manager could not very well give him the hook after one frame for acting wound up and strange — not after Windy Herring's big buildup. What a man's friends will do to him!

Even from up in the stands, Zeke's windup looked exaggerated. Either he put too much into it and almost fell off the mound onto his face, or he was so careful he pushed the ball toward the plate and covered up, in case the batter sent it back through the box like a shot.

But by some grace, Zeke got us out of that inning, too. I see a single, a force play, then a heads-up maneuver play to turn a single into the hole into another 6-4 force-out. Zeke watched his defense behind him as though they were playing in another game.

After the last putout I got up from my seat and walked down the steps of the aisle to the foot of the stands. I didn't know what I intended to do. Whatever it was, I'll always wish I had gone through with it. I got down to the first row of the stands, right above the Indians' dugout. The outfielders were trotting in with that easy stride they have, and in the middle of them was my father, stiff-kneed, overcontrolled. He was looking at his shoes.

The stands aren't high. I could have vaulted down to the playing field. I could have been at his side. He could have called me Toadfish or any old fool nickname I hated — I wouldn't have cared, as long as it helped him. But I never did it.

I leaned over the edge of the rail. The sleepy, lined face of Hector Torres, the pitching coach, peered around the edge of the dugout.

"Don't bother the players, son," he told me gently.

I drifted back foolishly to my seat next to Evangeline, who pretended she hadn't noticed I'd been gone in the first place.

We put up another run in our half of the second on a home run off the foul pole. Other people's luck. Two to nothing for the Indians. The lead was still not enough as the top of the third began and Zeke climbed the mound again to pitch to Al Pinkerton.

Pinkerton was major-league bound and everybody knew it. Usually he batted cleanup, but the Columbia manager had him at the bottom of the order because he had been spiked in the hand the week before. He looked at a couple of my father's pitches low and away. When Zeke released the 2 and 0 offering I thought *inside corner*, but the ball began rocketing up and in. Pinkerton was watching it coming, leaning in, looking for something to pull. At the last moment there was this disbelieving look on his face and he just froze. The ball caught him under the jawbone like an uppercut. His head snapped back and he went down in an awful heap.

The whole park heard his jaw shatter. A noise like a dry branch crashing to the ground. It was the worst sound I had ever heard.

"Holy fuck!" someone swore a couple of rows behind us.

I heard something spill and figured it was the guy's pop. When I looked back to see where it had landed I saw that the guy had thrown up.

My father had broken more than Al Pinkerton's jaw. He broke an unwritten Sally League rule. You never throw at a guy who's major-league bound. He had done it. His world, his rules, and he had thrown against them.

My mother was nodding her head, over and over, as if she had been expecting it the whole time.

Pinkerton was out cold on the field. The Columbia trainer waddled out and he and the umpire rolled Pinkerton onto a stretcher. The guy left Grayson Stadium feet first. A doctor hopped out of the stands and skipped after Pinkerton's stretcher, waving a vial of smelling salts in circles around his face. My father kept his back to the scene. I don't suppose he could bear to look.

No one in the stands could figure the pitch. You don't brush a man back on a 2 and 0 count. Pinkerton was good, but he had never hit my father hard. No reason for him to send Pinkerton a message pitch. There was just no strategy to something like that. Which made everyone think my father had thrown it out of sheer meanness.

Finally, Columbia put a pinch runner on first and the umpire hollered "Play ball" again. Outside the park, a siren was wailing down Victory Drive. And inside, the crack of Pinkerton's jaw was still echoing off the walls.

My scorecard shows that the runner advanced to second on a bunt and scored on a single to right. What it doesn't tell is that when the side was retired and he was coming off the field, Zeke Justice tried to apologize to Columbia's third base coach, and that it did not look as though the coach was having any part of it.

I knew it was going to happen. Everyone in the damned park knew, too. And though they all knew this thing, and knew it was bad, they couldn't, or wouldn't, do a single thing about it. Our second baseman, Azuma, singled up the middle. That put Zeke Justice up with a man on first and nobody out. A tailor-made bunt situation. My father walked to the plate with his bat. Everyone in the park figured they knew what was going to happen, then they changed their minds and said, No, they can't hit him now, it's too obvious. They'll save it till later when they really need it, at the end of the season or in a bigger game than this one, when they know it'll hurt more.

My father squared to bunt on the first pitch. His bat was chest high and he stood open stanced in front of home plate. The pitch came in at his head and he just stood there and made himself a target for it. He just watched it come toward him with God knows what on his mind — I would have given anything to know. He took it, as if it were just punishment.

The fastball rose over his bat and hit him in the batting helmet. The helmet splintered into a dozen pieces.

My mother leaped to her feet.

"The plate! The plate!" she screamed.

I looked toward home plate. I didn't see anything unusual about it. My father was getting up and dusting himself off. He felt his scalp for blood and rubbed his fingers together, then gave his head a shake. Then he trotted on down to first base without a glance at Columbia's pitcher, as if that kind of thing happened all the time. Runners on first and second, nobody out.

Evangeline stood up as the umpire was preparing to toss the Columbia pitcher out of the game. She was trembling. You would have thought she was the one who'd gotten hit by the pitch.

"I've had enough of this disgrace," she announced. "Help me find a taxicab."

I did not have too much choice. My feet were following her, but my eyes were looking behind. Pretty soon I'd be finding out what kind of plate she was talking about. It was a home plate in a way, but not the kind you find imbedded in the ground on a baseball diamond.

5

On the Isle of Hope and in town, the ball that broke Al Pinkerton's jaw had become public property. Two days after the pitch was thrown, Rags Scoggin pulled up in his pickup truck, the bed piled high with old shrimp nets and a cloud of interested flies buzzing above them. His truck looked more like a piece of driftwood you might comb off the beach. "Raggedy," said the front license plate. Usually, Rags strolled, or drifted, or shuffled. He was never in a hurry. There were lots of shrimp in the sea, and he knew where they were. But by the way he marched down onto the dock where my father and I were fishing, I knew he had business at our place.

My father slipped his rod into the stand and went to greet Rags. The two of them stood with their arms crossed, staring at the river, but neither of them was thinking about it.

"Things just aren't the same around here any more," my father said.

Rags didn't answer. He waited for what he knew was coming.

"You know, since I hit Pinkerton."

"Hit-by-pitch is part of the game."

"It is. But if you ask me, I've been getting a lot of strange looks lately."

"Yeah? Fish been giving you the evil eye?"

RAT PALMS

My father didn't laugh.

"Yeah, you know, like I'm some kind of a criminal. I went to Bo-Peep's. People give me lots of room at the bar. I'll never make it back into the Bigs again, not after this. They were looking for reasons? They just found another. First his curve's no good. Then he's too old. Now he's wild, he hit a man."

My father was talking faster, playing all sides of an imaginary trial.

"He hit a man who was going to the majors because he's not going. A spiteful man. There! That's what they'll say!"

Rags gave him time to cool down before he asked, "Why did you hit that Pinkerton fellow anyway?"

"I wasn't head-hunting. I just threw it up there. Okay, maybe I didn't have my good control. After Tybee, me and Toadfish here went over to Peep's establishment to place a bet. Me and Peep got into a little talking match, and I guess I had that on my mind. But that didn't used to matter. Booze didn't used to matter, either. I don't know . . . I just don't have the control."

He flicked his head back and forth, as if he was chasing away a cloud of gnats. But it was too breezy for gnats, and there weren't any flies, either.

"Pinkerton'll be back, don't worry," Rags said in a level voice, but you could see he was worried. "Everyone'll forget about it."

"I'm afraid to pitch inside," my father said.

"I've heard tell of that before. The guy who does the beaning hurts more than the guy that's been beaned. I wouldn't know, I was only a catcher. But if that happens to a pitcher, he's better off out of the game."

We listened to Rags's assessment hanging in the air. No one in Savannah or on the islands had ever let on to Zeke Justice that he might be better off doing something else. What else could he do? In the little silence that crowded in on us, we totaled up Zeke Justice's chances, each of us, Zeke included.

"You know, people are forgetting one thing," he protested. "I got beaned, too. In the head."

"Yeah. But it hit you on the helmet. That makes a different sort of sound in a park than a man's jawbone."

"But that helmet was in a dozen pieces!"

"Sure, it was. But the head underneath it came out in one piece."

"I ain't so sure of that any more," my father grumbled. He patted the side of his head, under his hair, as if he was still feeling for blood.

"If you got hurt," Rags reasoned, "maybe you ought to see you a doctor. A real doctor, not just some team trainer."

"I don't want no doctor finding things in me," my father exploded. "I've seen enough goddamned doctors in my life."

I looked down at the pail and inspected my take of toadfish for the afternoon. They were puffing and blowing out their gills. They were so ugly it was like having a bunch of your worst nightmares swimming around in a galvanized metal tub right there at your feet.

Then Rags Scoggin did the indulgent thing. He dipped into the back pocket of his loose chinos and pulled out a little half-pint of bourbon.

"This is your day off," Rags told my father. "You may as well loosen up some."

My father barked out a laugh.

"Is this your recipe for improving my control? Some battery mate you are!" He nudged Rags's bottle hand and motioned in my direction. "Besides, the kid's here."

Rags turned to me. "You forgive, don't you, son?"

"I've got to," I told him.

My father looked at me. His eyes bugged out a little, then he laughed.

"Listen to that answer! And they ask me why I drink! I drink for forgiveness, goddammit!"

Then he took the little half-pint from Rags and made a sizable dent in it.

Now, wasn't that some kind of wise medicine Rags Scoggin was dispensing? Take a man's fear of losing control, and domesticate it with some plain old sipping whiskey. I was relieved once the bourbon and the warm afternoon air conspired to make Rags's and my father's speech full of resigned wisdom and the agreement that the world was an unfair place, no matter if you won or lost its various games, and that a man's efforts were rarely, and then unpredictably, rewarded. First Rags had been rough on my father; now he was granting him indulgence. Inquiry and indulgence. It was something straight out of Father Dooley's church.

But since Rags's and my father's indulgence was so easy to obtain, I soon began to lose interest in it. After all, I had been party to such ceremonies before. I made a show of packing my gear as he and Rags carried on nostalgically before the Lazaretto. A half-pint is just a drop in the river and soon enough, I knew, they would be getting into Rags's pickup and heading over to the Negro package store in Sandfly Crossing, over Rags's protestations. "I don't give a shit if those people are black. No nigger's gonna outnigger me! I'll be as black as I wanna be! You stay in the truck if you're scared of the boogeyman," my father would tell him. It was a kind of reasoning only a half-stewed Yankee would use in these parts. And Rags would give in, and go off to the Quonset hut package store with my father. Then as sure as there was a God in heaven and toadfish in the Lazaretto, they would head over to the Thunderbolt dock where Rags's shrimper was tied up and sit on the deck and drink up their Sandfly purchases. With them gone, the dock would be mine again, to use as it was meant to be used: a place for reflection and toadfish catching.

When Rags's pickup had negotiated the bend of the Lazaretto Road, I heaved up the bucket of toadfish and dumped them back into the river. Lazarus fish, that's what they were. Consumed with a loathsome disease. Swimming up from the nasty bottom, mirrors of a sort. Messengers from the deep, or as deep as the waters got around here. I was beginning to develop an affection for them. I felt we had something in common. Not looks, apparently. Though I didn't exactly know what I looked like, I knew I wasn't repulsive like my gilled comrades.

The bond between me and the toadfish ran deeper than looks. And I was out on the dock to explore it.

The splash of water and fish falling into the river sounded like the flush of a giant toilet. When the rings of water had smoothed out and the fish were set free to swim away or die, I was hit by a kind of inspiration. I cupped my hands around my mouth, conjured old Paul Gant and began to sing.

Lazaretto, flow forth.

Lazaretto, flow on over me.

It sounded okay by me. I tried it again, with my voice higher this time. If you're not Paul Gant, if you can't go low and dignified and sound like God in His own sweet chariot, then you've got no choice but to go high and screechy.

Lazarus fish.

Lazarus House.

La.

Za.

Ret.

Toooo.

It was damned predictable. No sooner had I finished listening to my voice fan out over the marshes of Burntpot Island and fade away above the wading birds' nests, than the screen door of the house slammed. My mother emerged from inside, a moving white shroud in the dusk like the water ghost, and glided across the road down to the dock. She picked her way over the stone foundation of the old Marster store.

"I heard a noise," she inquired from behind me.

"The noise was me."

She nodded. "Have you been studying those men?"

"In a way. Since you mention it, there's something I don't understand. How come they're always blaming themselves out loud for their faults, so that everyone can hear them?"

"Boy," she preached to me, "there is nothing more glorious for some men than to admit fault in public. If you blame yourself, you make it hard for others to blame you. Your wife, for example. It is a way of striking against the enemy."

"Is that you?"

"Only secondarily, if that much. The enemy is yourself, boy, yourself. But don't you start thinking about that. It's too early for such preoccupations."

"That's like concentrating as hard as you can on not thinking about something."

She shrugged her shoulders in that delicate, hopeless way of hers. *The world is not made to my desiring*, that shrug said.

"Now walk me back across to my door, since your father isn't here to do it."

She offered me her arm. The king was gone, so the jack had to do his duty. We stepped off the dock and into the rectangle that the ruins of the old Marster store described.

"You like the dock. But I like this spot where the store used to stand. To each his refuge, I suppose," she said.

I thought of my father lying on his back on the deck of Rags Scoggin's shrimper at Thunderbolt, watching twilight descend. To each his refuge, indeed!

"It doesn't matter that the weeds have grown up, or that the ground has hardened. It is all still present, and it possesses us."

She spoke dreamily, as if to enroll me in her dream. But I wouldn't go. If it's all so great, I felt like saying, then why is it just a ruined foundation? Why don't we have a real building? Why does someone else hold the paper to our house?

"You are lucky, son," she accused me. "Lucky to grow up surrounded by this world. I know you disdain it. I know you favor your father's world. But one day you'll realize your good fortune."

"I wonder when that day will come," I mused.

She gave me one of her resigned looks she reserves for sinners and backsliders of all varieties. Then released my arm. She didn't want me escorting her across the Lazaretto Road any more. She glided across the darker surface of the asphalt and under the sheltering oaks alive with every type of chirping, singing insect. Shortly, in the house across the way, the lamps went out.

I did not much feel like practicing my singing any more. Let her call it a noise, I didn't care, but I was not going to have her pinning it onto the velvet board of the Marster family collection of sweetly anguished behavior. Why turn over my refuge? It was one per customer, even in this richly endowed family. Next time, I would go far out of her earshot. But to do that on an island, you need a boat.

Night, Isle of Hope night, I will put on your thick black cloak, that neither of my procreators may see me, that I might study and reflect upon them at my ease. I liked talking to myself in that made-up voice, half Scriptures, half Evangeline Justice, née Marster. It was a parody of both, appropriate somehow for a loathsome toadfish sinner sentenced to report upon his reflections if he wanted to be received again into the breast of the Academy.

In the dark my feet found the foundation of the Marster store. I assumed another voice: tour guide to Hurt's Landing. "Last century, with the people of Savannah packed in as tight as a dozen loathsome toadfishes in a metal pail, ignoring even the most basic precepts of human cleanliness and fine speech, epidemics of pellagra and other diseases too hard to pronounce raged like barroom brawls. The people fled the city, hoping for salvation from disease, and they settled on this high bank of the Lazaretto, so aptly named for a man who was saved. They baptized this place the Isle of Hope."

I paced off the foundation of the store. I was moving faster now, running that rectangle pattern like a maddened trained bear in the circus. I had to move fast if I didn't want the Marster roots to grow up all gnarled out of the stone and into the soles of my sneakers and fasten me to the spot. "And here we gaze, ladies and gentlemen, on Hurt's Landing, so named because . . . so named because . . . because this is where the hurt lands."

RAT PALMS

Marster, Justice and Hurt. The three masters of the Isle. I sang their names, but real soft this time. That night, I learned this about music: you don't have to screech or holler to fill a place with your voice.

A couple of days later, I was sitting in the first row at Grayson Stadium, leaning on the railing, watching the Indians go through a nonchalant practice before the game that afternoon, and thinking about the pleasure of admitting weakness in public. It was not exactly a religious act, like confession; the rules of confession were too straitened. There were times and places and listeners to be observed. Glory was constrained. The act as practiced by my father was akin to a military tactic: the preemptive strike. Maybe I should have paid more attention to my military science and tactics teacher at the Academy, where such practices were routinely studied in a calmer setting.

I embarked on an exercise in logic. Let us postulate that the enemy is oneself. I strike at myself before you can. I tried on the idea. It sounded odd, but the more I twisted and turned it and got used to it, the more plausible it became. On an island in hot weather, logic tends to soften and turn malleable like heated pipe.

Inappropriate thoughts, Evangeline had warned me. "This period of reflection of yours — and when you say those words I can't help but think you mean them as a joke — will only fill your head full of all sorts of ideas. And those ideas will sap you of your strength and youth. There will be no more freshness left in the world for you," she enjoyed cautioning me.

But what could I do? Reflection was a demon sown by Father Dooley.

Besides, she was wrong about freshness. This morning, the Grayson Stadium field looked as fresh and thrilling as ever, and everything about it made me want to feel happy. The line of shadow the deck cast over the first-base side of the field, the sound of the ball popping into the catcher's mitt as the pitchers worked out. The vibration in the air when the fungo hitter got the sweet part of the bat on the ball and sent it over the wooden fence where the local boys waited for just such gifts.

Then my father stepped onto the practice mound to get some throwing in. I had not seen him since that early evening two days past when he and Rags had climbed into the raggedy old pickup truck, hollering and joking about the boogeyman and heading for Sandfly Crossing. I had not seen him, but I'd sensed him in the house, the way you might feel it when an intruder breaks in. I opened my eyes in the darkness and felt him downstairs, moving through the rooms as solid and awkward and dangerous as a bear drunk up on berry juice. I closed my eyes again, too scared to wait for the rest.

Sometime during the night I had a dream. People are always going on about their dreams around here, taking them for signs, but I never dream. I try to make it my business not to. I leave that to other folks. But in my dream my father was sick. They were going to have to operate, and the prospect put me in a panic. *I don't want them to cut him open*, I protested. *I don't want them finding out about me inside.* I woke up and heard him downstairs again, feeling his way through the dark house, humming an old-fashioned square dance tune, a kind of music that didn't belong to the island.

I sat up in the dark room. The streetlight on the Lazaretto Road was wrapped in hanging moss. That's strange, I thought as my dream came back to me. Your father is supposed to be in you. Not you in him. Your father makes you. You don't make him.

I fell asleep again but the night was far from over. Sometime later I opened my eyes to my father standing in the doorway, a hand on either jamb.

"May I come in?"

His exaggerated politeness. The effort of control. He was walking that center line again.

"Yes, sir," I murmured.

"If you call me 'sir' one more time I'll put a frog in your bed!"

RAT PALMS

He came in and sat on the edge of the bed. A minute later he lay down full-length on top of the sheets, curled up with his back toward me.

"Can I sleep here?"

He started breathing easier, and I figured he did not need an answer. Slowly, the room filled up with a cloud of breathed-out alcohol and cigar smoke.

"I can't sleep in that bed," he said. "The conjugal bed. All the sleep in it's been slept out. It's like when you use up all the hits a bat's got in it. Voices in the mattress wailing and carrying on. Like sleeping on a bed of nails."

"You don't need to explain," I told him.

The truth was, I did not want him to.

"I love you, Toadfish," he mumbled.

Then he was out cold, unmoving, and for a panicked instant I thought he was dead. The next morning, this morning, he was gone.

On the practice mound below the front-row rail where I sat, my father put his foot on the rubber and started to throw. Easy warm-up pitches. After a couple dozen he began throwing harder, getting into a game groove. But it was there again, that strange tick: after every pitch he flicked his head irritably, as if he had a horsefly in his face. But he was the only one on the field afflicted by flies. Imaginary or not, they threw him off his rhythm. He went into his windup, then midway through it, he forgot what to do next, or what he was there for, or where that little white round thing in the palm of his right hand was supposed to go. How could a man forget something he'd been doing ever since he was a kid?

Then my eyes pulled away from him and I saw that the other players were giving him plenty of room, as if he were a time bomb, and they had no intention of getting hit when it blew. Leathery old Hector Torres was standing behind the mound, watching. I had never seen someone look that worried in a baseball park before.

Suddenly a man in an old-fashioned, shiny black suit came walking out of the outfield toward us, up the foul line. A black suit on a baseball diamond on a hot day. The man looked as though he had lost his way and somehow wandered onto the playing field of Grayson Stadium. But by the way he marched toward us, raising little clouds of lime dust with every step, you could see he knew exactly where he was going. As he came near I recognized that parchment-colored hair and and brick-red face: it was Jefferson Marster.

He walked up onto the pitching mound. As he did, I saw Hector Torres and the rest of the Indians players fade away. Grandfather Marster had a grim look on, like a manager about to yank a young starter who's gotten shellacked in the first inning. My father stood there with his hands on his hips, holding on to the ball, just staring at Jefferson Marster like he wasn't sure he was real or not.

Marster hooked a finger in my father's shirt. Then the old man cleared his throat like a politician about to unburden himself of a speech. He must have been rehearsing his lines all the way down from Pinky Marster's tavern to the Stadium, and nothing was going to stop him from delivering them.

"I am forced to retail alcohol to earn my keep and sustain those who depend on me, which includes you," the old man declared. "But that does not mean I will abide a son-in-law who advertises his failing and failures and those of his family in my establishment. If you want to drink, fine — it is a man's privilege, some even say his duty. But at least learn *how* to drink! And that means not carrying on in that dismal philosophical way of yours until all hours of the night. Do you understand me?"

Without waiting for an answer, Jefferson Marster unhooked his finger from my father's shirt and proceeded to march back across foul territory, past the dugout, where the railings were low. He put one hand on the rail and vaulted himself over.

"Spry old fucker," said Hector Torres, who had moved up behind my father on the mound. He spat a rope of tobacco juice into the grass. "Don't let him bother your concentration."

My father was standing in his hands-on-hips position, staring at the spot where old man Marster had so recently stood. He was transfixed.

Then he shook the imaginary gnats out of his face.

"Shit, does he think his is the only bar around? There's lots of wells in this town!"

6

I left the park, knowing I had witnessed a public shaming. It seemed that everything on this damned island had to be played out for other people's eyes. In a ball park, a sporting establishment, even over the radio waves.

I retreated to the house on Hurt's Landing in a state of expectation. Since there was waiting to be done, I did it the best way I knew how. I grabbed my glove off the front porch and smelled the good smell of neat's-foot oil, which can make an S & H Green Stamps glove into a real instrument.

I went around to the side of the house where there weren't any gutters and commenced throwing the hardball up on the roof, watching for it to come down against the sun, then gloving it when it did. Not much of a game. I did not make a very entertaining teammate.

After a dozen throws my mother came out on the front porch and stuck her head over the rail.

"Boy, my nerves are a little frayed this afternoon. Would you mind playing with that ball of yours somewhere else?"

I caught the ball as it bounded off the roof. Gloved it flawlessly. Defense always was my strong point. Then I looked up, past my mother, and saw what I knew was going to come. She knew it, too. It occurred to me then that she had probably put old Jefferson Marster up to it. My father was striding along the Lazaretto Road in our direction. It was a wondrous and terrible sight to see in the soft green midafternoon light under the live oaks: a man dressed in a white baseball uniform with the word *Indians* written across the chest, his uniform spotless except for two sweat circles under his arms and another triangle pointing down across his chest, his glove tucked under his arm and his cleats scraping on the asphalt pavement, and this, with no baseball park in sight to make a man in an Indians uniform make sense in the landscape. I wanted time to stop, but it would not. This inevitable thing was going to happen.

"Excuse me, son," my mother said.

She turned away, very deliberately, to keep from hurrying, then went on up the stairs to her room to wait.

I threw the ball up one more time onto the roof. I stood there in my defensive crouch by the side of the house, smelling neat's-foot oil and leather, and my own sweat going sour with fear on my body. My father closed the space between us and stood behind me. I looked up at him, and the ball came rolling hard off the roof and caught me in the cheek. A tear blurred my eye on the side that got hit.

"Never take your eyes off the ball, son," he told me.

Then he stepped around in front of me.

"We won, Toadfish."

What game was it? I wondered to myself. He reached into the narrow pants pocket of his uniform. There was green money in there, a whole lot of it, all rolled up and crumpled every which way. He put some into my glove. Three tens and a lucky two-dollar bill with the corners torn off.

"Distinct Intent," my father told me. "Sixteen to one. Just like in my dream."

Then he spun around and went up the front stairs onto the porch. I heard the slap of leather on wood as he threw his glove onto the porch floor. A bad sign from a man who taught me that a player's best friend is his glove, a thing made of the living skin of an animal. The screen door banged shut as he went upstairs.

I threw the ball high up onto the roof and flipped down my imaginary pair of sunglasses. Let me play a kid's game, please, just one last time, I prayed to the gods that ran Hurt's Landing. But they were as indifferent as ever. Before that ball had time to come down I heard my father slam the upstairs bedroom door against the wall so hard I could feel the metal screws yawning out of the hinges. My mother was screaming, "Zeke, Zeke, don't do that, you'll hurt your hand!" He started in yelling something about *you people*, and I knew he meant the Marsters. Then came the sound I feared would come, the one that no scream followed: my mother falling heavily against the commode in her little alcove upstairs where she prettied up, and the vanity glass shattering. The words *dead weight* flashed inside my head in red, explosive light, as if it had been me getting hit. I gloved the ball off the roof and sidearmed it right back up, too hard this time, and it was gone, down the far slope of the roof and into the neighbor's forsythia.

I stood there for a while till I caught myself at it. Standing there like a damned post, as if Father Dooley's God was going to personally reach down out of heaven and throw the ball back to me from the other side of the house, or some such miracle like that, that might save this day from being the worst one I had ever known. When I circled in front of the house my father was standing there on the porch, still in his Indians uniform. His face was unnaturally calm, but underneath it I could hear him taking short, sharp breaths to catch his wind. He was holding his winnings in his pitching hand.

"Thirty-two hundred green American dollars. Do you know how much that is? I've got to get to some place where I can't spend this shit."

He was talking to himself. Then he looked up and talked to me.

"Let's go for a little ride in the boat."

"I'll get the gear."

"We're not going fishing. We're just going for a little ride."

I tossed my mitt up on the porch. It landed next to his. I'd find that ball in the bushes some other day.

My father cranked up the 10 HP Evinrude and I sat down on the bait well. Water slopped back and forth on the floor, and I bailed it out with the half Clorox bottle. The bateau needed a good caulking. He revved up the motor, tipped it in, and we turned into the Lazaretto. I looked over my shoulder at the house. There was nothing moving inside, nobody watching us go. Then it disappeared around the bend in the river. Farewell, dock. Farewell, Marster foundation.

With the Evinrude laboring and putting out more noise than power, there was not much room for talk. It was low tide, and my father had his hand tight on the stick to keep us in the middle of the channel and off the mud flats.

"Distinct Intent," my father shouted over the Evinrude after a while. "Sixteen to one. Fucking Peep, he nearly choked on his fucking pink tie."

My father patted his pants pocket. "It kind of makes a wad, doesn't it?"

"What are you going to buy with it?"

"I'm not going to buy anything. I'm going to let it sit in my pocket until my pocket feels what it's like to have money in it. I've got to get to a place where there can't be any spending."

"What about here?"

I pointed at the wet fields of marsh grass all around, and on the hammocks, the scrawny rat palms waving and rattling in the wind.

He laughed. "Good choice, Toadfish!" Then his face got dark. "But you've got to dock sooner or later."

We started across the widening in the river where the Lazaretto and a few other creeks merge with the Channington River. To the left and inland is Savannah. To the right, the Channington takes all this water and empties it into Wassaw Sound and the ocean. We went straight. It looked as though we were going to run right onto dry land, or what passes for dry around here. Then my father eased up on the

Evinrude and steered us toward the mouth of a narrow creek. I did not think we would make it at low tide, but when we swung around the sandbar that guarded the entrance, I saw that the creek was deep and quiet, even at low water.

"What are you going to do with your money?" he asked me.

I took it as a joke at first, what with him having thirty-two hundred dollars in his pocket and me thirty-two. But he stared me in the face until I had to answer.

"I don't have anything to spend money on."

But that was a stall, or a lie, or both, because what I really wanted was a boat and a good outboard, but those things cost a little more than thirty-two dollars. So I said the next-best thing.

"Maybe I'll buy me a cheap guitar."

"A guitar?"

"Yes, sir. To sing with."

"You know how to sing?"

I could tell he didn't believe me, and why should he? "Listen to this," I told him, and I let loose my best Little Richard howl, which blew a cloud of snowy egrets right out of a nest nearby.

"Where did you learn to do that?"

My father was applauding, but underneath he looked a little uneasy. He had discovered that there was a stranger in his midst.

"I taught myself. Well, that's not really true. I heard the old train caller do it when I was waiting on you to come back from up North."

"And you went and did what he did?"

"It's not quite that simple."

"You're a crazy kid," he let me know. "You never told me you could do something like that."

"You never asked."

"But shit," he went on, "that sound kind of makes my brainpan rattle!"

He steered us through the shallow creek with the propellor all but churning up the muddy bottom. In his concentration, his face turned dark as swamp water.

RAT PALMS

"I'm sorry about the way this is turning out," he said. "I accepted to be Northerner in the South. I frequented the Baptists, and that's not easy for a Catholic who's used to forgiveness being as close as the nearest confessional door. I hate those naked church halls of theirs, all stripped bare! But I took it all, but no man can win against these Marsters. You can fight them, and you might win a temporary victory that'll cost you more than it'll cost them, but you can't beat them. When I went up to the Bigs I thought I was through with them till the season ended. Then I got sent down again!"

He stamped his foot on the bateau bottom and the little craft rocked. He was holding the side of his head where he'd gotten beaned.

"This fucking headache! Your mother's old man gave me this headache!"

"That beanball hurt you! I know it did!"

"Not as bad as it hurt the helmet." He tried to laugh it off. "You may not understand this till later, or you may never understand it if you're lucky, but it's always better to be the guy that gets hit, instead of the one doing the hitting."

Then my father shook away a cloud of imaginary gnats.

"The past is killing me — it'll kill you, too, if you don't watch out. Marsters every fucking place, leaving their little monuments all over town like a bunch of dry old turds. A Marster did this, a Marster did that, there's a Marster family plot you'll get a shot at if you die in time before it gets filled up. Tell you what, Timmy," he pushed on, "I know where we need to go. A place where we don't need to spend money. We're going to go to a place where people live in the present. Or if they do live in the past, their past is so past it's turned into something else entirely."

"Where's that? Doesn't sound like it could be around here."

"But it is, Toadfish, it is!" My father had switched into sudden jubilation. I was afraid he would start jumping up and down and hollering and capsize us into this mucky water. "The place is called Callibogee Island."

"Callibogee? Isn't that across the ship channel? Do you know how deep that channel is?"

"It doesn't matter how deep the water is, long as you stay on top of it. A man can drown in a saucer of milk. Shit, Timmy, I don't know how to swim, either! Not that it would make much difference in that channel. You just *picture* how deep they got it dredged out and you'll head straight for the bottom! Crabs'll eat you right up. So when we cross the channel, you just keep your ass good and tight on that bait-well cover so the ocean doesn't sneak up through it and start licking our behinds!"

He gave the Evinrude as much gas as it wanted and we moved out of that nameless creek into wider water. We headed through the Elba Cut and into the channel and the Carolina side.

"Look at how beautiful it is!" He gestured all around. "You won't find any Marsters out here — that's why I love it. There's no brass spittoons or cigar cutters out here. They've got the most beautiful nature in the world and they hate it, every last leaf of it, every stalk of marsh grass. It scares them — just the way they're scared of the coloreds. If I'd had some nature like this when I was a kid, I would have been somebody else entirely. I might even have had a better curveball!"

"Then why don't we just stay in here and forget about crossing the channel?"

"You want to be a singer? You want to have that guitar?"

"Well . . . sure."

"Then you've got to get out there and cross that goddamned channel!"

He goosed the motor and the front of the bateau raised up. We were getting close to the channel, I could tell by the way the water was chopping up and the wind freshening. How deep was the channel? Thirty, forty, fifty feet? If a one-story house was ten feet, could you put a five-story building in it and still not see the chimney? The water turned sea green and colder, smelling of the hostile Atlantic. I did what my father told me to: I kept my rear end good and tight on the bait-well cover. I didn't want anything from the deep coming up into the boat.

"You scared, Timmy?" he shouted over the wind and the outboard.

"What do you expect?"

Sure, I was scared. And happy, too, that he was calling me Timmy finally, instead of that fool nickname Toadfish. We needed fifty feet of water below us to get that much done.

"Then you just sing us across! Sing or we'll never make it!"

And I did. *Callibogee*, I sang, so we would get there. *La. Za. Ret. To.*, I sang, so my river would make us a road across this strange water. *Skid. A. Way.*, I sang, because I had no words of my own yet, and all I could sing were river names, and pretty soon I ran out of those. I figured my father would whoop and holler and applaud and profane my singing, but he did not. His face was dark and intent under his baseball cap and he had such a hold on the rudder stick that his fingers were white, and I saw he was scared, too. Maybe even more scared than I was, because he knew more of what was under that fifty feet of water.

"Sing, baby, sing," he pleaded with me in a voice so soft it went underneath the racket of the outboard to reach my ears.

"I don't know what to sing any more," I said weakly.

But my father didn't hear me, or else he pretended he didn't. I had to keep on singing. I had no more river names, so I sung marsh names and island names, but I did not sing the Isle of Hope. I sang *Half Moon*, *Runaway Negro*, *Burntpot*, *Cabbage Island*, *Romerly* and *Whitemarsh*. *Bloody Point*, *Tybee Roads*, *Thunderbolt*, *Sandfly*, *Rose Dhu*, *Beaulieu* and *Petty Gauke*. And *Callibogee*. I sang *Callibogee* so hard and so long that we actually started getting there. The island materialized, low in the water like an overloaded barge, with the great line of oaks marking the edge it made against the Atlantic. As we came upon the island I knew I had crossed through moments of the purest kind of happiness there was to know, the kind beyond reflection.

I did not want to dock. Docking meant sharing my father again. Being called Toadfish instead of Timmy. But we had to dock sooner or later. And the dock my father was steering us toward was the poorest, meanest-looking landing I had ever seen. A couple of poles jammed into the mud, with two or three planks lashed to them. A bass boat tied up on the end of a rope. A wide, grazed-out field where chickens were scratching and two Creole hogs fought over something one of them had rooted out of the ground. On the other side of the field were a half dozen stilt houses. Was this the place where the past was so past it had been transformed into something else?

"Callibogee," my father spoke.

For him, it was like a conjure word.

I saw someone come walking out of a stilt house, across the field and onto the landing, and when the figure was silhouetted against the sky I saw it was a woman. She had a turban wrapped around her head and on top of that a straw hat. She was tall enough to be a man, and thin enough to be a saint starving in the desert. She watched us ease up to the dock. My father was real gentle when we touched it. He didn't drive the bateau halfway up onto dry land the way he did at Hurt's Landing.

He cut the motor and tilted it out of the water.

"Mr. Justice," the woman said in a gravelly voice.

He climbed out of the bateau and I scrambled out after him.

"How did you know it was me? You always say you can't see a thing without your glasses. How come you ain't wearing the ones I brought you?"

"Maybe I can't see faces, but I sure can see colors. How many white men you think come out here?"

He laughed proudly.

"I brought my boy along with me this time. Timmy, this here is Mrs. Stafford. Her people all but own this island. They never were slaves. They had the sense to jump that boat before it hit Savannah. And they'll never be half slaves, either, not like your Grandfather Marster's Negroes who come shuffling around the side door once a year for some Santy Claus."

Mrs. Stafford led us off the dock and across the stubbly field.

RAT PALMS

Her silly, high straw hat had a kind of rightness here. A friendly she-goat came bounding up, with a swarm of flies interested in her hind end. Her teats were swinging as low as the sweet chariot, in dire need of a milking. Mrs. Stafford cajoled her, then gave her a kick in the ribs, and she skittered off to gnaw on some spiny bushes. The Stafford lady was as tall as my father, and wrapped in some kind of shapeless dress that could have been sewn together out of burlap bags. But there were three things I could see, and maybe some others I couldn't, that made her beautiful. Her color, her hands and her straw hat. She was copper-colored, maroon, some color that a name hadn't been invented for yet. And her hands: rough as a shrimper's, but with fingers long and tapering like church candles. Piano player's hands, they would have said back on the Isle of Hope. But here, there did not look to be any pianos.

She shouted something in the direction of her house. I didn't understand a word of it. Then she turned to us and spoke in an approximation of our language.

"Let me go into my kitchen and see what I can fix up for you men."

She strode away, and my father watched her. I watched him watching her, but I did not neglect to watch her for myself, too. We were like three players on a playing field, in some kind of game I didn't know the rules for. A six-foot-tall woman the color of a copper shield in the sun, wearing a turban with a straw hat riding on top, a woman thin and taut but not dry in the spinsterish sort of way you see on the Isle when one of the women there falls away from life. A man in a baseball uniform with thirty-two hundred dollars in his pants pocket, who happens to be my father, and who is balking at an invisible cloud of gnats and fleas gathered around his face. A man who has hit his wife, and has now brought his boy with him to a place of past-beyond-past, and that boy is me, a secretive, loathsome creature from the deep. Secretive, because you have to be that way on Hurt's Landing, for reasons too numerous to tell. Loathsome — it is harder to say why. The loathsomeness is of the place itself. Its hiddenness, for wasn't the way of our island to hide — or rather half hide, then half disclose — everything that drove you, and that you needed? Even the name of our river and the very form of its fish partook of loathsomeness. Nothing escaped. And since nothing did, wasn't it better to revel in it?

"This place is paradise," my father said to me in a low, confidential voice, as if he was afraid someone would swoop down and grab it from him. "No Marster will ever know Callibogee. They're all too scared of the Negroes. Shit, you can't blame them for being scared. Who wouldn't be scared of a bunch of people you've got hiding up in your woods, people you only see when you need a chore done or when they need you to go bail for them downtown? Thank God for them, I say! With them, a man can take his pleasure without having to sneak around and feel ashamed about himself because there's someone watching."

We walked idly up to Mrs. Stafford's shack, and sat down on a bench that seemed designed for keeping an eye on the landing. The bench was in full sun, and the wood gave off a sweet resin smell.

"But there's always someone watching," I told my father. "Even if you quit the Isle of Hope, and come to a place like this."

He cast an eye up to the clear, empty sky. "Of course there's always someone watching. But I've worked it out as far as *that* is concerned."

But I wasn't talking about God, or conscience, or the soul, or however you wanted to call that inconvenient visitor we seem to have lodged permanently within us. I was talking about *me*. Me, Timmy Justice, the reflective, ever-studious toadfish.

Above the field, bluebottle flies buzzed around the trails of chicken squirt. We inhabited the silence for a while. Sharing it with us was the matter of what had happened upstairs between my father and my mother. But we had come to Callibogee, the place without past, for the express purpose of not talking about the event.

Mrs. Stafford came out of her house and we both sat up stiff and straight, as if we had been discovered napping at church. She set down a big plate of deviled blue crabs and next to it an old-fashioned green glass bottle with a porcelain stopper. She was wearing her glasses now.

"Your favorite," she said to my father.

"Now this is worth crossing that cold green channel for," he told me. "You'll see."

The crabs were on fire with cayenne pepper, and better than anything I had ever tasted at any church social on the Isle of Hope. They made you want to drink something to wash the cayenne off your tongue, and I did. I poured some of whatever was inside the bottle into a chipped teacup. The stuff was sweet on top, but after you swallowed it, it turned bitter on your tongue and the taste stayed that way, even after the wine had gone down into your belly. I could not imagine why anyone would willingly drink something that tricked you that way.

"That's the best scuppernong wine you'll ever have," my father informed me.

He drank down his cupful, and it seemed to revive him. That, and Mrs. Stafford's return. He watched me sip at mine.

"That's your very first drink, son. What do you think?"

"Starts off sweet and turns bitter," I told him.

"Ain't that the truth!"

When our plates and cups and the bottle were empty, my father asked the Stafford lady, "Are you still charging the same thing for this feast?"

"It'll cost you what it always does. One dollar and fifty cents. We try and stay the same for you."

He patted down his pockets for change. He didn't have any. All he had was the wad.

He peeled off a hundred-dollar bill from it and gave it to Mrs. Stafford. She looked at it as if it were a cottonmouth snake.

"You know damn well I have no use for this kind of thing on Callibogee," she scolded him. "It only causes trouble. The bigger it is, the more trouble it causes."

"I don't have anything smaller right now," my father said. "You know how it is: feast or famine. The horses gave it to me. The way I look at it, even at a hundred bucks for a mess of crabs and a bottle of scuppernong wine, it's still cheaper out here than what it would have cost me back in town."

Mrs. Stafford folded the bill into little squares.

"I'll set this aside for you, for the day when you need it. You'll probably be needing it before I do. You see, I understand there's a lot of big money going to come down this way."

"Yeah? Something I should know about?"

The Stafford woman shrugged. "They say they're going to turn Hilton Head into a resort."

"How can they do that? The place is nothing but a swamp!"

"Silly fool! They'll fill in the swamp! They'll fill it in with bills like this one." She showed the folded-up hundred-dollar bill in the palm of her hand. "Money does what it wants to. You can't tell money, Don't go on that island, you'll get your feet wet. Money'll just buy itself a new pair of high boots."

"But that's Hilton Head," my father said. "What's that got to do with you?"

"I own a little part of it," Mrs. Stafford let on.

"You own? You own it?"

"Not all of it," she said modestly. "Just thirty-eight acres."

"You own thirty-eight acres on Hilton Head?"

My father was practically shouting. I was pretty surprised myself. Yankee developers from all over the world were fighting it out over there to see who was going to own what, and how many golf courses they could put in. Over there, pretty soon a hundred-dollar bill wouldn't even buy you lunch.

"What are you doing with all that land?"

"I got my stepson over there, him and his people. They got a pig on it, like here, and chickens. White folks want to put a tennis court on his pig field."

"Do you know what each of those acres is worth?"

"Mr. Justice, don't you understand anything about money? You're supposed to be white! Do you think those folks are going to give me and my people money for my pig field and my chicken-scratch ground?"

She showed the square wad of green paper money again.

"This is the most money I'm ever going to see. They won't pay us nothing. They decide that the land is worth so much, because they want to put a golf course on it, and then they raise the taxes to what it's worth to them, no matter if there ain't nothing but a pig on it. When we can't pay those taxes, because we don't have money and never will, no matter how many acres we've got, we'll have to sell that land to pay our taxes. They get the land, no sweating for them."

"Can't you do anything about it?" my father pleaded.

Mrs. Stafford laughed.

"Guess I'll have that stepson of mine back on Callibogee again, with all his damned kids."

She got up and cleared away the crab shells and threw them in the garden for fertilizer. It was hard to picture golf courses and tennis courts springing up where rooting hogs and stilt houses and the great, green wall of oaks stood. Money was restless, it seemed. It would go to the oddest spots to spend itself.

Miraculously, more scuppernong appeared in my cup. I was getting used to the dirty bittersweet trick it played on me. The sun was lowering and the sky was going from burned, hazy lead to deeper blue. My father rose with his cup in his hand and went into the house. I felt the heat leaving the wooden bench and flowing into my body, turning me to sun-softened tar. I heard a shriek of laughter from inside the house, then Mrs. Stafford went *"Shh!"* like she was shushing a child, but it was all too distant to care about. I knew a long and hostile passage stood between Callibogee and Hurt's Landing, back where they had electricity and such things, and that there was the minor issue of where we would sleep tonight, but all that had stopped mattering. Which is in itself a luxury.

So these are the effects of drink, I reflected. Now what happens? Do I begin to belong to others, as Evangeline warned? Do I invent imaginary baseball games on radio stations for all to hear? There are a lot more shameful things than that, I decided.

Of course, there is the genteel way to be when drinking, to polish and fashion and release fine words all day long, the way Evangeline did. Somehow, I didn't reckon I'd go that way.

7

I opened my eyes to the pig field under the early evening sky and, across the field, my father on the landing with two Callibogee people. I was cold, but that cannot be, not in early May in the low country.

I stood up, took a couple of steps forward and caught my foot in a gopher hole. This is what they mean by "befuddled by drink." Sleeping away the day, missing the object of my study. I had lost things. I felt cheated. The worst part was that I had cheated myself.

My father looked up and saw me as I crossed the field. He waved and called out in that enthusiastic way of his, "Hey, Toadfish, we're going hunting!"

He was with an old man and a boy my age, maybe younger. The bateau tied up next to ours must have belonged to them. I took a few steps onto the shaky planks of the landing.

"Going to catch us an alligator crocodile! Going with Mr. Otis here, and this boy, Tabby."

"Which one you want to catch?" The old man laughed.

His hair was pure white, and he was toothless. He was tinkering with the little outboard. On the bench next to him were some coiled-up lengths of rope and an ancient, mean-looking shotgun.

"Whichever one I see first," my father joked with him. "I don't know the difference anyhow!"

"Don't have no crocs down here," the boy said.

"Ain't we going back home?" I asked my father.

He looked up. It was that time of twilight when the sun has set but the sky is still full of light. He looked up as if gauging that light, and I thought he would tell me next that it was too late to go back across the channel and through the cuts and creeks in a bateau with a 10 HP engine hanging from it. But he did not. He did not make any excuses at all.

"You're whining, son," he told me. Then: "Did you have a nice nap up there?"

"Did I miss anything?"

"Just time passing by, boy. Just time passing by."

The two Negroes in the bateau laughed, Otis first, then the boy, to imitate him. The boy Tabby had a lantern on a hook up front and he was trying to comfort a whimpering hound dog that did not seem to like boats much. On the floor of the bateau were all manner of hooks and more coils of rope.

"Say you a prayer," Mr. Otis said.

"A prayer," my father repeated.

Mr. Otis yanked on the engine cord and the thing coughed to life.

"The power of prayer," my father pointed out when the engine was idling at a reasonable rate.

The outboard could not have been much more powerful than a lawn-mower engine. Maybe it had actually been one, on a white man's property on the mainland somewhere, before it found its way out to Callibogee and this man's bateau. I understood I was to get in and sit on the center bench of the boat, next to my father. Tabby used a pole to push us off from the landing, and we were under way.

We headed up the Hilton Head River toward the back-river side of Callibogee. There, they had the same puzzle of creeks and marshes as we did along the Lazaretto, but a hundred times more deserted, with no city of Savannah to stream the fishermen and picnickers and shrimpers into them. Where the Hilton Head River flows inland, into the low country, we cut right, along the Callibogee back river, into a maze of creeks so marshy we could not have made them if it hadn't been spring tide. The oaks hung low on both sides, and we lost the sky. The water was still and flat. No one spoke, and I understood it would be a mistake if I did. It was like being in church, but with the pulpit empty, and no one to lead or preach, and no moral to the story. My father drew out a pint bottle and passed it to Mr. Otis at the rudder. They drank in silence. There wasn't any talk about the whiskey the way there usually is, and how it burned their guts and mixed their brains up. When the pint came back my father put his lips where the Negro man's lips had been, which is something you would not see done at Hurt's Landing. The look in his eyes was as dark as marsh water, and when he raised the narrow little pocket-shaped bottle for a second pull, and I saw a tremor run through his hand. I was terrified to be there. Terrified, and proud.

"Gator be down there, last time," Mr. Otis spoke from the rudder after a while. "Little one, ought to be easy to take, that's what you want."

He cut the engine and it coughed black smoke. We drifted further in on the running tide. My father and Mr. Otis took their oars and steered us down the channel the old man had pointed out. My father was transfixed by something I had never seen before. Fear and eagerness, the need for something to happen.

Mr. Otis placed his oar on the bateau floor. My father did the same. They both did it without making a sound.

"Now, Tabby," the old man whispered.

The boy struck a wood match and lit the kerosene lantern. He hung it from a spoke hooked in the front of the bateau so the light swung low over the water. Five seconds later the fool mullet started jumping every which way at the light, and half of them ended up at our feet. The hound dog snapped at them as they flip-flopped on the floor of the bateau, and my father pitched a few of them out where they belonged.

Then the boy set the hound dog on his knees and gave the thing's ears such a yank I thought they would tear clean away from its skull. The hound squealed like someone had rocked a rocking chair over its tail, then it started in howling, a long sad howl that brought all kinds of protest from the marsh. Then just as quick he let go of the hound's ears and started petting it and whispering its name to calm it down.

Whatever it was, it worked. In the quiet that came up over the dog's howl, we heard a slippery, muddy noise and a soft splash. The gator was in the water, swimming.

Even the mullets stopped jumping.

The lantern hissed above the waterline. The gator swam closer, invisible in the water. Mr. Otis and Tabby picked up their coils of rope, and Mr. Otis got his shotgun ready. It was the only comforting thing in that bateau besides the motor to get us out of there, and even it couldn't be counted on.

Then six feet away, dead ahead, the gator broke the surface. The thing's eyes were as big as half-dollars, and they were blood red in the lantern light. Tabby gave the hound's ears another pull and dangled the squirming, yelping dog low over the edge. The gator lifted its head out of the water and unhinged its jaw for the kill, and I got set to see what a hound dog bit in half looks like.

But it didn't happen. Mr. Otis whizzed a rope past my ear, and the lasso closed around the gator's head. The gator twisted back and bit at the rope, but that only served to tighten the noose. As it fought, its tail lifted out of the water. Tabby dumped the hound off his knees onto the floor, then he threw his lasso and caught the gator's tail. He and the old man had a lasso around each end, and they flipped that gator and crisscrossed their ropes till the poor bastard was arched belly out like a semicircle right off the side of the bateau. Hooked on itself, like it wanted to swallow its tail. Then

RAT PALMS

Tabby reached right down for the gator and I thought *What the hell?* and he started in stroking its green, scaly belly. The gator eased up and fell asleep, just like that.

It was hypnotized. I had heard of such things happening, but I never believed they were real.

Nor will I ever forget the sound of a human hand running over a gator belly in a dark swamp off Callibogee. That was some new music for me.

Then Mr. Otis got the bateau motor running, and there was an extra one of us on the trip out of that swamp. There are sounds under sounds, I learned that night. A soft sound will travel under or even through a louder one when it's compelling enough. On the way back to the Stafford woman's landing, through the outboard's racket, I clearly heard the dry, rasping scratch of Tabby's hand over the hypnotized gator's belly, if a dry sound is possible in this world of water. The pint went back and forth between my father and Mr. Otis until there was no more inside the bottle. Nobody spoke, not with a representative of the dinosaur world in temporary suspension, grappled to the side of the bateau, with a pair of jaws on it that would bite right through the side of the boat if it awakened from its enchantment in the wrong frame of mind. We ran without lights, the lantern doused to save fuel and keep the mullets out of our face and from landing on the gator, because a counterstroke against the grain of its skin would wake it up. The moon was high and icy white by the time we came out onto the Hilton Head River. My father produced another pint from his Indians warm-up jacket and offered it to Mr. Otis. He waved it off with a tap on the side of his forehead. My father stashed the bottle in his overstretched pocket again.

The old man pushed the outboard to the highest it would go, and the louder the motor racket, the more insistent the gator scratch was. Like one of those dog whistles that let out a high-pitched scream that will drive a hound crazy, while a man standing next to it won't hear or feel a thing.

We came in sight of Stafford's Landing. Across the water the stilt houses were lit with yellow lanterns. Mr. Otis let out a high, yelping noise from the back of his throat, which sounded like a dog getting skinned alive. But it worked, because half a minute later an answer came from the Landing. Someone dashed across the dark pig field swinging a lantern. A half dozen more lights darted out of the stilt houses. The people were hanging their lanterns on the rusty hooks that jutted out of the dock to guide us home. What would have to stand for home, tonight.

We nosed up toward the landing all outlined in lantern light like Christmas candles.

"What you catch?" a woman's voice called. It was Mrs. Stafford's.

Mr. Otis answered in words I could not understand.

"Tabby, he all right?"

"I be scratching belly," Tabby said proudly.

"Keep on scratching!"

A voice howled with laughter, and someone clapped his hands. The planks of the dock shook and the lanterns swung.

My father tossed the rope out and we tied up. In the lantern light the gator's skin was cracked burnt sienna, like an old painting at the Telfair Museum, but a thousand, ten thousand times older, since the gator was a messenger from the dinosaurs.

I skittered out of the bateau and onto the rickety landing, raised up by Mrs. Stafford's hand. I must have held her hand a moment too long because she looked down at me, stern and penetrating. God only knows what she was thinking, though probably even He wouldn't know, for the only minds He could read into are skinny little white sinning ones like mine.

She looked away.

"Scratch, Tabby," she said softly.

Two island men were lifting the tied, arched gator on its ropes out of the bateau and onto the dock. Mr. Otis had his shotgun trained on its head. Tabby was underneath it, still in the boat, unperturbed, keeping up the belly-scratch rhythm, like a man playing drums on the beach in a hurricane.

"You ready?" asked Tabby from below.

And this is what happened, though I still don't believe it, even as I tell it. When the men had laid the gator out on the planks, Tabby left off scratching its belly and the gator sprung through its ropes, open-jawed and awake and ready to prey. At that very moment Otis blasted it with his shotgun in that dumb spot between its peeper eyes, where its brain ought to have been if it had one.

"Gator wake up to die," Mr. Otis summed up after the explosion had faded.

My father was still in the bateau below. He started clambering out after Tabby.

"Good work," he said. "The hide'll be perfect."

The Callibogee people had gathered in a half circle around the gator. The animal had the top of its head blown off. Something clay-colored was seeping out and running between the planks and into the water, to the joy of the loathsome, bottom-feeding toadfish, no doubt. The people were quiet, as if they were saying a prayer for its soul, or thanking their stars they had not been born alligators, at least not this one.

My father started to cross that half circle.

"You best stop." Otis motioned with his shotgun. "He no dead."

My father looked down at the gator.

"I don't know. He looks pretty dead to me."

You had to agree with him. An alligator with the top of its skull blown off and the contents therein emptying peacefully in lantern light does look pretty dead.

"He no dead," Tabby repeated.

"I've got my superstitions," my father said. "You've got yours."

That was the last cavalier, off-hand, jaunty, routine remark I ever heard him say. He was intent on crossing that dead gator. He almost made it. And the thing was dead as far as anyone could see, but when he had put one foot over it, the goddamned gator whipped its tail back and forth like someone had plugged it into a wall socket. The scales on a gator tail are sharp as knife blades, and they caught my father full in the shin, where there is hardly any meat to cover the bone.

He howled and went down in a heap. Mr. Otis pulled a shell out of his lumberjack shirt and reloaded his shotgun. He put the barrel right up against the gator's spine halfway down its back and blasted it again.

The shot set the Callibogee people howling along with my father. It was the strangest lamentation, like having the prophets right there on that dock with me. In the middle of their howling I heard Mrs. Stafford say to Otis, "It wasn't his fault," and I wondered if she meant the alligator, or my father.

"That be a bad gator," Tabby told her. "He never dead."

"Shush up, boy. Shush up your conjuring all the time."

I pushed through the Callibogee people to my father's side. He was trying to stand up, but I knew that would be a bad idea. I kneeled down next to him to keep him from doing it. His eyes were wild and he was pressing his Indians pant leg against the wound.

"My pitching!" he was crying. "Toadfish, it's the end of my goddamned pitching!"

I grabbed him by the shoulders.

"It won't be the end. It doesn't have to be the end."

Mrs. Stafford kneeled down on the other side of him.

"Don't you worry now, Ezekial. Everybody knows I'm the best seamstress on this island. I'm going to sew you up so straight nobody ever know."

Mr. Otis found a fishing knife somewhere and stuck the point into my father's uniform pants, just below the knee. He slit the cloth down to the ankle. Blood was pulsing out of the wound, and at the heart of it I swore I could see something white, like smeared ivory. I must have screamed because I felt Mrs. Stafford's hand over my mouth.

"Boy, not now. He needs you," she said into my ear.

The men on the landing made a fireman's carry and moved my father across the pig field to Mrs. Stafford's shack. I caught up to them and held his leg straight to keep the bleeding down.

"Scuppernong wine!" he was shouting, real crazy-like. "Scuppernong, scuppernong, scuppernong wine!"

He was casting his head from side to side. His eyes were wide from the shock, but they narrowed down when he saw me running alongside him with the Callibogee men, holding his leg out straight like a splint.

"Scupper — !" He blinked once or twice. "Oh, Toadfish, you're there." There was a flash of shame in his eyes at being seen like this. "Ain't nothing, ain't nothing but a little cut, just a little bitty gator-tail slash. Shit, I didn't mean for things to turn out this way!"

"It's just shock, Daddy. Just shock making you talk that way."

"What way? What way?" he demanded.

We streamed into Mrs. Stafford's stilt house.

"Lay him on the big bed," Mrs. Stafford told the men.

They carried him into the bedroom and spread him out on the enormous bed there. It had a fine wooden carved headboard and a wrought-iron piece at the foot end with somebody's initials woven into the metal.

"Scuppernong wine!" he started in calling. "Scuppernong wine!"

One of the men found a bottle in the kitchen cupboard and laid it in his hand.

"Now you drink, and you shut up now!"

My father was upsetting these people. White folks were not supposed to have misfortunes and turn crazy, especially not on this island where the Callibogee people might be held responsible. Besides, hadn't they told him not to step over that gator?

Mrs. Stafford was lurking over him with needle and thread. She shook her head.

"Too much blood. I can't see a thing."

Then she ordered everybody and nobody in particular, "Strip him down. Can't work with these rags on. Man catch pus and fever that way."

The men pulled off his baseball cleats and were admiring them, even though one was full to the wringing with blood. They struggled with his tight-fitting uniform pants, and in the process my father's undershorts rolled halfway down his thighs, and there was his pecker, all little and afraid looking, and I was embarrassed for him. He put his hand down there and weighed his balls and took to laughing out loud, and the men in the room laughed along with him.

Cursed be he that uncovereth his father's skirt. A lesson from the time of the Benedictines.

"Sew me up," he started to howl. "I'm ready, woman, so sew me up!"

Mercifully, Mrs. Stafford took the bottle out of his hand. "You ready to stop carrying on now and be a man?"

She poured a slug of scuppernong wine into the wound and he screamed. I gritted my teeth, because I know what alcohol in a cut does, no matter how good it is for you. Then Mrs. Stafford turned on the Callibogee men and waved her arms in the air as if she was shooing a flock of geese.

"Get out of here, all of you! What you looking at? You never seen a white man before? They all got blood, too!"

The room went quiet as a church, just like that. Everyone filed out.

"You, too," she said to Tabby, who was holding down my father's bad leg. "You too young to be here. Besides, you conjure. We be needing healers in here, not conjurers. Belly scratcher!"

Tabby skittered past me out the door.

Mrs. Stafford sat down on my father's foot to keep his leg still. She splashed the wound with water from a bedside pitcher mixed with her wine.

"There. We kill the germs. Now, don't you watch, Ezekial," she whispered to him. "First I give pain, then I heal you up. You don't like to rip, you can't sew, that's what my mama used to say."

She was humming to herself now, *Rip and sew, rip and sew, needle and thread*, going about her business, squeezing the lips of my father's flesh together and suturing them shut. Five minutes and it was over. She tied some lengths of cotton cloth around his leg to make a bandage, then turned down the bedside lantern. The room got smaller.

"Do you want to see your boy now?" she asked my father.

He must have nodded yes. She came toward me across the room to the doorjamb where I was leaning. Her shadow played big and dark over me.

"Go to him," she told me. "He needs you. He had his little crazy time, but now he's better. He's tired. He needs you."

I crossed the room to my father's bedside. She was right. Whatever had made him crazy had retreated. He was drained of it. Drained of everything. His face was gray.

"Timmy," he spoke.

"Yes."

"My fault. Shouldn't have taken that shortcut over that gator. Those old dead things can really rise up and kill you."

"Just like you told me on the way over here."

He smiled crookedly. "You remember everything." He paused. "You shouldn't, you know."

"I can't help it. People talk. I'm bound to listen."

"It's a curse," my father agreed.

I felt Mrs. Stafford's long fingers on my shoulder, shepherding me out of the bedroom. Don't rile up the patient, her fingers said.

"You're going to sleep here tonight," she told me once we were in the big front room. There was pity and kindness in her voice, something I had never heard before from a woman. "I give you the best bed. You sleep here. No haints'll come to bother you. I know them all by name. I call their names and they run. Tomorrow, you'll be back with your people."

She swung the lantern and lit up a stuffed mattress on a plank. That was the bed. Then she took my hand and made me feel a blanket folded neatly at the foot of it. It was rough, like a horse blanket, and heavy enough for a winter's night.

"You have this if you get cold, but I don't think you will be. Now, I want you to think sweet thoughts tonight. This is a peaceful place, most of the time."

I lay down on the bed with my clothes on. The mattress was stuffed with seaweed. It smelled of the ocean side of Callibogee, the good side where there was air and light and fresh wind. I turned my face to it and smelled the sea and sought sweet thoughts, as Mrs. Stafford had told me to do. People were forever telling me to think good thoughts, or no thoughts at all. But my assignment had been to reflect. It was one or the other, it seemed to me. Sweet thoughts and reflection did not visit hand in hand.

In any case, sweet thoughts were not abiding that night, and why should they be? I turned onto my back, put my hands behind my head and waited for Mrs. Stafford's haints to appear. Go ahead, copper lady, call them by name, scare them off if it gives you pleasure. Because they're your haints, you see, not mine. You don't find my kind of haints on an island like yours. Too bad; your kindly medicine won't help me a bit.

Must have been a haint woke me up. The perverse, ferreting haint of uncovering. It was the hollow of the night, the time you least want to wake up to. I heard the sea. The sea breathing, close by. I eased myself off the high bed and went toward the lighter patch in the darkness that the screen door made. The moon was way to the west, and the stars had come back over the ocean. I was not tempted to go out into the Callibogee darkness.

But the sea, I thought. The sea is too far across the pig field and down the end of the creek to hear so clearly.

I turned and faced the inside of Mrs. Stafford's house. There was lamplight in one of the rooms.

The sighing sound of the sea was close by now. I went to the doorway. The door was open, like all the doors in this house. Inside the room, I saw the endlessly long, bare, copper-colored back of the Stafford woman. She was squatting over my father, calling and cooing like a bird and humming to herself, as she had done when she was sewing. *How she can sing!* I thought, and closed my eyes to listen to her song, and when I opened them I saw my father's face behind her, tilted off to one side. His eyes were closed and his leg wasn't propped up the way it should have been, but there was no pain on his face. A little line of spittle was running out of the corner of his mouth, but he didn't seem to know or care. Then I realized that the two of them were fastened in the middle.

So this is love.

We forgot to be afraid crossing the ship channel on the way back the next morning. We came through the cuts and creeks in the silence imposed by the Evinrude. When we took the bend in the Lazaretto and came up to Hurt's Landing and our dock, my father said, "Timmy, your mother's going to be awful sore about us not coming back last night. If she asks you, you just tell her what happened. Tell her straight: the gator hunt, me getting cut, us not being able to get back."

I looked up at our dock, an accusing finger pointing into the Lazaretto.

"I will, sir," I promised him.

"Shit, I've even got the stitches to prove it! What am I worried about?"

There was plenty to be worried about. My father's skin was an alligator-green, suppurating color. And I was the boy who knew too much. We were quite a pair. On the crossing back, under a hazy sky and a fair-size chop in the water, he had put away a whole bottle of Mrs. Stafford's scuppernong wine before we even crossed to the Georgia side. "Goddamned stuff's got no guts to it!" he complained, and tossed the empty bottle into the channel.

You should have put a message in it first, I felt like telling him.

At Hurt's Landing, he limped up the steps that ran from the floating dock to the fixed one, still wearing his Indians uniform, but with one pant leg chopped off at the knee, and the other all blood-smeared, and the rest of the uniform reeking. I tied up the bateau and did all those things you have to do when you've been out on a boat for the last twenty-four hours. Did them with extreme, minute, time-consuming care.

Which did not spare me from Evangeline intercepting me at the doorway when finally I straggled up the dock and across the road to the house. She must not have gotten too far with my father. But there was always Timmy, a softer touch. I looked up at her guarding the door as I climbed the porch steps. Then looked away. She was wearing a shiner under her left eye. If there was ever a time for the Marster scuff, this was it. I took to studying the paint creases on the porch floor.

"What's the matter?" she demanded. "Ashamed to look your mother in the eye?"

"I looked at you," I told her. "I saw it. Now the both of you are hurt, okay?"

Like a trained bear, I recited my story. The hunt. The slash from the dead gator. The stitches. I told her all I figured I could afford to tell her.

"We had to spend the night over there on Callibogee. But now we're back."

I was getting to be an expert on studying what was underfoot. Porch floors, indifferently painted by hired help. Docks, sweating tar and creosote out of split wood. The tops of my sneakers. Fascinating things like that. My glove was right where I left it, next to my father's, underneath the porch swing. I edged sideways like a crab and swooped down and picked it up. With a little luck, my hardball would be waiting for me in the neighbor's forsythia bushes.

I made it as far as the first step.

"Timmy Justice!" my mother shouted.
All right, I said to myself. *I'll look at you.*
And I looked at her, good and hard. I saw the whole situation.
"I ain't your papa!" I shouted back at her.
Then I got out of there, down the stairs and out onto the road, as fast as I could.

8

I scuffed down the Lazaretto Road, past the empty ball fields. In the west the thunderclouds were building up and suturing together, preparing the storm. Early in the day for a big blow.

The drawbacks attached to a period of reflection were many. For starters, reflection separated you from other people. No one else was engaged in the practice, at least not around here. I suppose that was why Father Dooley gave me that sentence in the first place. A punishment that was sociable was no punishment at all. But I could already see it was not going to achieve its ends. These days and nights of reflection were driving me deeper to ground. I was becoming ever less suitable for the Academy.

I kicked along the road all the way to Shell Point. Everyone I saw was either going someplace with great conviction, or bad-eyeing me because I obviously wasn't going any place with any conviction. I got to the bend where the Lazaretto Road stops following the river and changes its name to Wormslow, then turns inland toward Sandfly Crossing and the mainland.

At the tip of Shell Point is Bud Bandy's marina. I walked up the gravel drive where all sorts of pickup trucks and cars were parked, two trucks, it seemed, for every person they had working in there.

RAT PALMS

Bud Bandy's was not a place of reflection. It was a place of talk, most of it big. Of talk, I say, not *speaking*. That suited me fine. On this morose afternoon, to tell the truth, I wanted to do anything but reflect.

Out in Bud Bandy's yard were all sorts of craft out of the water for repair, and empty trailers, and some sleek powerboats bobbing off the far end of the marina. Those boats meant money. Real money, not Marster money, which was only the memory of once having had it. Next to the powerboats, Bandy had a half a dozen bateaux for rent with little putt-putt motors.

I went into the office. Bud Bandy looked up when the screen door closed behind me.

"Hey, Timmy. Didn't you bring your old man?"

"No, sir."

He eyed me. "He all right?"

"Yeah. Well, not really. We went out gator hunting and he got his leg cut."

"Plumb cut off?"

"Just cut, Bud. Not cut off."

"Well, that's a good thing. He won't be down long, just you believe it. Indians need him too much. Shit, Timmy, wished I had a boy who cared whether I got a cut on my leg or not."

Bud Bandy's office was not quite like what a real office downtown would be. He had a desk by the window from which he could watch the work being done on his boats, the tide going in and out, and other important matters. In the room back of the office he had a few high stools and a plank that stood for a bar, and a cooler, and he was serving beer by the bottle in there. It was a semiprivate club. A neighborly version of Bo-Peep's.

I scuffed around his office, watching him pound on an adding machine. Finally, he got nervous with me in the room and said, "Why don't you go on in back? There's people you know there."

The Bandy sisters were perched on stools in the back, drinking

Colt 45 from the bottle, and wearing their blouses open with bikini tops underneath that looked like brassieres. The Bandy sisters did not have much to do in life except sit around their older brother's place and make fun of the dried-up old guy they called Stick, who took care of the bateaux that people rented for fishing, which they didn't do much of during the week. So, of course, everyone was happy to see me.

"Timmy, now what a surprise!" Madge Bandy said. "Come here and sit down. Hey, aren't you supposed to be in that military school of yours?"

"Got kicked out," I told her.

"Now isn't that a shame?"

She patted the seat next to her and I sat down.

Her sister Midge said, "You mean you're not going to be a soldier after all? Now, that *is* a shame!"

Madge said, "Midge here likes anything in a uniform. Even the guy that gave her a parking ticket downtown last week."

"I wouldn't talk!" Midge accused her sister.

Madge took to fidgeting back and forth on the stool next to me, as if she had an ant crawling up the inside of her blue jeans. She had a high smell on her. I stole a couple good long looks around the edges of her bikini top. She was all dusted over with talcum powder around her armpits, and a couple beads of sweat had worked little tracks through it.

"What'd you do to get kicked out of that fancy school, anyway?" Madge wanted to know after a while.

"When the hellfire preacher was preaching, I didn't like it, so I hid under the church, and listened to him from there."

Madge whooped and hollered. "Ain't that something! The preacher wants to send you to hell, and you already halfway there!"

"You've got it, Miss Bandy."

"Now, you listen, Timmy. Don't start taking what every preacher says as the gospel truth. They call that kind of thing a parable. They tell you a story, but it doesn't mean what it says, it's really supposed to stand for something else. That's how they work, making it complicated and all. The same thing goes for all that carrying on about sin. They don't really mean all that, not really. You understand?"

"I'll think about it," I promised her. "Only, how can you tell if they do mean what they say, or if it's just a parable?"

Madge shrugged. "You've got to pick and choose."

Just then Stick came sneaking around the side of Madge. "All this talk of sin make me unnecessary!" he declared.

Then he goosed her good and hard from behind, and took to howling like a hyena because Madge shot right off her stool. Midge grabbed him from behind and Madge jumped him from the front, and the stool fell on all three of them. They started squirming around on the floor like puppies, with the Bandy sisters trying to get into Stick's overalls from the side flap and goose him back where it counted.

It wasn't long before Bud Bandy stuck his head through the doorway.

"What the hay you girls doing? All that beer make you frisky as hell." Then he saw me sitting foolishly on a bar stool. "I can't have you contributing to this minor's delinquence."

"Shit, he's Zeke Justice's boy! We ain't contributing to nothing." Madge laughed.

The Bandy sisters and Stick scrambled to their feet. Stick made another move for Madge's crotch but she stiff-armed him in the face. He hooted with laughter, even with the cut she'd opened on his lip.

"Watch your tongue now, sis," Bud told her. "You're talking about this young man's father."

"He may be a father, but he's a man, too," she answered.

"Now, Madge," Bud warned her again.

"Yeah, just watch it," I repeated. "I wouldn't talk, what with you reeking like that!"

Madge raised her hand like she was going to slap me. But her hand just hung there in the air instead. Maybe she was too surprised to bring it down. Besides, with her arm up in the air like that she could clearly smell how she did reek. She stared at me with her mouth open and her eyes bugged out wide until her hand started shaking in thin air.

Bud Bandy chuckled and got in between his sister and me. He put his nose up in the air and gave a good long sniff like a hunting dog.

"You may be right, son, you just may be right. But those aren't the kind of words you want to use with a lady. You keep that in mind when you go chasing down that poontang."

In the meantime, Madge Bandy had lowered her hand. I told her I was sorry.

She shook her head and fidgeted her butt. "You're just jealous it don't belong to you."

"I guess I just am," I told her.

"That's better, son," Bud Bandy approved. "That's what you want to tell them."

He went and fetched a Colt 45.

"I understand old Zeke hit the jackpot at Bo-Peep's."

"I thought it was bad news that traveled fast, not good."

"Well, these things do get around. Your papa and I aren't exactly strangers."

"Did *he* tell you?"

"Not really." He squirmed.

"Well, let me tell you another secret: I won, too. Thirty-two dollars. My father placed the bet for me."

"Did he now? You're a wealthy man! What are you going to buy with all that money?"

"I don't know. A boat, or something."

I laughed at myself before any of them could. You couldn't buy shit for thirty-two dollars. But Bud Bandy took me seriously.

"When you get your boat, I'm going to help you look after it," he promised.

Outside, a flash of lightning jumped from cloud to cloud. It would probably blow over, the way it usually did this early in the afternoon, but I took the weather as my cue to leave.

"Don't want to get soaked," I said to Bud Bandy. "Thanks for the offer."

I walked back quickly along the Lazaretto. Gray curtains of rain twirled down out of the clouds ahead. It was raining into the Channington River, which meant the storm would miss the Isle of Hope and move out to sea. I thought of what my father had said about losing the war to the Marsters, and to the rest of the South. It was true, the way he teetered on the edge of acceptance here. Everyone loved him, even as they waited for his fall. He was public property, like a good piece of gossip. Only as good as his last game.

By the time I got back from Bud Bandy's that afternoon, the marsh grass was knifing back and forth furiously out on Burntpot Island, and our house on Lazaretto Road was full of hollering and cussing. Mrs. Stafford's medicine must have gone bad on my father. I could hear him all the way out on the road. He was yelping and moaning and carrying on like the righteous and the saved in the tent show outside of Sandfly Crossing.

I did not see Evangeline, but I sensed her in the house somewhere, preparing to materialize from behind a half-closed door or a half-thought reflection. I went upstairs, looked in the bedroom, then found my father in his den, where he kept a few books and his baseball souvenirs, a desk and a couch. Inlaid into the wood floor were the four signs of a deck of cards, the same lucky signs Bo-Peep had at his establishment. My father was lying on the couch wrapped in a heavy blanket, with his hands crossed atop his chest the way they fix a corpse. He was shivering, his skin was gator green, and his forehead and upper lip were running in sweat. Something did not smell too good.

He calmed down a little when I walked in.

"Shit, Timmy, where have you been?"

"Nowhere. I walked down to Bandy's."

"Don't go there. Why did you go there?"

"Nowhere else to go. I was just killing time, you know. Bud heard about you winning your bet."

My father threw his head from side to side. Right to left, left to right, casting, trying to get adjusted. He groaned.

"That's Peep talking, broadcasting my good fortune, that fuck."

"You still have the money?" I asked.

He patted down the right-hand pocket of his Indians pants.

"Yeah, still there. It's my lifesaver. I won't let go of these pants, ever. These pants are unlucky, but the pocket in them is lucky. How can you figure it?"

He went back to twitching his head, then an idea came to him.

"Shit, your mother sent for a doctor. He's going to cut these pants off me. He's going to cut my pockets. I don't want to see no doctor."

Right on cue, the doorbell rang downstairs and the screen door opened and shut. From the stairway came the solid, self-important tread of Dr. Fairchild, family physician.

"Don't worry, Daddy, he's only a leg doctor," I whispered as Fairchild plodded up the stairs. I got a stronger whiff of that smell: it was my father's flesh going bad under the covers.

I crossed Dr. Fairchild on the stairs as he marched up with my mother following, all in a flutter. He did not bother with me. I went into the kitchen and sat down at the table and chewed my nails awhile.

A few minutes later, Evangeline descended. She sat down next to me, shiner side toward me, exhibiting the hurt. I was grateful I possessed the Marster scuff. I looked down, examined the crumbs on the floor, the loose threads on my pants, anything but what my father had done to my mother. In the quiet house, we listened to him crying and calling, and Dr. Fairchild telling him how he should take it.

Before long the doctor came down, banging his bag against his pants. There was a cloud of disinfectant smell around him. He proceeded to the sink, threw on the hot-water tap and commenced scrubbing as if he had just shaken hands with a leper. When he got through drying, he held out the hand towel like it was a drowned rat.

"You'd better put this in the wash, ma'am. Right now."

"You just leave it in the sink, Dr. Fairchild. I'll look after it," Evangeline said laconically.

Dr. Fairchild came to the table and sat down.

"I've never seen anything like it! A wound sewn up with human hair. No wonder it was infected!"

"A man's hair or a woman's?" my mother inquired.

"Well . . . well . . . I don't rightly know," Dr. Fairchild sputtered. "It was long enough to use for stitches. Mind you, there was more than one in there. I couldn't really tell."

The doctor caught me looking at him. "What do you know about this, son? You answer me, now. Your father was in some real danger."

I did the Marster scuff, but with words.

"Some local people helped us out over there. I didn't really see what they were doing. They kind of had him surrounded. The medicine man fixed him up," I lied. "There really wasn't too much time to think about it."

Dr. Fairchild went back to his science. "I lanced the abscess and gave him a tetanus booster," he announced. "And something for the pain. He should sleep now."

He refused my mother's offer of iced tea. Then his eyes strayed across her face to her shiner. It had taken him that long to see it. For a doctor, he was not too observant. He looked hard, then looked away twice as hard, and you could tell he was trying to figure out what an alligator-tail slash had to do with a black eye on a respectable white woman.

He stood up. He must have decided it was time to move on before he discovered the connection, which would probably be something he would rather not know about, like wounds sewn up with human hair.

9

A leech is a black, shiny, slimy thing that lives in dead water in the swamp, and it'll suck out all your blood if you give it half a chance. So you can understand that I did not know what a leech was going to be doing in my house, with the picket fence and the widow's walk and porch swing, but I reckoned I would be finding out soon enough. I would wait, and the answer would come to me, whether I wanted it or not. I was on an island, and there is not much for a person who lives on an island and doesn't have the means to get off it to do but wait and watch.

After Dr. Fairchild left, my mother went up to make sure his pain shot had taken effect. I was sitting on the porch steps, watching the storm blow off over the ocean. My father's bateau rode low on the sucked-out, low-tide water of the Lazaretto, tied up at our floating dock where I had left it this morning, a year or two ago. I was looking at that little boat and plotting escape.

Evangeline stepped out onto the porch and closed the screen door behind her, carefully.

"Do you think I can go shopping for groceries like this?"

"Ma'am?"

"Don't be acting so vague-minded all the time! Do you reckon I can walk down Broughton Street in the light of day with a black eye?"

"I suppose not, ma'am."

"I am going to have to ask you and an acquaintance of mine, Mr. Calvin Fleetwood, to go see that yaller girl who keeps the leeches."

"Two people to transport a leech in an automobile, ma'am?" I inquired.

"Watch your tongue, boy!"

"Excuse me, just thinking out loud."

She went back in the house. I understood two things. That we were waiting for Mr. Fleetwood, and that fetching the leech was my punishment for having spent the night on Callibogee. I retrieved one of the baseballs from under the porch swing and rubbed it up, though it did not need breaking in. I practiced digging my fingernails into the seams. From the front room, I heard the squeaky door of the toddy cabinet open and close. I reflected on that squeaky door. Why was it not oiled, so that access to the toddies could be achieved without the entire house knowing it? Though going to the well was not forbidden, it was not something you need advertise, either, especially in the middle of the day. Which is what that squeaky door did. It advertised.

After a time of such reflections, none of which would ever get me back into the Academy, Mr. Fleetwood showed up. He did not care to come into the house. Mr. Fleetwood was a careful, squat, ruddy-faced man, the same burned-brick color as Jefferson Marster. But Mr. Fleetwood did not have a single drop of that fine tone of lamentation in his voice, the kind that ran in the Marster blood. Maybe that's what made him the ideal candidate for a leech-fetching expedition.

"I hope Mr. Justice is feeling better," he said to my mother, wringing his hands as though in despair.

"He's no different from before," my mother assured him. "Still sleeping."

We all stood around on the porch. Mr. Calvin Fleetwood was a floor studier like me. While he was studying the floor, I had an opportunity to study him. He was in no more of a hurry to eye my mother's shiner than I had been. Poor Evangeline, wanting to show it off, and everybody too polite but to look the other way. She lorded that black eye over him. Between her and Mr. Fleetwood, she ran the show. Why else would a grown man fetch a leech for a woman with a shiner put there by another man who happened to be her husband?

"Storm blew over, didn't it? Figure it'll blow back? It'll do that sometimes," Mr. Fleetwood speculated as he fretted with his hands.

Neither Evangeline nor I had much of an opinion. Anything could come out of a sky like this one, including leeches.

"Well, boy, looks like we'd better be moving along. We've got a job to do."

Wouldn't you know it? Calvin owned a Cadillac Fleetwood. I wondered whether he had named himself after his car. The Caddy was not new, but it had that new-car smell. He probably had a spray can full of it, and he sprayed it around the inside every time he came over to see Evangeline. He put the power windows up and we drove away from the river onto the Wormslow Road, off the Isle toward Sandfly Crossing where the liquor store stood. It was freezing cold with the air conditioner blasting away.

"No-count niggers," Mr. Fleetwood said, not unpleasantly, as we accelerated past a disorderly string of black men straggling along the road from Sandfly.

I looked out the window, and after a while the grounds of the Methodist boys' home went by. Well-kept fences and a stone gate, and fat cattle grazing in the fields. At the end of the oak-lined drive was the institution where the orphans lived. I pictured them peering out the windows at this rich man's car going by with a man and a boy inside, and wishing they could have a regular family life like the one they imagined we were having.

I was tempted to offer them a trade.

Mr. Fleetwood drove on, unperturbed, mouthing the words to a country tune on the radio and chewing his gum to the beat. After a time he slowed up his Cadillac and tilted us off the paved Chatham County road onto a red clay back road. We crossed a half dozen unmarked tracks going off into the woods and scrub.

"Nobody come out here but the niggers," he said gleefully.

That's the way these hard-shell crackers are. They all hate the blacks, but if they happen to find themselves straying onto their territory on some item of business, they get all excited. It's a big adventure for them.

"Nobody but them and the white people that do business with them," I put in.

That hurt Mr. Fleetwood's feelings.

"Now look here. I'm doing a favor for your mama, and that's a favor for you. You think I've got nothing else to do than drive up and down these old clay roads and wreck my muffler, just to get a leech?"

I shrugged and took to contemplating the landscape. Now and again there would be a rough shack half hidden in the pines, sometimes on red-brick pilings, other times slumped plain on the ground. Every shack was surrounded by fields of scrap and useless things that might be made to work again if you had the ingenuity of the devil and the eternity of God to repair them in.

Then the sky opened up. A leaden, dispirited rain came pouring straight down, like out of a faucet. There wasn't a breath of wind to stir the lines of water. I sneezed a couple times, then put down the electric window despite the air conditioning. Mr. Fleetwood took the hint and turned off the blower. The rain made a rotten smell rise up off the earth, half vegetable, half animal, a tired, heavy smell uncut by the breeze we had off the water at Hurt's Landing.

"Good weather for leeches," I commented to Calvin Fleetwood.

"You're strange," he told me. "But I suppose I'd have to say you're right. If I was a leech, I'd like this kind of weather, too."

The car bottomed out on a low spot in the road. A shower of loose red-yellow clay the color of diarrhea splattered up onto the windshield. Mr. Fleetwood swore inoffensively. A few minutes later he pulled off the road.

"Well, here we are. Good weather for leeches, but not for us. We'll just have to wait her out."

The rain fell so straight and flat I could leave my window open without having any water splash onto Mr. Fleetwood's upholstery. We were parked on the edge of a patch of scrub, a little pine and some water-loving trees like willow and cottonwood. It was a place where a rabbit might want to go to ground.

Or a toadfish like me, for that matter. Mind you, the piney woods were not exactly my element. There was too much nature involved. For me, nature was no more than a conveyance, a means of escape, the water that surrounded my island. I avoided nature; for reflection, I preferred the proximity of man's structures and devices of belief. Such as chapels, for instance, especially those on pilings. Shit! Had I known I'd end up in this banal, petty, motorized version of hell with a leech fetcher, my mother's panderer, I would have found another way to conduct my theological investigations, which would have spared me from detection.

I had the leisure to consider my crimes. Like all sinners worthy of the name, I remained unrepentant. I even secretly believed I deserved praise, not punishment, for my expedition beneath the Pax chapel. I descended there, I pleaded to some invisible arbiter, to examine the subject of my faith. Because I *was* a believer, believe it or not, because I took Father Dooley's words seriously. Literally. Which made me a believer in the worst, fundamentalist sort of way. If I didn't believe, I would have been up there on top of the oaken floorboards with the other young Benedictine soldiers, for whom Father Dooley's visions were no more than water off a toadfish's back.

A sinner unrepentant. A sinner convinced of the superiority of his sin. For to achieve belief, I had no need of efficacious illusion or splendorous places of worship. Belief is literally in every turn of phrase I use; it informs and forms my words. Belief is a natural outgrowth of my sin

RAT PALMS

of pride, of vainglory. I will believe in the manner I choose, and worship in the most perverse way, if my belief demands it. The rest of you, you can stay on your initial-carved pews and wrap yourselves in your farty robes! I'm going to confront the terror of literal belief, all by myself!

How's that for reflection, Father Damian Dooley? I thought as I watched the rain let up. You called for a written report? You'll get it, one way or the other! I'll reflect you right out of your church clothes! I'll reflect the way the sky reflects all the bitterness on Hurt's Landing. I'll reflect the way the sun reflects off a mirror — by blinding you with harsh illumination!

Then like a sign from the Lord, as if He were rewarding me for my revolt, the rain stopped and the road and scrub all around were lit up in leaden sunshine. In the steamy air, flies began landing in clumps on the Caddy's chrome bumpers to soak up the heat. I bailed out of Mr. Fleetwood's Cadillac a second or two before suffocating from farts, chewing gum, country tunes and air conditioning.

We stood on the side of the road and he looked balefully down at his penny loafers. They were already splattered with wet clay. He really was not dressed for a leech-fetching expedition.

"Path is up in there some," he said, pointing at a clump of cottonwoods.

He seemed to know the way pretty well. He must have been out here plenty of times to see the leech lady. On account of whose black eye, I had to wonder. We started in, him in the lead.

"You sure you aren't afraid?"

"No, sir."

"Don't call me sir. I'm Cal to you."

Cal the Pal. I hated this instant friend stuff. As if we were a couple of boy scouts out on a tramp in the woods, earning our merit badges in invertebrate collecting. I afforded myself a smile as his penny loafers turned a sick baby-shit color from the clay.

Then the shack appeared out of the woods, the way they do around here, with no other indication or warning that a human being might be living in the vicinity. There were no rusty cars around this shack. No road to get them in.

Mr. Fleetwood pulled up short.

"Hey, yaller girl. Hey, Theresa!" he shouted. "Got an order for you. Come on out of that place of yours and talk to us!"

There was not a human sound in the woods. Just a few birds hightailing it through the trees to escape Calvin Fleetwood's twangy voice. And the wind through the pines making that lonely sighing sound. I don't know why people build their houses in these piney woods, what with the wind blowing through them even on the stillest day, sounding like the voices of the dearly departed.

"Why don't you go up and knock on the door?"

Mr. Fleetwood shook his head in a rare moment of humility. "You can't do that here."

It turned out we didn't have to. The screen door of the shack slammed, and even from a distance I could see how beautiful the leech girl was. A thousand times better, if not more ideal, than the chalky white statue of the naked *Pudentia* at the Telfair. She was wearing a housedress. She moved to the top of the porch steps, dragging a withered leg behind her. It was polio. Somebody hadn't cared. They'd let this beauty's leg waste away.

She leaned on a porch post and pointed her walking stick at Calvin Fleetwood.

"You come on."

We moved across the clearing toward her place.

"She can work haints and hoodoos," Fleetwood whispered loudly to me. "But you don't have to worry, long as you're with me."

Maybe she could work a hoodoo on Mr. Calvin Fleetwood and make him disappear so I could have this girl to myself. We climbed up the porch steps, which bowed under our weight. Theresa stared openly at me, and this time I was not inclined to do the Marster scuff. I looked her right back. When I had had my fill, I moved my eyes down her body to her crippled leg, and across the floorboards of the porch and the front of the tilting shack over to the washtub where a hank of some kind of meat was soaking in black water.

A beauty with a crippled leg who kept leeches in a tub on the broken-down porch of her shack. *That* was what my mother had wanted me to contemplate. The punishment she had devised. Score one for the Marster education!

Theresa shifted her weight and went to the tub at the shady end of the porch. We followed. I looked down into the black soup. The leeches were fastened onto the meat like piglets to a sow.

"That's what you want?" Theresa asked Mr. Fleetwood.

"Sure is."

"You want to pick one out yourself?"

"Why, you impudent . . ."

"Then I'll pick one out for you."

She left her walking stick standing unsupported, and I had to catch it or it would have fallen into the leech farm. Theresa took a matchbox from one of the pinned-up pockets of her housedress and leaned down. Her dress worked its way up in back as she bent over and I had all the time I needed to contemplate that flawless, dark-honey skin over her atrophied muscles. A sight worthy of worship. But that all my worship could never correct. She unlatched a leech from the hank of whatever kind of meat it was and slipped it into the box. Then the box went into Mr. Fleetwood's hand.

"I chose a real thirsty one for you," she told him.

"That's mighty kind of you." He took out his billfold. "What can I give you for it?"

Theresa straightened up and took back her stick. She pointed it at me.

"I'll take him," she said.

I swear my heart hung dead in my chest like a lynched man from a tree. I know it's only superstition of the most primitive sort, but all of a sudden that stick of hers seemed to positively run with magic. I took a step toward Theresa.

Then I heard Calvin Fleetwood gave a big, greasy, hateful chuckle.

"Oh, he'll come sneaking back here to you and dirty up his shoes, the way they all do! But not today, girl. If I leave him out here with you, his mama'll never forgive me. And we can't be having that!"

Theresa nodded. She saw the whole thing.

"That's who the leech is for," she stated.

Mr. Fleetwood answered her with a rolled-up bill. I could not catch the denomination on it.

The money answered her, but it did not silence her.

"You folks have no right to bring him out here. He didn't hurt nobody. He didn't do the hurting, I can tell."

Then she touched me with her stick, in the center of my stomach. She didn't say a word. Her eyes were grave and understanding. Hers was a magic touch, supposed to ease the hurt. But it worked the other way around. It was the touch of knowing, and with it came more hurt.

On the Lazaretto Road, my mother made a show of accepting the matchbox from Calvin Fleetwood, as if it held a diamond ring and not a bloodsucking, spineless, invertebrate parasite. Mr. Fleetwood fretted and wrung his hands and inquired after my father's condition, then drifted off toward his clay-spattered car.

That night, in my little, clean, white wooden house, I closed my eyes and saw Theresa standing on her slanting porch. Her beautifully sculpted face, her almond eyes, her honey skin, her leech farm in the black water in the tub. Evangeline, I addressed my mother, for the sake of administering a moral lesson, you sent me out there. You took a foolish risk, exposing me to so much beauty. Not that you'd ever see her that way; not that you've ever been out there in your life. But I have, and now that I know what I know, now that I want her, there'll be no unknowing it.

10

The next day began with dramas private and public. The Savannah Indians put my father on the fifteen-day disabled list. A hunting accident, the sports pages reported. The private drama was that after spending the previous day in her room with the contents of the matchbox, my mother came downstairs, her shiner all sucked clean and leeched away to a smudge, and told me she was going up to Broughton Street to do some shopping, then sped down the Lazaretto Road in the car through the waves of heat. I went upstairs to take a piss, and what do you think I saw? A leech floating in the toilet, as big as a balloon. Well, maybe not that big, but a lot more consistent than it had been when Theresa had slipped it into Cadillac Calvin Fleetwood's hand. Leech in toilet. Who might that demonstration be meant for, I wondered, my father or me? The latter pupil, I wagered. The Marster education was taking on some new, desperate and imaginative methods.

I flushed the toilet and forgot about the piss. I could hold it a little while longer. Maybe I'd go outside and pee off the dock into the Lazaretto.

I went down the hall and knocked on the door to my father's den.

"I heard how they put you on the disabled list."

"Gator poisoning." He laughed.

It looked as though Dr. Fairchild's treatment had done him some good. He was almost cheerful, though in a feverish kind of way.

He shook his head. "It wasn't too much fun, I'll tell you that. I hate to think of the things I might have said. Shit, do I have to be responsible for everything? I thought my brains would fly out the hole in my head."

"You were going on about home plate."

He frowned. Then he kicked off the sheet and said in a change-the-subject voice, "Let me show you my battle scars."

Mrs. Stafford's hair had been replaced by standard medical stitches. His leg was still discolored, but at least it looked like human flesh now. I told him that, then took a look around the sickroom. There was a deck of cards open on the floor, and a stack of books on the bedside table.

"Not too much to do in here," I commiserated.

"More than you'd think. I'm reading about the Civil War. I've always had that gentleman Caton's books. Now I've got some time to read them."

"What do they say?"

My father shrugged. "Not finished yet. Neither the books, nor the war."

He laughed, showing me his sugar-eating stumps of teeth.

"Civil war's the only kind to have," he added. "Saves you all kinds of traveling time."

"You can laugh. But it's not funny and you know it."

"I'm sorry, Toadfish. I know you're watching everything, and you're frustrated because you can't do anything about it."

"I suppose it would be better if I could blame myself for some of it," I told him, trying out my mother's logic. "That way at least I could share in the glory."

"Oh, I'm sure you blame yourself enough as it is. That's the way all innocent children are."

He threw the sheet back over his bad leg.

"I can tell you've been listening to your mama. I'm not going to waste my time undoing the damage she's doing. I don't have that kind of time anyway, or inclination, to tell you the truth. You're old enough to judge for yourself. And actually, I've got some talking to do myself. Are you willing to listen to me?"

"Yes, sir."

"You see, Timmy, there are times I'm afraid I might be going on the permanent disabled list. In case I do, I want to get a few things straight between us. First of all, I want to give you my bateau."

"Why, thank you, sir."

"Would you kindly stop doing the goddamned Marster scuff!" he thundered. "I'm trying to execute my last will and testament and give you the means to get around, and all you can think to do is go polite on me. Do you want that boat or not?"

"Of course I do."

"Now, I don't suppose you know why my bateau's called what it is?"

"I've wondered."

"You've wondered in silence," he corrected me. "Then listen to my little story. It might not be one hundred percent true, but that doesn't matter. Never let the truth get in the way of a good story.

"My folks came from Canada, I know you don't know that. They were just a bunch of French pig farmers, from Sainte-Perpétue in Quebec, the Holy Perpetual I called it when I was a kid, and they were just as poor and dirty as the slop they fed their pigs with. And when there wasn't a job left in all of French Canada, they went down to Massachusetts and sold their goddamned Catholic, Jesus- and Mary-loving souls to some factory. Now, everybody knows that story, right? People are always on the move. Especially the French in this part of the world. You scrape the surface off a lot of words and a lot of people's names and names of towns down here and you get French. But half the time you can't tell any more, not the way people say them."

"Speak some French to me," I asked him.

"Oh, no, I couldn't do that. I forgot it all a long time ago. I had to work to forget it, and I'm not about to start remembering it again. I believe I succeeded. No use remembering it if you want to be a regular American. Now, what was I saying?"

He shifted from side to side, trying to get his head at ease with the pillows. But the pillows seemed to be made out of stone.

"Picture a Massachusetts Yankee factory, in the shadow of which I was born, Elzéar Lajustice, Elzéar the Just, and so baptized, fucking amen. In Massachusetts, I wanted to be a regular American. It was too late for my parents. Not much chance of being American if you can't hardly speak English. I wanted to be a Massachusetts American, and I had a gift for mimicking the Americans around me, so pretty soon I became one. And that American got himself called Zeke Justice, the way you know me to be named. Well, shit, Toadfish, I should have stopped there. Being somebody at all is hard labor. Becoming somebody different is absolutely exhausting. But I didn't stop there. I came down here to play ball, met Evangeline and got right down to the business of making you. Your mother's family has got skin as tough as the *Merrimac*, and to fight my way through that armor and get myself accepted and all, I had to become a Southerner, too. Well, I discovered it's a lot harder to become a Southerner than a Massachusetts American, especially because I was older then. When you're young, a kid, like you, you're more flexible. I failed. I lost the Civil War. I was defeated at the battle of Callibogee by a dead alligator. So if you want my bateau, I'll ask you to keep her name, the *Elzéar*, until she ends up at the bottom of some creek."

"Once a boat's baptized, that's her name," I promised him.

"Just like a person." He laughed bitterly. "So you swear?"

"I swear. But are you sure you're feeling all right?"

"No. But does that mean what you swear is any less solemn?"

"No. On the contrary."

"Good. At least you understand that much. Now, son, you'd better go on and leave me."

I did what I was told. I made myself scarce. I went and stood on the downstairs porch and looked at the river. *All this belongs to you*, I heard the voice. As if the Marster story was not enough, now you have the wanderings of Elzéar Lajustice. They are not the kind of things that, when offered, you can decline: *No, thank you, I don't care for this past. I would prefer another one or, if possible, none at all.*

At least with my father's past, I got a boat out of it.

I walked down to the floating dock, then to the *Elzéar*. I would have to say it different now, to go along with the man's new name. Not new, actually; original. Not *Elzeer. Ell-zay-ahre.*

But whatever the bateau was called, the main thing was to get in it and get the hell out of Hurt's Landing. I gassed it up from the big can in the boathouse and checked the oil level. It took me a couple of tries to make the Evinrude work. The motor was like an old mare. It had to recognize your hand before it would cooperate.

I got me and *Elzéar* out into the current of the Lazaretto. And it wasn't until I turned and saw how the houses of Hurt's Landing were getting smaller and falling behind that I realized the leap I had made. I had always been possessed of a heavy island, dense and choked with the parasitic moss of the past. Now I had a boat to get off that island.

In the midst of my hallelujahs and rejoicing I nearly got myself caught in a floating crab trap. When I steered free of it and had the leisure to turn back again I saw nothing. Just the flowing, black-green Lazaretto and trees and marsh grass on both sides of the bank. Hurt's Landing had disappeared. Once I had the outboard laboring and raising a hell of a racket, I commenced to sing, all kinds of yelps and howls just to get my voice back into practice because it had been a while since I had sung. After a time I got a little dissatisfied with that noisemaking, but what could I do, I didn't have my own words yet. But today, that didn't matter. The important thing was that no one could hear me, way out on the creeks and marshes.

The new Hurt's Landing motto: To each his refuge!

The next day, I was passing time with that Caton gentleman on the Civil War, reading in the front room. In the very midst of Shiloh, Rags Scoggin knocked on the door. He had the whole Savannah Indians infield with him. They filed in, all of them wearing their uniforms except Rags, who was dressed like a shrimper and smelled like one, too. It looked as though they were going on a picnic. Rags had his cooler, which he carried under his arm as easily as a loaf of bread.

"We're the cheering-up section for your daddy," he explained. "I was having a cool one with the Indians trainer the other evening over at Pinky's, bitching about my knees like I always like to do. The trainer confides in me that Zeke here is suffering from listlessness. Now, I don't know what listlessness is, but I knew it couldn't be a good thing if a medical man told me about it in that medical voice they tend to get. Since Zeke can't come to the team, I reckoned I'd bring the team to him. As much as I could muster up, anyway. They got together and packed them a lunch."

The infielders hung back a little and inspected the oak staircase and all the Marster pieces that weighed down the front room. Some of the Indians players could have been ten years younger than my father, and they looked around with reverence in their eyes, as if they were at Cooperstown. Judging from the aroma, the boxes they were carrying had Johnny Harris barbecue inside.

"I don't believe I see Mr. Justice here," Rags remarked, making a show of looking around the room.

I pointed upstairs. "He's in his study."

Rags turned to the infielders. "His study," he told them with great significance in his voice, as if the word itself explained something of Zeke Justice's case of listlessness.

RAT PALMS

They trooped upstairs. Rags in front, beer cooler held high like an offering, the infielders balancing their boxes of Johnny Harris barbecue on the palms of their hands like Italian pizza waiters. Halfway up the stairs, they burst into that old song:

Take me out to the ball game
Take me out to the crowd
Buy me some peanuts and Cracker Jack
I don't care if I never come back.

Never did that song seem to contain such foreboding as I waited downstairs for that shrimp-pink, simple man who loved my father to try and work a cure based on the fraternity of baseball players, plates of barbecue and the contents of a beer cooler. I waited, and paged idly through Mr. Caton's account of who won, and why, and how Mr. Lincoln's vision was the most shining one of all, which justified his victory. Upstairs, behind the closed door of the study, I could hear a lot of elbow jabbing and backslapping and church key working, but could not tell who was slapping whom, and to what effect. I prayed and prayed they would stay up there all afternoon. *I prayed* — take note, Father Dooley, you old unbeliever in me. I prayed that the whole infield would descend at five o'clock for a six o'clock game, too stewed to play the game, and that my father would set a heroic example by downing a couple cups of scalding black coffee that would cut through the malt-liquor haze that hung over the low country this evening like a sea mist, then take the Grayson Stadium mound to lead the Indians to unexpected victory. *Poetic Justice*, the sports pages would write. *Justice Triumphs over Gator's Tail*. Lazaretto Justice unwrapping his bandages in public once again and rising up onto the mound. And though he stinketh, and is sewn together with thread resembling nothing less than cunt hair, he is truly saved.

My optimistic reverie, along with the drone of that Caton gentleman and the heat, must have lulled me to sleep. I woke to a heavy tread on the stairs. Rags Scoggin was leading the infielders down again, minus their barbecue boxes, and the way he was dangling the cooler from one hand, you could tell it had been relieved of a considerable part of its burden.

But Rags Scoggin was wearing a worried look.

"I can't figure it, Timmy," he said to me at the bottom of the stairs. "He doesn't even want to take a drink. That's a bad sign in a man of your daddy's kind — you'll forgive me for putting it that way."

"What did he say?"

Rags squinted up his eyes and shifted his weight.

"Say? I don't really know . . . Crazy stuff I can't quite figure . . . Stuff about the Civil War. You know I'm not exactly a schooled man."

Rags was playing dumb. Something somber had transpired up there. You could feel it from the way the infielders were itching to get out into the fresh air.

"Mr. Scoggin," I told him, "You've got to do something."

"I'll be back," he said. "I got to think on it. I'm not used to this kind of thing, you know."

"Come back soon," I said. *"Please."*

Rags promised. As he closed the screen door behind him, gently, as if exiting a hospital ward, I felt the uselessness of good intentions.

With Evangeline gone, buying up all Broughton Street to make up for her convalescence, and the infielders returned to their game, I sat in silence in the house on the Lazaretto Road, feeling it grow fuller and fuller of my father's disorder. I feared the pressure would grow so great the walls would burst, like a diver's skull in deep water. I never knew a house to be so empty, yet so inhabited.

It was six o'clock. I knew because a Marster grandfather clock had just tolled the hour. I went upstairs and knocked on my father's door and heard a muffled noise. I took that as an invitation.

The room was a mess from Rags's mercy mission. A dozen cans of Colt 45, some in the wastebasket, some out. The stack of Johnny Harris take-out boxes with the sweet brown sauce interesting the flies. And in the middle of it, my father in bed, with covers up to his chin on an eighty-degree day.

"I've been doing the Marster scuff outside your door ever since Rags left," I admitted. "It tires a person out after a while. I decided to stop scuffing and come up and see you."

The Caton volumes were on the floor, each open to a different page. From underneath them, the lucky signs inlaid on the floor peeked out.

"How's the gator poisoning?"

"It's not just the leg any more." He tapped the side of his head. "I believe it's spread to the home plate."

Somehow I figured he was talking pitching. Shit, what else could I have figured? I was no more schooled in these matters than Rags Scoggin was.

"You always had good control," I told him. "You always stayed around the plate. That was never your problem, not here, not in the Bigs."

"Once you get plate problems, you lose your control. Nobody wants to believe me. I keep telling them that."

I had no idea what he was talking about. What do we call people when we can't make sense of them? Crazy. Mad. Zeke Justice, my father, was a madman. His voice was dead and toneless. All that good piss and vinegar that had made him such a raconteur and tavern man was gone. With it, my life on Hurt's Landing was draining away. I wasn't the son of a Savannah Indians pitching star any more. I was the son of a madman. I was losing my inheritance. My belongings, which were my sense of belonging.

I tallied up the losses: the privilege of idle reflection with my river playmate, the Lazaretto. The odd excursion to the Telfair to form my appreciation of ideal beauty in the company of Grandfather Jefferson Marster, who considered me but a half step up from bastardy, the son of a Yankee sandlot star and the last shredded line of Marsterdom. The dolorous schooling on the widow's walk, the teacher of which was even more eager to play hooky than her sole student.

Poisoned gifts, all of them. Dubious inheritance at best. But they had made me who I was, and I did not want to lose them until I knew who I was going to be next.

"Let's go," I told my father, so loud that he jumped. "You've got to get up and practice. You have to stay in shape. Throw some pitches. I'll catch you."

"You can't catch me."

"I got a mitt, I can catch you. Come on outside."

I stepped up to the head of his bed and pushed aside his bedside table. A sheaf of papers and a fountain pen fell onto the floor. I saw what was written there: lines and lines of letters in fine loops and flourishes. The useless repetition of a sad, nostalgic mind stuck in a convent school from another time. He was heavy and inert, with the springiness of stone. I yanked him into the sitting position.

"I can't wear this," he complained, tugging on his uniform. "All torn to shreds by that witch doctor Fairchild. Look in the closet."

A whole teamful of clean uniforms was hanging from the rod in the closet. His equipment bag was on the floor, and inside it his Rawlings glove and a few new unscuffed balls. I spread a uniform out on the bed for him.

"Let me see you stand."

"I don't know if I can. Haven't tried it for a while."

He threw off the sheet and blanket, and I had no choice but to contemplate what he had become over the past few days. Why does everyone in this house insist I see everything? Why can't they unwrap their bandages and dispose of their leeches in the privacy of their own lives? My father was horribly thin, his skin had a pale green cast, and his hair was plastered against his skull from being in bed too long. I don't think he had eaten since the deviled crabs on Callibogee. He hadn't changed clothes since then, that much was for sure. His left pant leg was cut off at crotch level and his wrinkled pecker peeped out. His right went down to his ankle, but it was all frayed at the end, as if scavenging fish had fed off it.

He dug into what was left of his uniform pants and held out a crumpled handful of bills.

"The money. You better look after it. Think of it as your inheritance."

"It's your good luck. I kept my winnings, you keep yours. Put it in the pocket of your new pants. You might need it sometime."

I left him there to get dressed with his fistful of hundred-dollar bills and went downstairs. Outside, I scratched out a home plate in the sandy dust in front of the garage. If he was wild, the garage door would serve as backstop. I walked off what I figured was sixty and a half feet down the drive and put a brick on the oyster-shell pavement for the pitcher's rubber. Then I drew a mound around it with my toe.

The screen door slammed and my father came wandering along the side of the house, limping, looking stunned in the sunshine, his Indians uniform so clean and white it threw out harsh reflections like a mirror. He wore his cap with the bill bent up, and I could see his face plainly, twisted into a squint of concentration. Then he walked out onto the mound I had devised for him.

He rocked his rear foot against the brick and frowned.

"It ain't much of a rubber," I agreed from sixty feet and six inches away. "But it's only practice."

"Only practice." He nodded.

He pulled at the bill of his cap. He flicked his head a half dozen times, shooing flies. Then he went to work.

He rocked his arms back for the windup, brought his left leg up for the kick, his right hand that held the ball was going to rocket across his body for the delivery, *curveball*, I guessed and got ready to adjust to that little twist and jump the ball will take on you just when you think you know where it's going. My fingertips tingled and my skin felt alive, because this was the real game, the only game, and I was playing it with my father.

Then he stopped. He just stopped dead in his tracks, and I felt the effort that stopping in mid-movement takes. There was no delivery. At the last minute his right arm flopped loose and he dropped the ball. It rolled off the oyster-shell pavement onto the grass.

I pounded my glove with my fist. "Come on, show me your stuff!"

My father stared at the ball. Snatched at it to pick it up, but missed it.

"I can't get it right!" he hollered down the driveway.

"Don't worry about the windup. Just loosen up first."

"Sure thing, coach."

He climbed my imaginary mound again. Paced. Smoothed the imaginary dirt. Rocked both arms back to commence the windup, but I could see his balance was all wrong. He didn't even get into the leg kick. The goddamned ball was in the wrong hand.

He looked disbelievingly at his right hand and found it was empty. The ball was in his glove, not his throwing hand. He must have gone through his delivery a hundred thousand times without making that mistake.

"Forget the windup," I encouraged him, but encouragement was a futile business at sixty feet. "Man on first on a fielding error. Pitch from the stretch."

He paced the mound, jerked his head left and right, shooed the invisible flies. He got set again. He was going to try again. That was all I could ask for. That he would not give up. He was taking my suggestion. He was going to pitch from the stretch, no windup or leg kick. He brought his hands together at his belt. The ball was in his right hand. He paused and flicked his eyes. He's checking the imaginary runner at first, I figured. But the pause turned into paralysis. I saw it all as if it was a snapshot taken from above: my father in our driveway, as still as a statue, tense to the snapping point, hands clasped together at his belt, elbows out, staring down at me for a sign, and tears running down his face.

Then he threw the goddamned baseball. It was not any particular pitch at all. As soon as it left his hand I knew it would be wild. It sailed in at me, rising, rising, and I leaped for it and caught it in the

RAT PALMS

webbing of my glove before it could fly over the garage roof.

I trotted out toward him, the way catchers do when they want to settle their pitcher. When I got halfway out he started in wailing.

"I can't get it right! I can't find the plate! I don't know what my hands are for!"

I went to toss the ball back to him.

"I don't want that fucking thing!"

How long does it take to cover sixty feet and six inches when your father is standing on an imaginary mound you've drawn for him, crying helplessly under his baseball cap on a calm summer evening? Forever, I think.

"Come on, let's play catch. Forget about pitching, just throw the ball. Try to loosen up."

"I've lost the plate," he wailed.

"You have to try. Just *try*."

I popped the ball into his glove, and his glove fell right off. He stood there with naked hands.

"Just try!" I begged him.

"I'm sorry, Toadfish. I can see it clear as day, and I want it to be different. But wanting just doesn't seem to help any in my case."

Then he gave a smile. There was something rotten, sheepish, ashamed, unapologetic, complacent, self-accepting about that smile. I had had enough.

I slammed my glove down on top of his.

"I don't want your explanations! I just want you to pitch the ball! Don't you understand?"

I ran past him to the end of the driveway, then stopped short under the live oaks. All around me, Hurt's Landing was breaking up like a dock in a hurricane. I swear, if I was going to have to mother Zeke Justice, my own father, I'd sure enough take something in return. No one in this house was going to hold me in thrall any more with their antics or their manners. I crossed the Lazaretto Road and went to the river. Under the trees it was cool, almost evening, but the sun was still shining on the marshes on the other side. Plenty of daylight left to get somewhere in.

I ran back into the house and went up to my room. Flashlight, fresh batteries, a knife, a sleeping bag, a windbreaker. Peaches from the fruit bowl on the dining room table. I could buy provisions at any landing and fish for the rest. From the front room sofa a broken-spined volume of that gentleman Caton's history. And a sheet of paper and a pencil to begin my report for Father Dooley.

I had to laugh as I folded the sheet neatly into my pack.

The creeks and marshes are for escape, not reflection. But whatever they're for, shit, I'd rather take my chances with the haints and the spirits of the dead out on the river after dark than with the living ones here on Hurt's Landing.

11

By the time I got past the bend of the slack Lazaretto and free of the spectacle of human inhabitation, I was cursing myself for having demanded so much from a sick man. If he took sicker, would it be because of my demands? True, I did ask him to step out of himself, if only long enough to throw a baseball. But it was for curing, not to torture him with his own incapacity.

Which is probably what I succeeded in doing.

Burntpot Island came up on my left. Burntpot was no more than a marsh with a raised hammock in the middle that let people call it an island. It offered no anchorage. Half of it disappeared at high tide, and at low tide if you stepped out of your boat onto its banks, you'd sink into mud up to your knees.

Around here, you're safe only on the water. But today, not even the Lazaretto was far enough, not with Bandy's marina peeping out of its cove ahead on the right. Docking place of Bud Bandy's knowing smile and Midge and Madge's knowing reek. It was enough to make me want to get good and lost.

Though I don't suppose I would have protested had Midge appeared out of the Lazaretto like one of those Telfair beauties, Venus on the half shell, except, it being the Lazaretto and all and not some ideal spray of water from a museum painting, she would come to me all clothed in algae and marsh grass and garlanded with toadfish with a necklace of barnacles around her neck, and her breasts strapped tight by her bikini top. Midge upon the waters, all deployed, and we'd do it on the slimy river bank offered up by low tide, or in the bottom of the *Elzéar*, ass over teakettle on the bait well in full sight of all of God's creation, and afterward she would say, *You're better than your father, boy.* And I would say, *I do not wish to be known.* Then Bud Bandy would sail up, chewing on a plug of Red Man and spitting out little flecks of tobacco for the fish to feed on, and he would advise, *You might think that, and you might be right, son, but it ain't the kind of thing you say to a lady, not if you want to get some poontang.*

What with all these comic reflections — who says reflection has to be solemn? — I nearly missed the cutoff to Runaway Negro Creek and the back river marshes, all quiet and strong-smelling and propitious to report writing for Benedictine fathers. I slowed up the Evinrude and inched forward into the creek, listening for that sick churning sound when your propellor hits the bottom mud. I kept to the center of the channel, green-black and opaque, and finally I got skittish, or smart, and cut the motor and tilted it out. There was hardly enough draft for the oars, and I ended up standing in the bateau, pushing off the creek bottom.

In the evening breeze, the marsh grass whispered its knife-sharpening sound. I put on my mock-Biblical voice and intoned, Hear the racket of the plague locusts, Father Damian Dooley, hear the sound of the elders readying their blades to put down the sacrifice. Poor Father Dooley, because of your priestly station, you are but a puny observer of the sacrifice of the young, which is how we serve the plague here among the islands. Had you been wiser, you would have counseled escape, not reflection. Besides, deep down I believe I'm a Hebrew, found floating among the marsh grass on Runaway Negro Creek by my parents out on a Sunday crabbing expedition with a couple of crab lines and a bag full of green chicken necks. After all, I do not care for the saints. I am not moved by Jesus' mercy. All those apostles scurrying about the known world at the time like chickens with their heads cut off — they lack grandeur. Secretly, I prefer the oldest of the Good Books, composed back when God was cruel and admitted it. Give me the primitive church, the terror of naked belief. Because, you see, that is how our landing came to be named. Not after Mr. Hurt. There never was a Mr. Hurt. It is named for the hurt that flows through us as surely as tides flow through the water. Since God is a master of hurt, I say, God, follow my example and damn Hurt's Landing!

I was right on top of a nest of snowy egrets when the white birds exploded airward, practically from underneath me, and I swear I could feel the plumes on my cheek as they shot up. Some punishment! Blasphemy rewarded with a flock of graceful pure-white water birds. I watched the egrets circle overhead, sounding their high-pitched alarm as they guarded their territory. I drifted further along Runaway Negro Creek with the egrets descending behind me, assured that I was no predator. All around, the marsh hooted and popped and crackled. In this world free of human scuffling, I felt something that might be called a moment of peace. Note that, Damian Dooley, Grand Inquisitor of my toadfish soul: blasphemy can be followed by peace.

With these reflections, I drifted from channel to channel through the marsh, using the oars to keep from bogging down in the grass. Wading birds cocked their heads and watched as I drifted by. I took a peach from my pack and broke the skin with my front teeth and ate it down. I sucked the filaments off the stone, then dumped it overboard. Bass surfaced for a bite, then were gone. If I could have any woman out here, away from inquiring eyes, it would not be a white, powdery Bandy sister, who was no more than a vulgar representation of the *Pudentia*. It would be Theresa. Theresa, who turned over the rock of our family's secrets with her hickory stick.

Unfortunately, I couldn't get to her in the *Elzéar*. I had achieved the boat; could I get the car, too? It was that, or ask Calvin Fleetwood to drive me to her shack in his Cadillac and have him wait in his refrigerated car while I went inside to her cabin, and him sitting there all the while with his pair of hands lying dead across his crotch, as if he had just gotten through pulling his pope, then return to his jovial jokes about high yaller pussy, and how it don't matter what color it is on the outside, 'cause it sure enough is pink on the inside. Calvin Fleetwood, family panderer, a leech in more ways than one!

It took a few minutes of gazing across the infernal sameness of the marsh before I realized I was utterly lost. I had escaped Hurt's Landing a little too well. I had mislaid Runaway Negro Creek somewheres back a while, or it had mislaid me. I reckoned I was in the Cabbage Marshes, a place I knew for a maze, where all the channels and creeks look the same, and where all but one will lead you into a shallow dead end.

This is where philosophizing in a marsh will get you.

Mind you, anyone can get turned around in a marsh. Turn around and panic. That's what marshes are made for; the world delights in making places like this. The evening breeze freshened up and the marsh grass commenced that plague-locust noise that will whittle your nerves down to thin, transparent points. Don't lose control, boy, I told myself. Remember the sun, it'll guide you. It sets in the west, even out here.

I got the Evinrude started again and revved it hard. There might not have been enough draft for a toy tugboat on this stretch of the creek, but I tilted her in anyway and blew out of there, going too fast for the water I was in. Who cares? Force the issue, make it fate's fault if I ground the *Elzéar* and bust her propellor. I'd do like any other man and shrug and say, Well, goll dang, I was moving along okay, how could I have seen that sandbar, then all of a sudden she hits it and the whole shooting match goes ass over teakettle. I didn't know whether to shit or go blind.

And goddammit if I didn't bust out of that scummy little creek and pop right into the Lazaretto, not all that far from the mouth of

Runaway Negro Creek. I must have circled back to where I'd started from, the way lost people always do. Around here, escape isn't as easy as it might sound at first. You have to study and plot if you want to get it right.

I stayed on the Lazaretto this time and passed the mansion on Shell Island, where talk said the man who built the Brooklyn Bridge had once lived. The mansion stood all alone on its private island, with the landing all washed away and never replaced. The man's name had fallen into disrepute, talk said. Once the island was all strung with lanterns, and the man's kids rode ponies in circles around and around the yard, like in a carnival. And when the kids and the ponies weren't enough, the man brought in a barge loaded with bone-white cattle to graze on his land so he would not have to drink the milk that came from off his island. The barge was negotiating the big curve out in front of the Isle of Hope. There were hunters in the marsh, or someone poaching deer on the Wormslow grounds, but whatever it was, the gunshots panicked the cattle and they all took to one side of the barge. And the thing capsized on top of the poor animals, and at high tide in the center of the channel, with no one to lead them, they had no chance to make it to shore. The waters there are part of the Intracoastal Waterway, so the Army engineers came out to drag for the corpses. But some of them got away and surfaced down the river a couple days later, great big stiff, gas-filled carcasses come up to get the sun's warmth.

That was the end of the lantern parties at the Shell Island mansion.

The Lazaretto began angling toward Wassaw Sound and the ocean. The open water of the Atlantic was no place for a bateau. I cut inland toward Jones Narrows and The Branches.

The Branches were five fingers of water that ran behind the old Wormslow plantation, where deer were sighted and poached on fall mornings. I swung into the center of the shoaled-in creek so as not to disturb a couple of Negroes my father's age who were fishing in the shallow water. They looked up as I passed but did not wave, as the rules of river courtesy tell us to do. For them, there was no sense running the risk of waving to a white stranger. Them niggers didn't even wave at us, Jefferson Marster would have said had he been in this boat. The blacks provided endless hours of shouted conversation and spoiled friendships and family relations on the Isle of Hope. When some member of the family or visitor to the house would start in about the damned niggers, my father would jump in and stop the proceedings. "Now, I don't want to hear that kind of talk. You just give them a bateau to fish from and a plot of ground to grow their greens on, and you won't have to worry about them for the rest of your life." And whoever was there representing the Isle would shake his head and grumble, "You ain't been down here long enough to understand," which in that polite way of talking meant, *Shut your mouth, Yankee*. Because to have black folks catching their own fish and growing their own vegetables without having to skulk around begging for the magnanimously bestowed Marster charity was more than these white men could imagine.

Then my father would push his Isle of Hope visitor a step further and say, "Shit, I don't mind going out on the river with some of those boys and sharing a bottle with them, long as they show me where the fish are biting." And everyone in the room would bite their lips and shift their fannies on their chairs at the thought of a white man drinking from the same bottle as a black. Then some old member of the Marster clan would slip me an eye as if to say, Now, *you* don't really hold with that, do you? But the eye I would give him back was blind.

What did I feel about these people who lived all around us, but never with us? I was afraid of them. I did not like them. Not because of their color or their speech or smell. Because of how my father used them. Because he thought they were a people without a past, like on Callibogee. Because he thought you could take your pleasure among them without having to sneak around. Because he thought they weren't watching. But that was no more true than that dead gators don't move.

RAT PALMS

In The Branches, the water was opaque with the sun as good as set, but I knew I had at least five good feet of draft beneath me. On one side were the thick but well-tended woods of Wormslow. In the center of the fingers of water was an island that reared up like the humped back of a bottle-nosed dolphin. A little bluff, surprising in this flat land, a place shaven of bush and scrub and all but the most orderly of trees, willows and oaks, with a little cove where flagstones had been laid down to make a landing. This was Bonaventure Island. The cemetery island that held the Marster family plot. I knew I'd been heading here all the while. I steered the *Elzéar* gently into its cove.

Once, my mother and I had come here in pilgrimage, for instruction, when my father was up North. She was carrying flowers, and we had been ferried over by Freeman Prince, one of Jefferson Marster's half servants. It had been a memorable visit. Not because the Marster dead had risen up to greet us and offer consolation, but because I had *repudiated* her, as she had put it. We debarked as I would today, and walked gravely up the rise that kept the feet of the dead out of the water. At the top, we stood before the stone of her grandfather, a man I had never known. Evangeline was in a transfixed state. I hazarded a glance at her without fear of detection. On her face was a baleful stare. There was something evaluating in her eyes, the kind of look men preparing for a fistfight in a tavern have, a challenge, as if she were inviting the occupant of the tomb to come out with his dukes up, like some kind of pugilistic Lazarus, and show her just what kind of stuff he was made of. I was shocked. Where was the reverence for the Marster past? Shocked and delighted, secretly, to realize that she, too, was at war with the Marsters, and that she had enough hatred for all of them put together, the living and the dead alike. Only this Marster, being a poor defenseless corpse, was a lot easier and more painless to hate than her own father.

After a while she remembered I was there. In that instructional tone of voice she told me, "You must not be afraid of the cemetery. Only superstitious people are."

This is a baseball family, I noted silently. Baseball is founded on nothing if not on superstition. So don't tell me not to be superstitious.

"Do not loathe this place," she went on. "It can provide an odd sort of comfort. Bonaventure has always been a comfort to me. Look at the way it rises out of the water. This island has never been washed over by flood. How could it be? It would be an abomination, the dead buried under water. Do you understand that?"

Whether I did or didn't, it didn't matter to Evangeline. I was merely an attending ear. I looked from my mother's face down the slope to the bateau where Mr. Freeman Prince was waiting for the white folks to finish with their cemetery business so he could ferry us back. As I watched, he took out one of those sneaky little half-pint bottles from his shirt and drank a good pull off it. He saw me watching him, went to slip the bottle back in his shirt, then changed his mind. He flashed me a big wink and a quick smile, as if we were a couple of playmates playing a trick on the mistress of the house.

For a moment I desperately wanted a pull off that bottle. It was the appeal of having something real in my hands here on this island of spirits, the way I imagined a bottle warmed by a man's jacket on a late spring day would be.

I watched that man satisfy his thirst, and his boredom, too, most likely, and listened to my mother drone on in her grand, dolorous manner.

"The dead do instruct," she was telling me. "They instruct more than the living."

Was it watching Mr. Prince take a drink that loosened my tongue, as if I'd been the one pulling on the bottle? I went and asked her, "Don't you think these dead folks miss being up here with the living?"

Evangeline turned on me. I had broken the welcome spell that this place cast on her.

"You *repudiate* me. You repudiate all those on this island! Well, I suppose I can't be expecting too much of you, not with your mixed heritage."

RAT PALMS

I stared at the ground, so richly fertilized with the Marster dead. It was only a matter of time before she accused me of taking my father's side, and of course, she got around to it.

I mumbled my excuses, but to no effect. Though the only thing I was sorry about was having set off her tirade on an island — a place I couldn't walk away from.

And now today, I was tying up the *Elzéar* in the sandy cove where Freeman Prince had sat pulling on his bottle. Tying her up good and tight, because you don't want to get marooned in a cemetery. Everything that had been under the surface on the afternoon of that pilgrimage had come to light. Now, there was no one left to tend to the dead but me. And I had not come here in tribute.

When I had the bateau secure, I walked up the rise, dragging my pack behind me, toward where the gravestones of the great Marster retailers tilted. *Okay, you ghosts,* I addressed the stones, *what do you have to teach me today?*

Everything in this world is give and take, so I hear, even when you're dealing with the dear departed. You've got to give something to the dead before they'll bestow their wormy knowledge upon you. I had no flowers, and I didn't figure they could do much with the peaches in my pack, though all the pictures I'd ever seen had shown the dead in full possession of their teeth, if nothing else. I had my bones, but I was not about to lay them down.

That left my voice. I sang:
Marster be dead, Timmy be quick,
Timmy jump over the Marster pit.
Then I read their names:
Pharris
MacKinley
Dewey
Jeremiah
Waller
Jefferson

Evangeline
Elzéar
Timmy
Gotcha!

Then I heard it. A high-pitched, raspy howl from the other side of the rise. I promised never to take the dead's name in vain again. More howling. I listened: too hysterical and undignified for the dead. Someone else was using the cemetery island of Bonaventure for some odd kind of reflection.

Then I saw her. *Old hag*, I swore at her under my breath, though as she came closer I saw she was not much older than my mother. She came over the rise of the humpbacked island, picking her way through the long grass among the graves. A cleaning lady's dress and lank, hanging hair. A white woman who looked as though she spent a greater part of the time out in the weather. I caught an animal smell off her as she approached.

I knew who she was. The crazy lady who lived on the grounds of the Wormslow plantation. They kept her there in a cabin to scare away the kids and poachers and the couples who went there to lie down.

I don't know why I wasn't afraid of her this time. I guess because I'd already seen one crazy person today, and it had been a lot worse than this. I'd had my scare. There wasn't room for two in my soul today. When she figured she was close enough, she let out her crazy-woman's shriek again. I just stood there and held my ground and let her come.

"You're not scaring me, ma'am."

"That you singing?" she accused me. She was more afraid than I'd been. "What're you thinking, making that kind of a noise?"

I smiled. I had conjured a haint, just like Mrs. Stafford said she could. Not bad for my first time out on the water.

"This is my island," I told her. "You're in my graveyard."

"You're living, boy. Graveyard belongs to the dead."

"That's not what my mother says."

The crazy woman raised a claw in the air.

"Your mother," she said, and I got a feeling somehow that she knew Evangeline, and I wondered what she had against her. "Fuck your mother."

I got a high feeling of elation and freedom from those words. I tried them on for myself, and felt higher. Crazy woman not so crazy after all.

I took a step toward her. "Anyway, what are you doing here?" I teased her. "You're supposed to be back in the Wormslow woods."

She gave me another shriek and showed me claw number two. Maybe she didn't like anyone getting too close. I backed off, but I wasn't frightened. Nothing frightening about a crazy person acting crazy.

She pointed at a stone nearby. "They're my dead, too."

"Oh, yeah?"

It was like playing a kids' game, except here we were, fighting over the rights to a bunch of moldering corpses. Evangeline would have been proud of me.

"What's your name?" I asked her.

"McQuithy."

"Don't see no McQuithys around here."

"We're related by marriage," she defended herself.

"Well, then, who knows? Maybe you and I are related, too. They say everyone is around here."

It was a joke, but she didn't laugh. That's the problem with crazy people: they have no sense of humor.

She waved me off. "I'm not related to anybody."

"A person who ain't related to anybody doesn't skulk around old graveyards, communing with the dead," I pointed out.

My logic, so dearly acquired, was lost on her. Then, praise the Lord, the few shreds of it that did remain after the beating it had taken disappeared when I got a good whiff of the animal smell she gave off from under her cleaning lady's dress. The smell of the woods, a matted-fur smell. The smells of perdition had always been leather and bourbon and cigar smoke, and the green smell of fresh money and billiards tables at Bo-Peep's. The smell off the McQuithy woman was a new one in that catalog. But familiar, somehow; I recognized it from underneath the chapel, with Father Dooley thundering on above, all of which had started me on my path here in the first place. Rabbit rib bones. The termites going about their eternal toil, the moisture and rot, the good animal earth.

Praise the Lord, I blasphemed joyously a second time, because I saw how the McQuithy woman's dress was open in the middle like the clothing of an innocent, where a couple of buttons were missing. I could see one of her titties tilting up at me, and how her skin was not nearly as weathered there as it was on the rest of her body. The woman of my dreams was someone like Theresa or the crazy McQuithy lady, a freak or a cripple who carried the earth smell, and not the Shell Island kind, those cow-murderers. And glory hallelujah for that!

I stood there, smelling and staring, and forgetting altogether to talk, which is what humans think they must do when they are cast together in a place like this. The McQuithy woman got fed up with being ignored.

"Boy!" she shouted at me.

She turned around and stalked away, then disappeared down the other side of the rise. Just as vain and touchy as any other female. Not crazy at all, really. That was a little disappointing.

I checked the sky and saw I had put myself on Bonaventure Island for the night.

I went to the water and pulled the ropes on the *Elzéar* to make sure she was tied good and tight. *Be there tomorrow morning*, I implored her, then got busy picking a spot to spread out my sleeping bag. I had my choice of a half dozen live oaks and as many willows to protect me from the dew, and I tested the ground for rocks beneath each one, sidestepping the graves as I had been taught to. Never walk on dirt under which the dead are buried. They don't like it.

RAT PALMS

Plainly, the McQuithy woman was gone. Swam back across The Branches, or flew away on her broomstick. I gathered up whatever fall wood was around, dry enough to make a fire.

Bonaventure was not exactly wilderness camping. The island had nothing to do with nature at all; it had been stolen back from nature by the Marsters. Built up and cleared and sculpted to make a monument. A night in the woods on Callibogee would have provided other ghosts, the Stafford kind. On Bonaventure, the dead were civilized. They could be studied like the pages of a book. I was acquainted with their needs and weaknesses and reasoning. If, at the stroke of midnight, the graves on this cemetery island popped open and the old Marsters came thumping up, I wouldn't be scared, and I certainly wouldn't be at a loss for words. *Why?* I'd ask them. *Why did you make such a mess of it? And why did you make me?*

That would send them scurrying back into their holes! We'd see who was scared of whom!

I lit a fire and it burned a circle of dry air out of the humidity. I dined on three peaches and a chocolate bar, and threw the pits into The Branches for the trout, the bass and, of course, the faithful toadfish. I considered my world at that moment. Underneath, the unquiet Marsters were moldering in their graves. On Hurt's Landing, my father stood in an empty house, in an Indians uniform, clean and white but for the spreading sweat stains under his arms, thirty-two hundred-dollar bills in his pocket, winding up in front of a mirror and refusing to take a drink. Evangeline was still shopping in the stores on Broughton Street, despite the fact that it was long past shopping hours. A crazy woman in the Wormslow woods knew of my existence.

These were things beyond my changing. But for now, I was in a sleeping bag on Bonaventure Island, suspended and unhurtable.

I opened my eyes into darkness. My face and hair were soaked. A low-country ground fog had rolled in thick as soup as I slept. In that fog, I sensed movement.

I slithered out of my sleeping bag and reached for the flashlight, then thought better of it. A light would give nothing but reflection in fog this thick. I felt my way to the nearest live oak but the trunk was too thick to get my arms around, and there were no low branches. I ran, bent double like a man under fire. The next tree was a young willow with a low crotch. I started in climbing. When I was six feet off the ground the fog turned luminous, as if there were candles planted in it. I followed the trunk upward, climbing easily toward the light. Another couple feet and I was out of it.

In the clear sky above, a half-moon burned pale, lighting up the carpet of fog below. Up here, the air was warmer. I considered the rootless treetops of Bonaventure, anchored in fog. The atmosphere was still and hollow, the way it gets to be in the small hours. In this relative warmth, I made myself comfortable in the crotch of the willow's main branch and watched the night. The head of the night, above the mist. The feet and trunk and soft parts were below, wound in a sheet of fog.

A nighthawk broke the cover, a field mouse protesting stupidly in its beak.

Then, in my dream, I was back in Grayson Stadium watching a game. Zeke Justice was pitching. The batter popped one up in foul territory, right in front of my seat, and the players converged to catch the ball, including Zeke. The infielders gathered by the railing with their gloves up, and their faces were frozen and waxy. I realized then that they were dead men, and that all their faces were my father's. My father went to jostle them out of the way to catch the ball but they would not move, they were as heavy as stone. Suddenly my task was to help him keep the ball from falling to the ground, for that fall would mean his death. I strained over the railing to shag it, then had to catch myself as I started tumbling off my willow branch, through the fog, onto the tombstones below, back on Bonaventure Island.

I shinnied down the trunk, cursing the mind's stubborn capacity to dream. I went back into the ground fog, where it was less frightening than in that tree of nightmares. Can you sleep to forget a dream? I don't know, but that's what I did for the rest of the night. I didn't dream that dream again. I didn't need to. I had gotten the message the first time.

By the time I awoke, the thickest of the fog had burned off. The McQuithy woman was sitting on the ground next to me in the sunlight, her arms around her knees, her dress spread out on the grass next to her. I sat up in my sleeping bag. The zipper was open along the side. I doubted I had slept that way.

She put her hand on my arm to keep me from speaking. Then lay down on the wet ground beside to me, and I saw what it was all about. Her titties with their two wide, walnut-colored nipples and her round belly and a good tangle of brown fur right in the middle. She didn't have that tight, screwed-up crazy woman's mouth any more. The hag had become glorious. Her mouth was soft and with her eyes closed I could look all I wanted. She was beautiful, I realized painfully.

This was the glory. This was what people died for.

I don't know what came over me. I jumped out of that sleeping bag and ran down the soft slope to the sandy cove where I had tied up the *Elzéar*. She was there, floating easy and untouched. A kingfisher was perched on the bait well. I stared at that goddamned bateau, so tightly tied up, then looked up the hill. *You fool. You foolish child, I cursed myself.*

When I got back to the grassy spot, she was gone, of course. I rushed to the top of Bonaventure and saw her stalking down to the water on the Wormslow side. Naked, her dress in her hand. Her body had gone clumsy and clawlike again. The crazy McQuithy woman's body. I had done that. I sprinted after her.

She hit the water of The Branches. I called out, "Don't! Stop! I've got a boat. I can take you over!"

She plunged in awkwardly, stumbled, then found her feet. The green-black water foamed around her fur spot.

She turned and shouted, "I don't need your tardy graces, boy!"

Then she let herself go, kicked and began swimming toward the far bank. Her dress trailed behind her like the outline of a drowning woman. She skittered up the bank on the Wormslow side and crashed through the brush like a panicked animal, which was all wrong, because I was the panicked animal, not her, but it was too late to tell her that.

"You look like a backwoods nigger," my mother greeted me when I tied up at Hurt's Landing later that morning and came walking across the Lazaretto Road with my bag in my hand.

I knew something had happened to my father. He would not have her saying "nigger" around the house, not when he was there.

"Where the hell have you been?" she asked.

"Over on Bonaventure. You told me a cemetery could do a lot of instructing. It did."

It was obvious I had earned no grace in her eyes for having made the pilgrimage. I looked past her and saw our white Chrysler New Yorker backed up to the house with the trunk open. Mr. Fleetwood, the Marster family leech gatherer and handyman, was carrying out some heavy-looking bags. The New Yorker's trunk was as wide open as the grave. Stow them coffins, Mr. Cadillac Fleetwood.

"Looks as though someone's going somewhere," I commented.

"We can't be staying here any longer."

"What's Daddy say about that?"

"They took your father away yesterday evening, while you were out on the river."

"Took him away? Where did he go?"

"To an institution. To a home for those who have lost their lucidity."

I felt shock, but no surprise. His complacent smile and plea of helplessness had generously prepared me for this.

"It's not his lucidity he's lost," I told my mother. "It's his will."

RAT PALMS

"If you take comfort in philosophy at a time like this, when your own father has just been taken away to the insane asylum, well, then, may you be the stronger for it."

She pulled out a Viceroy from the pack she had been cradling in the palm of her hand.

"Now, you go upstairs and see if I haven't missed anything. While you're at it, get yourself washed up. You stink. Of what, I'd rather not know."

I went up. The front room was still inhabited by the heavy, hostile Marster pieces, but everything personal had been swept away: the paintings, photos, plaques and trophies. The house had become characterless, like a furnished apartment offered for rent, where one of the conditions for rental was that the place be stripped of personality. I went upstairs. My room had suffered the same fate. Furniture exactly in place, but the drawers and closet emptied into the suitcases that I had seen Calvin Fleetwood lugging out.

I took in the silence in the upstairs hallway. Then entered my father's study and sickroom.

The study had not been packed up. Disrupted, but not swept clean. It showed signs of a struggle. The crushed Colt 45 cans kicked into the corner, the Johnny Harris cartons scattered, the Caton volumes on the Civil War thrown down and their spines broken. I went to the closet. Everything was gone. The equipment bag, uniforms, glove, shoes. Everything that said *baseball*.

I wanted a memento from the Battle of Hurt's Landing. I wanted his glove, or maybe a uniform, something to start my own hall of fame with. But everything had been pillaged, wrapped and boxed, squared away. Then I saw the thing. A quarried blue-granite plaque with a perfectly round, seamless granite baseball set into it. How could they have overlooked something like that? I picked up the plaque and read the inscription. *To the kindest white man in Savannah.* I knew I couldn't get both the plaque and the ball to safety — they were too heavy — so I chose the ball. It felt good in my hand.

Odd, ungraspable, with no seams. You can't control a ball without seams. It would have to stand for my father till I caught up to the real thing.

I didn't bother with my room, or with washing, either. There was nothing to wash off. I went on downstairs with the granite ball in my gym bag, and from the front porch I saw Calvin Fleetwood fussing over the New Yorker's oil and pulling on the fan belts. Evangeline was standing beside him, watching him critically. In the silence, as Fleetwood glared at the dipstick, I picked up the merry jingle of ice in the amber-colored toddy my mother was holding on to. There's a certain sound ice makes in a glass in this air, my father used to say, though he never did say what that sound was. He left it up to the imagination.

Ting-ting, went the drink. The tinny, icy knell of Hurt's Landing.

"What happened in there?" I asked Evangeline.

"A disgrace," she told me. And then: "We will have time enough to talk about it."

Calvin Fleetwood gave her a chaste kiss of peace on the forehead like a goddamned priest. She got into the New Yorker and positioned herself behind the wheel ceremoniously, checking her mirrors and her lipstick, tying her scarf. I understood it was my turn to get in.

I settled in on the seat next to her. Take one last look, boy, I encouraged myself. It's your right, it belongs to you. I turned back and saw Calvin Fleetwood watching us go, his hands clasped together, wringing each other, crotch high. I saw the white front of our former house. And beyond all that, parked on the road in the shade, Jefferson Marster's creme-colored Buick, the driver's face shielded behind tinted glass.

I knew the way. Down the Lazaretto Road, skirting Wormslow, over the bridge that fastened the Isle of Hope to the American continent. At Sandfly Crossing we took a new way, straight west to pick up the highway for Atlanta.

And I swear, I was not entirely surprised when Evangeline

announced that the two of us were driving to California.

"What about my report for Father Dooley?"

"You can write it if you feel the need to. Though I doubt he'll ever see it."

II
DESERT TONGUES

12

"What's in Californa?" I asked Evangeline once we were on the mainland and heading west across the state of Georgia.

"California," she informed me, "is a place for people who have overstayed their welcome everywhere else."

We rocketed through a crossroads town where some old geezers were rocking on a swing in front of the general store. In the sideview mirror, I saw one of them let fly at our comfortable automobile with a brown rope of tobacco juice.

"How can you overstay your welcome in a place where you've always lived?" I asked her.

But my reasoning did not have any more chance of moving her to speak than the old geezer had of hitting our speeding car with his tobacco juice.

"We will have time enough to discuss such things," she told me. "You will forgive me, but I'm not in the mood for philosophy just now. It's the same with this so-called reflection of yours: simple toying with words, if you ask me. That priest Dooley said it himself. 'The sin of pride, vainglory in words' — though I must admit you do put your own twist on it. Now, please leave me alone, I'm busy driving."

Goddammit, I thought. If I sing they call it noise. If I reflect they call it wordplay, pride and vainglory. Where am I supposed to come up for air in this deal?

Evangeline clamped her hands on the wheel, thrust her body back in the seat and concentrated on the boring business of driving. A vision of self-absorption in her shade glasses and scarf. Behind the tight little line her mouth made, she ground her teeth together. I could see, for the time being, that I wasn't going to get any more answers about my father out of her than I would have from the wax dummy that belonged to the make-believe gypsy at the Chatham County Fair. She could have been a statue for all the movement she displayed over the next hours. From time to time, her fingers would tense and relax on the wheel and her knuckle joints go white, then red again. That was the extent of it. Otherwise, she might as well have petrified and turned to stone right there next to me.

Though once, abruptly, in the midst of the road noise that passed for silence, she said, "After all, I do have people out there."

I eased my hand into my athletic bag, which held all my personal effects for the foreseeable future, and got my fingers around the granite baseball. Odd to derive comfort from a stone, but that's where things stood this morning. I cast my eyes sideways to see if Evangeline was watching me; her face was as expressive as a sphinx's. God only knows what she would have done had she discovered me rubbing up the granite baseball that had belonged to my father. Accused me of shrine building, idol worshiping, side taking and morbid attachment to a man we were driving away from at the rate of one hundred miles an hour.

And who knows, she might have been right. Look at it from her side. My father travels across dangerous waters to sin, gets hurt in the process, I come home the next morning with Mrs. Stafford's blanket hairs clinging to my jeans and cover for his lies, and tell lies in the process. Then when it's Evangeline's turn to suffer, I apply the whole weight of my impudent, questioning mind to her suffering. I even refuse to contemplate her shiner. For a minute I wished I could forget my trip to Theresa's shack and the sated leech in the toilet bowl. I resolved to love her, simply love her, and not just study her.

We traveled inland. The temperature rose. The air, the little that did seep into the car through the air conditioning, was unbreathable. We drove through miles of pine scrub, then cotton fields, then woods where the trees stood knee-deep in black water that flashed in the leaden sunlight. Savannah is not the South, my mother used to say, implying we were somehow above all those land-bound, backward people who grew the food we ate. Now I had to admit she was right. Nothing I had seen among our past-besotted, dignified squares downtown, or on our salt-stained landing where nothing moved but the tide, had prepared me for this landscape. I felt its heavy hostility toward us, two desperately fragile creatures in a fast car, as if I really had caught that old geezer's rope of tobacco juice full in the face. And all this coming at us at a tremendous rate of speed, things that seemed to be far in the distance throwing themselves at the windshield as if to say, Here, this is the world, this is how it will come to you.

I looked down at the map across my knees. Evangeline was right. There would be time enough to discuss such matters as there were before us. The country made it so. We had driven like hell all morning and hardly made a dent in the state of Georgia. Let alone the South. Let alone the United States.

I dropped the granite ball into my bag and dozed off. I prayed for dispensation from dreams in which my father was offered up to me in all the cruelty of his predicament, and this I was granted. Something else replaced him in my vagrant thoughts: the crazy McQuithy woman. She must have crept into my mind, though I didn't realize it until I felt the bone-on I had lying down along my thigh. Remember this much, I addressed myself. Next time a crazy woman wants to lie down next to you, don't worry whether your bateau's tied up or not.

These vain reflections were interrupted by a siren whooping behind us. I turned around. The siren belonged to the Georgia highway patrol.

"Well, how about that?" Evangeline said. "Another one of life's little miseries."

A minute later a Georgia state trooper with fresh razor nicks on his neck stuck his head through the car window. With his head came an oven-hot burst of air off the road and a turpentine stink from a distillery somewhere back in the pine scrub.

"You in a hurry, ma'am?" he asked in a pinched, nasal voice.

Evangeline turned and punched the lighter button on the dashboard.

"You was exceeding the limit by a good thirty miles an hour," he took to lecturing her. "And that's if I'm being generous to you all."

Evangeline did not give him the grace of an answer. The lighter button popped up obediently and she lit a Viceroy.

"You could catch yourself a hefty fine for that kind of speeding." The trooper took a look at our long automobile. "Yep, mighty hefty. Payable to the justice of the peace of McClintock County, on the spot, up there in the woods someplace."

He pointed off in the distance, to nothing in particular.

My mother inhaled the smoke from the Viceroy without blowing it out afterward. I never knew where that smoke went. I suppose it just became a part of her.

"Young man," she finally said to the state trooper. "Yesterday evening, I had to commit my husband to a home for the insane. This is a time of great distress to me. I hope you will take that into account as you prepare to write up one of those tickets you surely intend to give me."

The poor trooper stared into that mask of a woman with her old-fashioned scarf pulled over her hair to keep it in place, and the shade glasses she would not take off, smoking a cigarette with the filter end as flattened as a squashed animal on the highway. The policeman took a step back from the car and rubbed his sweaty forehead. Evangeline had sacrificed herself, and won.

He looked at our car again, but with new eyes.

"In a big heap like this you don't feel the road, I reckon. But you'd better pay you a little more attention to the limit. Next officer down the road might not be so bighearted as me."

Evangeline sat with her hands on the wheel and her eyes set straight ahead, even once the trooper's car had disappeared into the heat haze that ended the road.

"Well done," I told her.

She turned on me. "Well done? What was well done?"

"Handling that trooper the way you did."

"Just because we are on the road, in an automobile, in this vulnerable state, does not mean that you're free to speak to me in any way you wish."

A pair of trucks barreled by and rocked us as we sat on the shoulder. Evangeline swung out onto the road in their wake, and before long, she had us traveling at a hundred again.

"What did he do that was so bad, anyway?"

"He?"

"My father, who else?"

"If knowing is of any comfort to you, your precious father stood out on the corner of Bull and Broughton, acting like he was pitching a baseball and speaking in some kind of language that no one could make head nor tail of! Isn't that insane enough for you? Or would you have preferred him to chop us all to bits with an ax and feed us to the crabs?"

"He must have been speaking French."

"I don't care what language he was speaking!" Evangeline burst out, and the car veered as she jerked the wheel unintentionally. "He might as well have been talking in tongues for all that it mattered! Acting the fool on the corner of Bull and Broughton!"

"But everyone knew who he was," I pleaded. "Couldn't allowances have been made? Couldn't someone have just led him away from the street to somewhere quiet where he wouldn't have made a spectacle of himself?"

"Maybe someone could have. I don't know who that someone might have been. But whoever it was, that person certainly wasn't on the corner of Bull and Broughton when your father commenced carrying on. And, yes, everyone knew who he was. That was part of the problem, don't you understand?"

Another minute, another mile or two.

"Meanwhile," Evangeline added, "you were lucky enough to have been out on the river."

I knew what had happened to my father. Why he had started in speaking French. He was like a jukebox that gets kicked in a barroom brawl, and starts in playing old tunes that no one even knew were in there, and it keeps on playing them, over and over again. And because no one wants to hear those old tunes, someone gives the machine another kick to shut it up again so they can get on with the business at hand.

That kick is called the men in the white coats. On the corner of Bull and Broughton.

And, yes, I was lucky enough to have been out on the river at the time, dear mother. There is no sense in regretting that, not when you're rushing away from the place of regret at a hundred miles an hour.

The heat and road must have lulled me, along with the lack of sleep the night before. I slept through the afternoon and awoke to a slanting sun and the state of Alabama. I glanced at Evangeline. Nothing moving there. Our speed had dropped down to almost the legal limit.

"It feels like we're standing still."

"I see you've decided to accompany me on this trip after all." She rubbed at her temples. "This sun is giving me a terrible headache. I'm afraid we're going to have to be stopping pretty soon."

She pulled off her shade glasses a minute to massage her eyes, and I saw what her face had become after a day behind the wheel. Her eyes were red and there was a vertical line cut between them, as if a suitor named Mr. Worry had stolen in while I was sleeping and put it there with an awl.

We slowed for the next town. I watched a feed and seed, a used car concession and a Holy Vineyard Deliverance Center roll by. And a motor court consisting of a handful of cottages scattered around a grassy plot where a swing set stood. Evangeline touched the brake pedal, gave the motor court an evaluating glance, then replaced her shade glasses.

"We're going to have to stop somewhere, sooner or later," she warned as she accelerated us through the outskirts of the town.

"Somewhere, ma'am," I agreed with her. "But not right here, and not right now."

"We can't just drive right across the country."

"No. It looks too big for that."

We both knew what awaited us, and neither of us wanted it. A single room in a low, blockhouse motel, or a cramped cottage, with two soft beds in indecent proximity. The kind of lodgings we would allow ourselves. Not that we didn't have the money for something better. But since it was against the Marster code of dignity and proper showing to be out on the road in an automobile in the first place, with no more notion of a destination than a compass point, looking for the kind of lodgings you'd expect to find among the cotton fields and scrub pine of Alabama, then while we're at it, let's spend the smallest possible amount for the meanest, sorriest room. Let's punish ourselves for being what and where we are — even as we protest that the entire trip was forced upon us in the first place.

You just can't beat that Marster logic!

Dinner at Skeeter's Big Biscuit.

"So this is what people eat," Evangeline said when the cream-colored plate of biscuits and sausage gravy was set before her on the mustard-colored Formica table.

"You wanted to go to Skeeter's," I reminded her.

"I had heard of it. I was curious."

She fenced with the biscuit with her fork, then proceeded to mash the lumps out of the lumpy gravy. Her fork made an alarming noise when it hit the plate. The lumps she was persecuting turned out to be bits of sausage that wouldn't let themselves be flattened. Those lumps didn't bother me. I had dined on three peaches, a candy bar and a mindful of ghosts the evening before, and had eaten nothing all day. I was hungry, and not about to imitate her sensibilities. I put away my biscuit, then most of hers. Besides, they weren't that bad.

I shoved away my plate.

"What if California is like this?" I teased her.

"Like what?"

"Full of doughy biscuits and lumpy gravy. We don't know anything about California, except where it is on the map. What if that's all there is to eat out there?" I pointed at the quarter biscuit that lay prone in her plate, awash in brown sauce. "Are we going to turn around and come back?"

"Nothing," Evangeline declared in her grandest, most wounded manner, "is ever going to make me return to the Isle of Hope."

The waitress in her uniform starched with spilled biscuit gravy delivered us our bill, and we stepped out of the violently air-conditioned restaurant. There was still a good streak of light in the west, and the sky above us glowed with warm, moist twilight. For a moment we stood watching the little stand of pine on the far side of the parking lot, where a noisy cloud of songbirds was rising and alighting again, settling in for the night. This is all the world affords us of peace, I reflected. A few minutes between Skeeter's Big Biscuit and the interstate highway. To earn it, you must stand in a place of no support: a strip of asphalt, a nameless town, a cloud of birds announcing the night. And a terrified stranger beside you, who is your procreator.

RAT PALMS

When I went to pick up my feet and trudge over to the New Yorker, I found they had sunk into the heat-softened tar. That's what happened to the saber-toothed tigers, who once lived in California. They got mired down in the tar pits and became easy prey. Came out of Skeeter's Big Biscuit with their bellies full of sausage gravy and bang! Instant fossil. Just like Evangeline and me. A pair of fossils from the Isle of Hope museum.

When I got to the car I was alone. Evangeline was still standing in the middle of the parking lot, staring at the car as if it were a coffin.

"I don't suppose there would be a decent motel in this biscuit-eating town."

"I suppose not. But I can always drive."

She thought that over.

"You don't have a license," she told me.

"Don't need a license to know how to drive."

"I suppose you know how to?"

"Driven plenty of times."

"I see."

She considered the darkening sky and the streak of light in the west growing ever paler. And the road stretching from Skeeter's parking lot all the way to the Pacific Ocean.

"Where have you done all this driving of yours?"

"Driving Daddy back from the beach, for example."

"That was back home," she countered. "When the world would make allowances. That's not the case any more."

"It could have made a lot more allowances than it did. If it had, we wouldn't be where we are."

Together, we looked at the brightly lit, anonymous restaurant and the road.

"Maybe so," she admitted. "Still, you can't keep going to the well of forgiveness. Even on the Isle of Hope."

"Especially on the Isle of Hope."

She put her hand in her purse and gave me the keys, as we both knew she would. I took them and settled in behind the wheel under my mother's watchful eye. Just point it, I reminded myself. Go where the road goes.

"Remember, this thing needs gasoline to run on. You'd do well to stop pretty soon."

The next town I came to had fewer lights than the ones on the New Yorker's dashboard. I coasted down the main street in search of a filling station sign. The place was a thousand times sorrier looking than even Sandfly Crossing, and that was saying a lot. Men were squatted down on their haunches in front of the outside lights of a pool hall, black and white together, as if the town was too beaten down to bother with such divisions, spitting on the sidewalk and waiting for nothing, or something, a fight, maybe, or a girl in a short dress. My father would have appreciated this town; it did not look as though you'd have to sneak around if you wanted to sin. You just made yourself available, and it came to you.

There was a filling station at the end of the main street, past where the lights ended. I pulled up in front of the Super pump and waited. It was the kind of gas station where people lived around the back, by the looks of it, with a store set up in the living room.

A few minutes later a boy came trotting out in shorts, no shirt and barefoot, with a rag in his hand.

"Mister?" he asked anxiously, scratching his head, which looked freshly shaved.

I spotted his family standing in the doorway of the shack. It was a black filling station, and their eyes let me know it. I had never had to concern myself with such matters in Savannah. The Negroes just naturally knew that my daddy was the kindest white man in Savannah.

"Do you mind filling it up with super?"

The boy looked me over, just to make sure I was white. And once he was sure, he looked me over some more, as if he still could not believe I was willing to put black gasoline in my white automobile.

RAT PALMS

Evangeline emerged from the car as the boy started filling the tank. She considered the family peering out the screen door at us by the cool blue glow of a neon beer sign.

"Like your poor daddy used to say, ain't no nigger gonna out-nigger me. I'll be right back."

She marched into the store. The family scattered, recognizing her for one of those crazy white ladies who won't accept any rules, and who can bring misery to all rule-abiding folks of any color if they're not careful. A few minutes later, she came gliding out of the shack with a rattly paper bag under one arm. She paid the boy for the gas and tipped him appreciably. Once we were past the town limits, she reached back to her overnight bag on the seat behind and drew out a brandy snifter all nicely wrapped in tissue paper.

"I asked the gentleman to give me whatever he had hidden up behind the counter. And do you know what? He obliged. I thought I would end up with a milk bottle full of moonshine, but look — these charming little miniatures. I took all he had."

She had that childish, gleeful voice that drinking people can get when they come into possession of a bottle. She half opened her rattly bag and a good dozen miniatures of Christian Brothers brandy peeped out, those little toy-size drinks. Just how Christian that brandy was, I couldn't say. Then again, the Benedictines were known for their liquor, too. Perhaps it even had some connection to the reflection process as prescribed by Father Dooley.

Evangeline snapped the seal off a couple of miniatures.

"Now, if I should doze off, and you happen to see an adequate motel for the night, don't you forget to stop. I don't intend to sit up in this old car all night."

I heard the brandy splash into my mother's snifter in the dark automobile. She dropped the empties into the map compartment on her side, and constructed a little platform for her glass out of a map of the Southern states. The drinking person's balancing act. The fumes from her Christian Brothers floated over to my side of the car.

"Medicine," she said, and took a drink. "My after-biscuit-and-gravy cordial and consolation."

"I hear tell it makes you belong to someone else."

"You do have a memory to go along with your impudence," she told me, mixing scolding and compliments. "But since you ask, I belong to myself. Entirely," she boasted, "until I choose not to."

Manifestly, she was in one of her moods to speak. To instruct. It seemed to come with the first sip of whatever particular hooch was on the menu. Who was I to deprive her of that pleasure, especially with a long night ahead?

"When you choose not to belong to yourself," I queried, "who do you belong to?"

"The arms of Morpheus," she declared, reaching down and activating the seat-recline lever.

"Morpheus?"

"Sleep," she specified. "That's a little word I picked up from your daddy, him being a Catholic, and well versed in all sorts of worthless Greek and Latin things that sound so pleasing to the ear. Must be where you get that tongue of yours that takes up so much room in your head, your . . . what did that poor Father call it?"

"Vainglory in words," I supplied.

"Oh, yes, the sin of pride."

She snorted with laughter, then took another sip. Then waved her hand in the air in summary fashion, as if giving a quick, derisive sketch of the sin of pride, as if it were hardly worthy of the lofty title of sin at all. In that gesture, I swore she could have been old Jefferson Marster himself there on the seat next to me, and I marveled how, given the differences that sex imposed, a daughter could imitate a father so faultlessly and detest him all the while.

"Morpheus. I remember once your father started in talking about the arms of Morpheus. Must have been back when we still talked. I was on the point of throwing a fit of jealousy over this Morpheus until he took out one of his dusty old books and showed me a picture of just who this Morpheus was!"

She opened her mouth and laughed long and hard.

"You two used to talk like that?"

"Oh, yes! When we loved each other. Before we discovered we enjoyed talking so much we stopped listening to one another!"

This time, there was no laughter. Just the tops of a couple more miniatures being wrenched off, then joining their empty companions in the map pouch. After she'd watched the white line for a time, her voice, dreamy now, broke the dull pattern of wind and road noise.

"It's the strangest thing, hearing myself talk that way. Sounding so much like Zeke and all. It's like, having your daddy gone, I've got to do the talking for him. I've got to say all those things I never could when he was around, what with him saying them for me. Me and everybody else, for that matter."

"That would take a brand-new tongue," I told her. "But then again, he's not really gone, is he?"

Evangeline tilted her glass and swallowed.

"We'll have time enough for that discussion," she said stiffly.

I didn't know how much Christian Brothers it would take before she would lose her resistance to my impudent, ferreting, toadfish questions. But she wasn't anywhere near the required amount. She reached back to her overnight bag and found a delicate little blue box that could have held a pair of earrings or a wedding ring. It did not. It contained earplugs, which she slipped into her ears. Then she went back to her bag and pulled out a pair of eye patches on an elastic band. She adjusted them over her eyes like a Halloween mask and turned her face to the window.

The session was adjourned for the night. Talk about twisting the arms of Morpheus! With a strategy like that, he couldn't help but come!

Mind you, there was no shortage of motels, motor courts, motor inns and bide-a-whiles on the road across the states of Alabama and

Mississippi that evening. The night was not that far gone that most of those places did not still have their outside lights on. In some of them, I could see the owners and the owners' wives sitting up in the offices, watching television, and hoping for some driven-out traveler like myself to come dragging in, desperate for a room.

But tonight, I would not be driven out. It's true, I had slept through the afternoon, but that was not the real reason. I was driving out of vengeance. You want to go to California, Mother? I'll get you there, all right, so fast you'll be sorry you plucked me off the river and coffined me up in this automobile! Do you want to have a new life, an unknown life? Free of the claws of the Marster dead but, most of all, far from whatever shame Zeke Justice was supposed to have perpetrated? Then let's get the hell on with it! I'll roll up this country like a bath mat and stow it in the trunk! Besides, I have not so generously partaken of the forgiveness of the Christian Brothers. I have the Benedictine fathers, and let me tell you, they do not lend themselves to sleep in any manner. They have preached to me never to forget the past, and to study the ways of the world. The ways of the world? Hell, if that won't scare off Morpheus, nothing will!

Not only did I have the Benedictines in my head, I had Hoss Man Allan on the radio, broadcasting for the account of Randy's Record Shop, in some border state. Now, Hoss Man Allan was nothing but a white man pretending to be a black man, which is an illogical thing to do considering the distribution of privileges between the two, and Allan did it in order to sell insurance over the radio to black people. But none of that mattered to me as long as he kept on playing those records, music that was half dignified like Old Paul Gant, half screechy like Little Richard. I sang along with those real singers, I chased them up high, I chased them down low, and more than once I even caught myself sobbing the length of a two-and-a-half minute tune by somebody called Bobby Moore and the Rhythm Aces. All this singing was made possible by Evangeline's toadfish-proof earplugs that preserved her from the disorder of her only son and chief combatant, now that Daddy was gone.

I headed in the direction of Meridian and Vicksburg. My, how time is flying. Not flying, I corrected myself. Speeding to the point of distortion. Remember how it was, before this morning, when time had been like a six-foot cast net thrown from a bass boat? Opening slowly and perfectly into full ripeness, until it all but hung suspended in thin air, the way you'd hold a breath for fear of breaking a spell. Time on the Isle of Hope. Discrete, separate, countable, a possible object of study. It won't be that way any more. Think of time as that glittering, silver, perfectly thrown net. Now, remember what shapes that net: lead sinkers sewn into its very fabric. Those sinkers seek the bottom and snatch up the prey, and when you hold them in your mouth to cast for the scavengers you are trying in turn to take, they taste of swamp muck. Remember that: the destruction of the world you knew was sewn right into that world. Which is why you are in this goddamned car in the first place.

Besides Hoss Man Allan and Benedictine reflection, I had the empty miniature bottles. Now, I am unaccustomed to conversing with empty one-and-a-half-ounce bottles, but that is exactly what I did that night in the great state of Mississippi. In their map pouch and under the seat, they rolled and tinged together at every curve of the road or deceleration for a town. They were sending me a signal. They were possessed of — how else can I describe it? — a voice. So it was only logical that I would want them to tell me some of their secrets. After all, they had been around, and seen some people I knew in their more private moments. I inquired this of them: why a person would insist on paying extra money to purchase brandy miniatures from under the counter at a Negro filling station, especially when money was advertised as being in short supply, when that person could have had a pint or more at the same price?

At the next curve in the road, and they were few in this land of straight, black, fertile fields, the miniatures sent back their answer.

For honor, they said. For it is more seemly to partake of us, with our intricate little toy labels and quaint seals, than to crack a vulgar pint from a package store. Especially where an Isle of Hope lady is involved. The price is higher, you say? Honor always costs more. Expenditures of all kinds are called for.

Not only for honor, I tried my hand at lecturing the empty bottles. For ceremony, too. There must be some pleasure to be had there, in the breaking of those puny seals.

The miniatures corrected me at the next available opportunity, which turned out to be a rotting grade crossing. What you call ceremony is really measure, they said. Or the ceremony of measuring, if you prefer. *I have taken this much. I have this much left to take. The night has this many hours left. The country, this many miles.* Calculations of this sort.

I had to trust the miniatures' opinion. They had seen that which I could only conjecture. Besides, they made the most engaging travel companions, better than any of the ghostly hitchhikers who rose up for a moment in the Chrysler's headlights, then turned into darkness. I hated to refuse those hobos Christian charity, but on this kind of errand, I did not need their company to stay awake. I had the miniatures. And it was important to stay awake, and away from those rented motel rooms, and get to this place called California, where I did not want to go. If I had to turn little liquor bottles into oracles of knowledge, so be it. You claim, Mother, that Father Damian Dooley will never see my report, even if I do stay pigheaded enough to want to write it. You underestimate me, as usual. I won't write the report, Evangeline: I will become it.

I flicked open my eyes to the Chrysler's right front tire on the gravel shoulder and saw the US 80 sign rushing at me with the drop-off and ditch and field behind it. I threw the wheel to the left and shot off the shoulder onto the pavement again, into the oncoming lane where the merciful Lord arranged for no one to be coming. There was a black-bile taste of fear in my mouth, and I retched. My foot was insensate on the gas pedal. It was time for a break, I had to admit.

On the west side of Meridian was a truck plaza, all lit up like a little town. Though Evangeline had blinded and deafened herself, I took no chances. I circled the gas islands twice and backed up to the far pump to keep the light from falling across her face. Even an innocent like me will just naturally become a strategist when pushed to it by circumstance.

It wasn't until I finished gassing up the car and went into the plaza to pay that the consideration of money occurred to me. Money was always something I had done without on Hurt's Landing, something I had personally never needed, though it was at the forefront of nearly every conversation in our house. I patted down my pockets as the pasty-faced starchy woman behind the cash looked on, and there they were, my three lucky tens and a two. Distinct Intent. I laid a little of that money down, not very much, really, when you considered how far it would carry me. I took a coffee and a Reese's Peanut Butter Cup out of the silver.

I sat down in the booth nearest the door and began work on biting a hole in the plastic cover of the coffee cup. I had my share of the winnings, but where were the other thirty-two hundred dollars? Make that thirty-one — Mrs. Stafford had kept one for a rainy day. Mind you, if ever there would be a rainy day, this was it. I didn't begrudge her a single hundred-dollar bill, not when there were thirty-one others just like it out there. But where? When a man is transported to a place for those who have lost their lucidity, or will, or both, do they not have their pockets cut and the contents removed since, supposedly, they are no longer responsible for those contents, and know not what to do with them, except to harm themselves if at all possible? Not that I wanted that money for myself; what did I have to spend on? But they were my daddy's winnings. They still belonged to him, lucidity or not.

"You having some kind of trouble with that old cover, aren't you?"

A man in truck-driver clothes hanging off his scarecrow frame was standing and watching me wrestle with the plastic cover. He was smiling kindly, and God knows I needed kindness just then. I looked down at the cover. I had managed to gnarl it into the shape of a sneering lip.

"Yes, I suppose I am."

"Let me show you how it's done."

He tore along the line on the cover to make a half-moon opening, and the hot coffee spilled over his greasy fingernails. I wasn't so sure I wanted it now.

"You've got to get used to it," he told me.

"I don't know as I want to."

He screwed up his eyes and squinted at me.

"You out on the road kind of late."

"I'm driving my mother to California. Trying to do it as quick as I can."

He glanced at his watch. "I don't reckon you're going to make it tonight."

"I would if I could," I told him. "Just get the thing over with."

The truck driver looked quickly around the plaza coffee shop. It was nearly empty.

"You keep a secret?" he asked me.

"Been keeping them all my life."

The man let out a bark of laughter.

"I don't know if that's funny or not, but I'll laugh just in case it is."

Then he reached into the breast pocket of his shirt and took out a capsule. He broke it in two and poured half the powder inside into my coffee.

"That'll get you as far as you need to go tonight. But I want you to promise me one thing."

I told him I promised.

"When you feel this stuff run out on you, and it will, too, because it really ain't that strong, I want you to stop. I don't want you to go a single mile further. Even if you're sure you can. I don't want to have to hear about some poor kid crashing somewheres in Louisiana, and knowing it's my fault."

He pointed to my cup. "Now drink some of that stuff."

I did. "Tastes terrible."

"Tastes bitter. Nobody likes the taste. It's one of them necessary evils. But, of course, nobody's making you drink that coffee."

I took a big slurp of it so as he wouldn't think I was being ungrateful.

"I've got to be driving on up the coast now," he told me. "I want you to remember what I said about stopping."

"Yes, sir."

What coast? I wondered as I walked across the parking lot to the car. We're plumb in the middle of the cotton fields. I slipped in behind the wheel and put the coffee in the drink holder my father had had installed above the ashtray. Evangeline had not stirred the whole time, and it occurred to me that she must not have slept much either last night. Probably even less than I had on Bonaventure.

As the truck plaza disappeared in the mirror, I took a sip of the coffee, which was hot with bitter, sulfurous residue, almost intolerable. I reached across to Evangeline's side and found her sack of miniatures crumpled on the floor between her feet. My turn to snap some seals. I emptied a couple of bottles into the coffee, then took another drink. The Christian Brothers brandy cut the bitterness, but the sulfur was still lurking under the sweetness.

If you could be quick-witted, at ease, confident, intelligent, skillful — in short, the king of the world forever, why would you choose not to be? Especially if all that power was as close as a scarecrow truck driver at a truck plaza? If you could have the process of sleep and wakefulness at your command, why not take it, except out of chicken-shit fear, and perhaps the suspicion that these powers were not natural? But what's so natural about my state anyway?

What's natural and right about sitting bolt upright in a speeding coffin whizzing across the state of Mississippi in the middle of the night, with one-half of my procreators who has willfully blinded and deafened herself?

I know why this bitter powder and others like it were invented. They were designed for people like me, to put an end to the reflections that torment them like shit flies around an open wound.

I commenced to sing without the aid of Hoss Man Allan or any other station, singing about the times I had sung to make myself a refuge on the Lazaretto or on Bonaventure or the crossing to Callibogee, places I knew I'd see again, but when, and under what conditions, I did not know. I ate up the miles, terribly enthralled with the center line and the reflectors marking the curves in the highway. A gospel hour drifted on to the radio. Numerous were the poor souls in need of Jesus tonight, but fewer were those given the grace of belief. The reflectors twisted and turned and led skyward, where they were transformed into the constellation of Draco the Dragon. At first I followed the upward curve with pleasure, for who does not want to drive his car up into the sky? Hours went by in this blackness. But then I started losing speed. For a horrible, petty demon of reason had insinuated itself into my path as I drove: if I am moving uphill, into the sky, then I must be going slower, for is not such a grade extremely steep? I checked my speed. It was constant. Since it could not be constant on such a steep climb, I eased off on the gas pedal. With satisfaction, I noted the speed dropping to seventy, then sixty and fifty. It was uphill all the way now.

By the time I entered Vicksburg, I was rolling along at forty miles an hour, and had once considered getting out of the car to push. That nagging suggestion of nausea in my gut, put there by the sulfurous coffee, had bloomed into a fountain of sour juices. Vicksburg, at least stay awake for Vicksburg, I told myself. Hadn't that gentleman Mr. Caton written about this town? A battle had taken place here, if I recall, and we had won it, and the tide was turned in our favor. No, that wasn't it. A battle had taken place here, and we had lost it, and the tide was turned forever against us. Or both those things were true. Yes, that's it. We had won the battle. And as a result, had lost it.

Please, Daddy Zeke, no more jokes about the Civil War! They're not funny and you know it!

Desperate fatigue. Overstated, unusable energy. The civil war inside the body. How do people control this stuff? Who do they ask for guidance? Slowly, I began to recognize the gospel singers on the radio. The MacIntosh County Shouters. I knew them, they were a friendly point in this otherwise unfriendly night, they had come to Sandfly Crossing only last year, six women in gingham caps and dresses and a seven-foot-tall Zulu with an oaken cane beating out the rhythm. The MacIntosh County Shouters had scandalized the Deliverance Center and its preacher by maintaining through song that Daniel in the lion's den was nothing other than Rastus the slave boy who had slipped down to Master's smokehouse and was just now making off with his smoked loins of pork, and that God didn't have anything to do with the story, no, sir. Then here comes Master, up in the front of the church where they were singing, a black man painted up in sloppy whiteface and dressed in a shiny-kneed black suit, looking every which way and shaking his fist, and all the gingham-clad women singing, *Why, there he go!* and pointing right, and old Master goes running off that way with his rusty squirrel gun in his hand, while Rastus comes creeping along the left side with over his back a big bleeding side of pork scheduled to be barbecued for the evening's festivities.

I was balancing on top of the bridge over the Mississippi River when I saw him. My father. He was standing on the white line in the middle of the road. Right at the foot of the bridge on the Louisiana side.

I hit the brakes hard. The back end of the Chrysler fishtailed and the car began to skid down the slope. He just stood there, unmoving, absent, self-satisfied, smiling that complacent smile. *Go ahead and hit me if you must*, that smile said. It was all I could do to hang on to the wheel, and too late to steer around him. I was crying as I slid broadside into him, readying myself for the great wave of red-purplish blood to splash up from his body and wash over the windshield.

Then, nothing. No more resistance than an airplane wing slicing through a cloud. That man I hit? He was a ghost. The car continued its lazy slide down the bridge and came to rest on the shoulder.

I bailed out and started back up the bridge, trotting under the buzzing, orange-colored lights. "Daddy! Daddy Zeke!" I called. No one answered. Down the Mississippi some sand barges hooted in the darkness. My father was a haint. A man with no reflection.

I kneeled down on the pavement. It was warm and welcoming to the touch. It was made of tar and little stones, and some of those stones shone and winked at me. Lie down with us, they urged. But I did not. I am a man of rigor, I retorted.

Instead, I did what I had been wishing I could do for the past couple of hours. I vomited up a stream of sulfurous white powder, coffee and Christian Brothers brandy. When that was done, I looked east, to where I had come through the ghost. There was a little spot of more intense emptiness where it had stood. Then west, the territory to which the ghost had introduced me, like a signpost. I have had some experience in interpreting haints. I know their ways, and what they are for. You are leaving me here, Daddy Zeke's haint had meant to say. Travel on without me if you must. This is the border of my domain.

What could I answer to that? His haint was right. I was leaving him. But before I did, I promised to be back just as soon as humanly possible.

The car waited at the foot of the bridge, askew, front end nearly nuzzling the guardrail and the back end on the road. In it, my mother slept an obscenely innocent sleep. I didn't bother starting up the engine. I shifted the lever into Neutral, cut the wheel hard and coasted down the rest of the slope. I turned off where a brown sign studded with buckshot showed a pine tree leaning over a picnic table.

The car came to rest, nose against a bank of picnic tables. Before me flowed a great expanse of moving mud. The Mississippi River. *There*, I addressed Evangeline. *You wanted the West, here it is. And you, perverted spirit, cowardly spirit, bad mother, not even awake to enjoy the crossing!*

I stepped out of the New Yorker. In the glow of the dome light, I gazed upon my mother's plugged ears and masked eyes spoiling her pert and vivacious features. It was touching, was it not, the sheer vain hope of shutting out the world, if only for a night. Except I was not in the mood to be touched tonight, not by willing ignorance. Each to his refuge, did you not say that once, Mother? Then why do you need so many of them? I thought it was one to a customer! Besides, your refuges will never work. I will see to that!

I closed the door softly. If all the sleep in a bed can be slept up, as my daddy had claimed it could be, couldn't the same thing be said of a car? Especially since there was precious little sleep in a car in the first place. I went toward the bank of picnic tables, stumbling in the process, disturbing the pigeons nesting in the girders of the Vicksburg bridge above this roadside park. On that bridge, I knew Daddy Zeke was waiting, a spot of concentrated absence, as he would be at the end of every bridge. I'll be back to get you, I promised him again, just as soon as I can acquit myself of this rather lengthy errand. And in the meantime, do not take offense if I ask you to keep the fuck out of my way.

I scratched away some gray pigeon droppings from the tabletop with a twig and lay down. How could the entire careful, furtive, compromised way of life on Hurt's Landing have come apart so quickly and so completely? How is it that I am lying on top of a picnic table in a roadside rest stop next to the Mississippi River, when just a day or two ago I was being instructed on the many possessions in my domain? But what did I really own? Marsh water! Satiated leeches! Leaky bateaux! How else could anyone explain the sudden and total collapse of life on the Isle of Hope?

And the worst part is that I believed in all that, in spite of myself. And even though the world has since conspired to display to me how false my beliefs were, I still cling to them, out of human habit and need, I suppose.

I threw my windbreaker over me, then commended my sorry, shivering toadfish soul to the dirty river gods.

13

"Timmy Marster Justice, what have you done?"

I sat up on the picnic table, a bad taste in my mouth and a pigeon dropping on my sleeve.

"Where in the hell are you?"

The passenger-side door opened and Evangeline got out, wrestling with her clothes. She gave her underwear a good snap to let some fresh air in. I waved to her. She scowled.

"Over here, Mother."

She walked toward me, patting at her face, obviously not liking how it felt. Unwashed, stiff, greasy.

"I'm not exactly used to sleeping in my clothes. I thought we were going to stay in a motel, not this car. We might not be wealthy, but we can afford that much. What was on your mind, anyway?"

"I was driving along, making good time. Then all of a sudden I got so tired I just had to stop. I crashed."

"We crashed?" Evangeline looked dubious.

"Not literally."

"I see. Another one of your word games."

My mother considered the landscape. In the early morning, hazy sunlight, the river showed a burned mustard color. The cars clicked over the bridge above us. There were a lot of them, everyone going to work, probably, leading ordinary lives, and certainly not going to California. We were the only ones at the roadside stop.

Evangeline shaded her eyes. "Just where are we, or don't I get to know?"

"Don't you recognize it?" I motioned toward the river.

"That water? No."

"It's the Mississippi. Where the West begins."

"So?"

"The West," I insisted. "California. I thought you wanted to go to California! I got us all the way here."

"We're not in that much of a hurry."

"Funny. Yesterday we were."

I jumped off the picnic table and said a silent goodbye to the Mississippi River, and all the Southland beyond it. Behind the wheel, the keys were still dangling in the ignition. Keep leaving them there, I told myself, and maybe some charitable thief will come along and steal the thing, and your mother with it.

Evangeline got into the car and slammed the door wearily.

"Take me to some decent restaurant where they have hot running water at least, so I can make myself presentable."

"Presentable?"

"Yes, presentable. To oneself. To the world." She gestured irritably at everything on the other side of the windshield. "Now, you're such a good driver. Drive me there."

I favored the two-lane road over the interstate, figuring we would hit some breakfast spot soon enough. Though the thought of smoky links and eggs scrambled in bacon grease made my unquiet stomach do flips this morning. Evangeline busied herself by cleaning up her area, emptying the stale Viceroy butts from the ashtray into a bag, plumping up her traveling pillow, taking inventory of the miniatures. A brand-new day in northeast Louisiana.

"I am missing a miniature," she announced after a few miles.

"Actually, you're missing several. I drank them."

"You don't drink." She eyed me from her side of the car. "At least, you never showed any inclination."

"I always have turned down the invitations."

"Then don't tell me you're going to catch the disease. Here, now, with me. I'd never forgive myself, let alone you."

I considered the chances. Such a charming, sociable disease to catch. What a world of camaraderie and excuse-making it opened up. But such an utterly facile disease.

"I saw a haint last night," I told her. "Drove right through it like it was a fog."

My mother sniffed. "A couple miniatures enough to make you see ghosts?"

"It was my daddy's haint."

"Now you leave Zeke out of this!" she yelled. I thought she would leap from her seat and make a grab for my throat.

"How can I leave him out? He *is* my father."

Evangeline sank back in her seat.

"I suppose he is," she admitted. "But you're just playing. And the situation is nothing to play with."

"You can't tell someone they didn't see something they saw, even if you didn't see it. Even if no one else has."

"I suppose you believe in talking in tongues, too? Get consistent with yourself, boy! First you tell me about reflection, then haints! You can't have both at the same time. You've got to decide between the two. They're too different from each other."

"That's not my opinion," I told her. "One tends to lead to the other. At least, that's what I've found."

"I think," she said with exasperated finality, "that I have to use the washroom. Would you mind finding us a place to stop?"

"As if the road depended on me, Mother."

A short while later I steered the car into the parking lot of the Big Wheel pancake house. It was funny how, even as we streaked across the country, we were still fighting over Zeke Justice's name and the right to judge his actions. Inside the Big Wheel, Evangeline marched straight into the ladies' room to make herself presentable. When the waitress came with the acrid-smelling coffeepot, I ordered dry brown toast and a glass of water with no ice.

On that second day, Evangeline and I hardly spoke. She drove, and I slept. We were like married people who have learned to avoid each another by sleeping days when the other sleeps nights, and vice versa, so as not to have to breathe the same air. Or maybe it was the road's fault that we did not speak. The road dulled us, as it dulled the landscape through which it passed. I had never suspected that, in this family, it would be possible to sit side by side for hours at a time in utter silence. Maybe we were simply gathering strength, if it can be called that, for the next assault.

I dozed through hours of unrelieved scrub. The swamps and wet fields dried into grazing land as we headed west. Early in the evening I opened my eyes to the New Yorker idling and the heat needle pushing the overheating point, on the outskirts of Sweetsburg, Texas. The western outskirts. I looked across at Evangeline and saw twin sunsets glowing dully in her shade glasses. She pulled off her glasses and displayed those narrow, tired slits to me.

"If you're tired," I said, nodding in the direction of the great dusty sunset, "I can always drive."

She gave me a sidelong glance, then replaced her glasses. "There will be no more of your excesses at the wheel, boy," she informed me.

And with that she swung the car around and headed back through Sweetsburg, as if she could have possibly missed something on her first pass through it. Together, we gazed upon the town. Three motels, a chicken-fried steak place and, to my surprise, a movie theater. We reached the eastern edge of the town, identical in every way to the western border, save for the sunset. Evangeline did not want to enter any of the three Sweetsburg motels, where intimacy would be forced upon us, any more than I did. But even less did she intend to be sped through the night by a maniac driver who was her son.

For a moment, there was something close to understanding between us. *Neither of us wants this*, ran her appeal. *So let's not torture each other over it.*

"I say the Wishing Well," she said wearily.

"I vote Sleepy Hollow."

"Well, then, why not the Nite-E-Nite?"

"You know how much I love words, Mother. I can't stand motels where they can't spell."

The Sleepy Hollow it was. Home of Ichabod Crane and his eternal tormentor, the Headless Horseman. As I sat in this car in Sweetsburg, Texas, I would have gladly thrown my head away, as far as I could, and I had me some kind of arm. Son of a pitcher! We sat in the Sleepy Hollow parking lot a moment, my attention taken by the buzzing of the white line of neon that ran the length of the motel, along the roofline. Why is that neon tube there? I asked myself. It is there, I answered, to separate the edge of this building from the miles of nothingness on all sides. It draws a line against it.

When Evangeline switched off the engine, a scrawny man appeared at the motel office door, delight and disbelief on his face. Apparently, he did not get much in the way of trade. Though the country was full of restless people, they must have been too restless to stop, at least this early in the evening, in Sweetsburg.

Judging from the room keys hanging on the board behind the desk, we had our choice of accommodations. Evangeline asked for a single room with two beds.

"Yep," said the owner. "For the young man and his mother. Cash mighty hard to come by these days."

"I should say so, at least out here," Evangeline retorted, her eyes coming to rest on a stuffed coyote's head with the fangs missing.

She dug into her purse for her pocketbook and I slipped out the door to inspect the grounds. There was the regulation motel swing set and a giant sky-blue planter that might have been a kids' wading pool in an earlier life. It was obvious that Sweetsburg was a perfectly desperate place, but no different from any other place, probably no different from the Isle of Hope, had you been dropped down there against your will. I laughed out loud there in the dust and open sky, imagining back to the time when Hurt's Landing, and I boatless, had made me feel stranded. That was nothing compared to this.

Evangeline came and stood beside me. Her copy of the room key, I saw, was attached to a plastic cutout of a hillbilly outhouse.

"What do we do now?" I asked her.

"Now? We stay at this motel, unless you want to find a picnic table somewhere."

"No, I mean *now*, with all of *this*."

I pointed to the straw-dry lawn in front of the Sleepy Hollow, and beyond it the tractor-trailer trucks passing on the highway before us with a roar of tires and hissing of brakes, and the dustdevils they raised that came sweeping into our eyes. *Distance*, those trucks said. You are perfectly in the middle of nowhere, an equal distance to both ends of your journey, at which point the nothingness you inhabit will be given a new name. At the Benedictines, I had been exposed to the reflections of Pascal; he had been part of that parade of gloomy philosophers inflicted upon us by Father Dooley's legions, auxiliary punishment for our souls. Despair, according to their pedagogy, was the tool for teaching faith. Now, standing on the hardened ground and yellowed grass by the swing set at the Sleepy Hollow motel in Sweetsburg, Texas, I finally understood that gentleman Pascal's dread of the infinite.

What *do* you do with this? I asked myself.

Though I did not drink, I had studied drinking, and knew the principles. What you do with *this* is drink.

A shame I forbade myself such an easy way out. Not loosening up can kill a man.

"This?" my mother queried, and I realized she had been carrying on the same silent quarrel I had. She gave a desultory wave of her hand, and there was disdain in her voice. "This? We cross it. It's just something in the way. Unfortunately, there does seem to be a lot of it. It's the damned country's fault."

"It's not something in the way. It is the way."

"God, I certainly hope not!"

She laughed and lit herself a Viceroy. I slipped the key off her finger.

"You go and get the things out of the car," she told me. "I'll just finish up here, and watch the scenery go by. I know you don't want any of my smoke in the room. Sissy!"

The motel room lived up to my fears. The two soft beds were indecently close; only a night table separated them. The television was the centerpiece of the room, perched as it was on a metal shelf bolted into the painted concrete-block wall. I put our overnight bags on the luggage stand and went to explore the bathroom. His and Hers, read the pair of thin towels hanging by the shower stall. The drinking glasses were wrapped in paper with a picture of a nurse on them. For Your Protection, the paper read.

I used the bathroom, then replaced the paper ring on the seat. When I came out, Evangeline was sitting on the bed closest to the bathroom, staring at her unopened bag as if it contained a dead skunk, or worse. She looked utterly defeated. Maybe the true essence of Blaise Pascal in Sweetsburg had come to inhabit her as she stood out on the grass, finishing her cigarette. Or maybe she was just tired. She had put a lot of miles behind us, I had to admit. It looked as though she had swung around to my way of thinking: we may not know where we're going, but we're certainly not anywhere now, and since we don't know where we're going we might as well get there as fast as we can and find out where it is, and get it over with, and get the hell out of here in the process.

"Could you bring the miniatures in from the car?" she asked as I walked through her field of vision. "I would take a cordial at a time like this."

Odd how her language changes when she discusses drink, I reflected as I brought the paper bag full of little bottles from the car. She gets so delicate, so ladylike about it. *A cordial.* As if by referring to the toddies in that fine way, she could talk all the evil out of alcohol, and leave nothing but the sweet stuff.

Night two, after Lazaretto. It looked as though I would not be able to elude this one. No sleeping bag on the cemetery island, no crashing on picnic tables at roadside stops. Night, in all its dreadfulness: an airless motel room with Evangeline Justice, née Marster. At the Sleepless Hollow, as I had already renamed the place.

The night began with supper at the King of Chicken-Fried Steaks. The marriage of meat and fowl. The King of Steaks, the Big Wheel, the Big Biscuit. Everything seemed to be outsize off our careful little Isle of Hope.

Once she'd placed her order, my mother breathed to the waitress, "I'll have a Manhattan with that."

"Sorry, ma'am," the waitress loudly twanged. "This here's a dry county."

"Goddamned hard-shell Baptists!" my mother burst out. Before the waitress had time to recoil from the frightful blasphemy, Evangeline added, "I should know. I'm one myself."

The waitress was having trouble believing that claim. "County line's just another twenty miles down the road," she advised, then fled our table as if from Satan himself.

"Sounds like an invitation to me," I told my mother.

"Twenty miles," she repeated, as if the waitress were ordering her to drive another twenty years.

I ate my steak hurriedly, and half of hers, and we exited. The movie house, which had offered such hopes of escape, was open only on weekends. We retreated to the room, where we sat up and watched the local news, straining our necks to see a television that was practically bolted to the ceiling. Apparently, the newsman informed us, coyotes were devouring the land. Meanwhile, Evangeline forgot my dislike of smoke and began chain-smoking Viceroys as we watched the news of a place we would never see again. She went and fetched a For Your Protection drinking glass from the bathroom and emptied most of the remaining miniatures into it. There were a few cream drinks mixed in with the brandies, and they made a nasty-looking mixture, grasshopper green and locust brown, in with the Christian Brothers. I had a sudden and unbidden memory of childood on Hurt's Landing, as unwelcome as a dream that tells you things you do not care to know. It was a memory of playing with one of the black boys whose fathers was over doing some repair work on the house or the bateaux, maybe even the son of Freeman Prince, and we were in the garage, mixing up the paints and varnishes and weed killers and whatever else we could find there, stirring it together in an empty Folger's can with a member of my swizzle-stick collection and calling it poison. And me horrifying my playmate by lifting the can to my lips and beginning to drink the contents. "Yum, good poison." I smacked my lips after an imaginary mouthful. "Just like Daddy."

When a commercial for farm implements came on, Evangeline rose and went into the washroom. I reached up and turned off the television, and when the door was closed and the water good and running, I pulled off my clothes and got into bed.

After a time, the water stopped and my mother called from the privy, "Ready or not, here I come!"

I was at a loss. Is that why we were here in Sweetsburg, to play hide-and-seek? Besides, there wasn't anywhere to hide. If there had been some secret corner, I would have located it by now.

"I said I'm coming out now!" she called again.

Her teasing voice had turned irritated. Coquetry gone sour.

"All right, come out!" I shouted back.

That was not answer enough. Evangeline flung open the door, but stayed hidden.

"What I want to know," she specified, "is whether you're decent or not."

"I'm in bed," I groaned.

"Well, bully for you! Now pull the covers over your head."

I did as I was told. I smelled thin, chlorinated sheets and my own sour crotch. My mother's nightclothes rustled as she walked into the room and put her hands on her hips.

"If we're going to have to live like this, and it looks as though we'll be having to for some time to come, then you're going to have to be a little more cooperative."

"Yes, ma'am," I promised through the sheets.

I started to come up for air, figuring my purgatory was over. Not so.

"I didn't say you could come out now," Evangeline called gaily. "And remember, no peeking."

"I wouldn't dream of it."

I heard the plasticized crinkling of the bedspread, then hangers tinging together from the other side of the room. Then I was treated to more rustling and loosening and adjusting. I prayed fervently for deliverance from my cage before I suffocated on my own scent.

The room went dark.

"Olly, olly, ocean free!"

I crawled out from under the sheets. Behind our vinyl curtains, the Sleepy Hollow's sign buzzed and flashed, and in the parking lot a floodlight protected us against Mexicans, or coyotes, or the haint of emptiness, or whatever people in the middle of Texas were afraid of these days. In other words, darkness in this room was a relative thing.

"Good night, Timmy."

Then came a time during which we waited to see who would break the silence first. Or what would break it, for it was the click of Evangeline's lighter that I heard next. The tip of her cigarette glowed. Words would follow that brief flame, I knew, just as surely as night follows day.

I was not disappointed. Once again, I had occasion to marvel at my mother's ability to change from flirtatious merry widow to dolorous keeper of the Marster book of lamentations.

"You don't think I loved your father," she said plaintively in the dim room.

"I don't think I want to know about this."

But she wanted me to know, of course. According to her, I had to know, if not for my sake, then for hers. When the need to speak traveled over her you could not stop it, any more than you could ask the tide to wait so you could bait your hook.

"I gave myself entirely to your father," she informed me. "Before, then during our marriage. For as long as he was interested. I know you don't want to hear this. No one does. They are indecent things to say, and even more indecent to have happen. But I have to tell you because I know what you think: you blame me for everything that happened to him. Everything he did."

"I don't blame you. He didn't blame you. He blamed the Marsters."

"And aren't I a Marster?"

"You are. But if I remember rightly, you've done your share of blaming the Marsters, too. That seems to be a family trait."

"Have you ever heard me speak against my own family?"

"No. But I thought you were going to punch out those tombstones that time we went to Bonaventure."

"You have quite the imagination!"

"Thanks for the compliment, Mother. You only have yourself to blame. What with all these grand notions and stories about the past floating around, I was bound to start wanting to make up a few myself."

I gave her a shit-eating grin, which was wasted in the dark. Too bad I didn't have fluorescent teeth. "It's not my fault."

"Of course not. You're just a poor innocent child."

Evangeline shifted in bed, trying to get comfortable. She did not seem to be succeeding. A regular princess and the pea here in the

Sleepless Hollow. And I was the pea, the stone in the shoe, the fruit of Zeke and Evangeline's early passion. Passion? I questioned myself. Perhaps not. More like the fruit of Evangeline's rebellion against the Marsters. I could picture it now: since no Marster girl could be blamed for her willing misconduct, her rebellion must have been laid straight at my father's feet. And so, Jefferson Marster's hatred of him.

"Well, at least you've been putting this so-called period of reflection of yours to use. But for studying — not reflection. Don't go thinking they're one and the same, you amateur philosopher, you. I understand the meaning of words, too. Reflection means looking inside yourself. But this study of yours seems to be more dedicated to cataloging other people's weaknesses. Well, congratulations, you've come to the right place! But just don't think that true reflection and this list-keeping of yours are the same thing."

"Not the same, Mother. But one can't help but lead to the other. Studying just seems to come with the territory. I believe that's part of belonging to the glorious Marster line."

In the flash of the Sleepy Hollow sign, I saw my mother's arms sweep across our meager room.

"Do you really think being a Marster means anything in a place like this? Do you?"

"Yes," I said quietly. "It must. I would think it would mean even more in a place like this."

"A fat lot of good it did me. Has it ever occurred to you that maybe that's why I took us out of there? Because I was tired of being a Marster all the time, day in and day out?"

It hadn't occurred to me. It should have. She lit a Viceroy, then kept her lighter lit to guide her way toward her overnight bag on the floor by her bed. She rummaged through it, cursed, then the room filled with the acrid scent of singed hair. The Sleepy Hollow sign chose that moment to go out for the night, and suddenly our room was wholly inhabited by my mother's outsize shadow, cast upon the vinyl curtains, as she tore apart her bag in search of a few miniatures

RAT PALMS

she might have missed earlier in the evening, or a half-pint that might miraculously be resident within the very fabric of the bag, something she had hidden from herself and me, saved for just such a rainy day. And sure enough, there came the happy chirping of glass on glass and cup on lip. The calm that came over her was as palpable as the humidity on a summer's day on the island.

Newly fortified, she propped herself up on her pillows. Then had the unfortunate inspiration to turn her lighter in my direction. There, she found herself face to face with her ever-studious toadfish son observing her through darkness-piercing eyes.

"I don't have to. I *want* to." I could tell by her gesture she was displaying the For Your Protection glass. "I enjoy a drink too much to waste it in abuse."

As proof, she took a dignified, ceremonious sip, as if the stuff was communion wine.

"I am not an abuser," she insisted. "Have you ever seen me grab one by the neck, knock its top off, turn it ass up and kill it? Now, that's abuse!"

She laughed with sudden self-indulgence. "That used to be your Daddy Zeke's favorite joke. Now, just listen to me, repeating his tired old jokes. If that's not love, what is? Oh, I know, you accuse me of negligence, you think I should have saved him. But I loved him, I gave myself to him completely, as us women are taught to on the Isle of Hope, as if we had no other purpose on that island but to attach ourselves to love like a leech!"

She laughed again, uncomfortably this time, having uttered one of the many unmentionable words in our itinerant household.

"Anyway," she said darkly, "none of that did any good."

"I don't know. At least you won."

She opened her arms wide, embraced the motel room. "You call this winning?"

"You're here, free, and he's back there in an institution, among strangers. In the order of things, the way they stand now," I told her in that reasonable, evaluating voice I knew she hated, "you'd have to say that this is winning."

"It's always more glorious to be on the side of the wronged party. Next best thing to being the wronged party yourself, when you can't manage the real thing. That's strategy, boy. I thought I explained that to you already, a long time ago, on that goddamned dock you used to haunt."

I pulled the thin white sheet around me and displayed my back to Evangeline. Yes, I could have told her, I do accuse you of negligence. But I accuse my father of other things, some of them far worse crimes according to my well-filled book of family misconducts. But don't expect to hear about them. That complaint is between him and me.

Unfortunately, for the time being, we were moving at a great rate of speed from the very place I would need to go to seek a remedy.

There was movement in the house. My task was to determine whether it was that of friend or foe. If the moving spirits are in this house, they must be friend, for is not the house a construction for the friendly? But why would the friendly move in so furtive a manner, in the hollowest part of the night? They must be foe.

I opened my eyes and was blinded by the flash of my mother's lighter. Her face flared up and was gone.

Then I made the mistake of the night, one even worse than impudence or side taking. I shifted in bed. And she discovered me out.

"You are awake," she declared in a loud, flat voice.

If I hadn't been, she would have made sure that I soon was. I recognized she was suffering from one of her needs to speak. Let me tell you, there is no sharper hell than that of being sequestered in a motel room with someone who cannot sleep, and who insists that you share the curse. She positioned herself at the foot of my bed, cigarette tip glowing, she gloating and triumphant, with a predatory glint in her eye visible even in the darkness. The door to the outside looked a hundred miles away, and besides, even if I could reach it, it led to nowhere useful.

"I'm awake now. What's going on? What time is it?"

"It is eternal motel time," she slurred.

"Jesus Christ, I thought this was a dry county! Or is this room an exception to the rule? What about the arms of Morpheus? Didn't they open for you?"

"You've got a hell of a tongue in your head, and I just hate myself when I think I helped put it there! And just when I need your help!"

I watched her come wheeling around the edge of my bed in the glow of the parking-lot floodlight.

"Don't those toddies help a little?"

"Miniatures, maxiatures, nothing works any more!" she wailed.

She took a step toward me, but neglected to put her front foot down. She hovered over me on one leg like a great pitiful, flightless bird. She was holding her glass in her hand, and I noticed she had started using it as an ashtray. So this is what the likes of Zeke and Evangeline do when the lights go off: they stay up and wonder and mope. Loudly. Conspicuously. It did not look like much fun. It was like being at a party that you could never leave.

Then she resolved to set down her front foot. At which point she struck something unexpected on the floor that made her lose balance. She pitched forward, her nose in my blankets, valiantly keeping the ashtray level.

"In case you're wondering, I'm not decent."

"You never were," she grumbled. "What the hell is this?"

She righted herself, sank to her knees and started groping around under the bed in search of the object that had waylaid her.

"Now how in the hell did this get here?"

She held up the granite baseball.

I shrugged. I didn't even feel like displaying embarrassment. What the hell, I thought. What else does a mother expect to find on her hands and knees in the wee hours of the morning under her son's bed in a motel room in Sweetsburg, Texas? It could have been worse.

"It's a baseball. A souvenir of Hurt's Landing. I brought it along for the ride."

She rubbed it up between her hands. No one could fail to be taken in by a ball like that.

"Are you intending to torment me with this?"

"Honestly, no. It must have slipped out of my bag."

"It slipped out, all by itself? Do you think it has magical powers?"

"I don't know. Maybe so."

She turned the ball loose and it crashed to the asphalt-tile floor, unnaturally heavy and destructive, as if it really did have a haint inside.

"And you accuse me of being enslaved by the past! And here you are, carrying around this . . . souvenir. I suppose you know where this comes from?"

"For the kindest white man in Savannah," I quoted the inscription.

"And do you know how you get to be considered the kindest white man by the colored people in Savannah?"

"No, ma'am, I don't."

"Well, it's better if you don't know."

"I know enough things already," I told her, "that the things I don't know yet don't scare me any more."

"Good for you. I wish I could say the same for myself."

I slumped down in the bed and prayed for dawn, and deliverance. The former came before the latter; the latter has still not arrived. When sunlight slipped around the vinyl curtains into our room, I gazed upon my mother stretched out on the plasticized bedspread, half wrapped in it, thoroughly unconscious. That's the trouble with Morpheus. He does not come when you want him, and when he finally does, he won't go away. Hateful reflections for a son to admit to. You should love her, poor sad victor, spoiled parent. You should love her even if it won't make any difference.

After all, think how much we have in common. Here we are, both suffering from the shock of discovering, mile after mile, that our world is not the real world, the way we always believed it might be. That the world does not stop at the bridge that connects the Isle of Hope to the mainland. That the Marsters are of no concern nor consequence to anyone else, any more than a bluebottle buzzing over a trail of chicken squirt is. When I considered this new knowledge, which so richly contradicted all my previous instruction, I felt a kind of melancholy exhilaration. Call it freedom, for lack of a better word. My mother, however, was taking it harder.

Is this the moment when love, mixed with pity, will settle over me like a state of filial grace? I asked myself that question as I watched her sleep, scarcely breathing, so obviously exhausted by the effort of the procurement of sleep. Perhaps I would never love her. Perhaps I would never love anyone. Perhaps the Isle of Hope had disqualified me from love.

I went outside to look at the sunrise. Its beauty was lost on me this morning.

14

For two days Evangeline was sullen and silent and would not touch the wheel. That morning at the Sleepless Hollow, she rose late, dragged herself to the car, then waited there while I picked up the room. I could not blame her for refusing that chore; it would have been cruel to ask her to help me. The room looked like a barroom after a brawl that everybody lost. Tipped ashtrays, a drinking glass full of butts floating in some warm brown liquid, empty miniatures hither and yon and tiny shreds of paper that could have been her last will and testament for all I knew, but that no one would ever reassemble. And in the midst of it all, the seamless granite baseball, fully intact.

Evangeline had spurned the passenger side of the front seat and was now firmly established in back. I got in behind the wheel, in the chauffeur's position. You can run but you can't hide, I felt like reminding her, since I could follow her every tick and disagreement with herself in the rearview mirror. Through the mirror's reflection, I watched her vainly, fastidiously and uselessly setting out her traveling things. Her map, her scarf, her compact with the little mirror, her handy pad for tallying up the trip's expenses — though whom she would attempt to claim them from, I had to wonder.

At one point during the day I made some passing comment on the landscape, nothing of any consequence, on how beans seemed to have replaced grits as the starch of predilection. She did not grace me with an answer. I glanced in the mirror and saw she had inserted her earplugs again.

She removed them for the truck stops. You cannot place your order with the lady behind the counter with plugs in your ears. Inside these establishments, she discovered in herself a taste for trinkets. She bought beer mugs, road maps for states we had no intention of driving through, illustrated pen and pencil sets, pennants for a variety of college football teams. At one stop, we made our only two purchases of permanent real estate during the entire crossing: a Styrofoam cooler for a dollar and forty-nine cents, and a pair of sunglasses for me. I filled the cooler with beer and even tried a few myself, once I could twist the cans off the tenacious plastic strap that held the six-pack together.

"That will make you unfit for driving," Evangeline told me listlessly.

"I'm thirsty."

And I was. I tried the air conditioner, but in this desert heat the car ran so hot with it on I had to give up on the artificial climate and open the windows. Great gusts of overheated air carrying dust and sand blew in. Conversation would have been impossible, had we desired it.

At one point in our desert crossing, I heard singing from the back seat.

What'll ya have, Pabst Blue Ribbon
What'll ya have, Pabst Blue Ribbon
What'll ya have, Pabst Blue Ribbon
Pabst Blue Ribbon Beer.

She was singing to her beer can, gazing fondly at it as if it were the Virgin of Guadalupe in person. In her ears were her two rubber earplugs. With spiteful, raging heart, I pressed the accelerator to the floor and sped past a large, sun-bleached sign that warned, No Services Next 100 Miles.

I know it's wrong, even perverse, but I confess I enjoyed the inevitability of driving out the rest of the fuel. With the warning sign and the Colorado River bridge growing ever smaller in the mirror, I looked down at the odometer and made a quick calculation: how much gas, how many miles, how to roll to a stop in the exact middle of a desert without services. I glanced up to the rearview mirror. Evangeline had disappeared. I turned and took a leisurely look back. She had fallen asleep on the backseat, surrounded by the day's collection of PBR empties and corn chip bags.

The landscape outside the car was a miracle of emptiness, a positive consolation for the eye. Rock and baked sand, an occasional bush as dry and dead-looking as the mineral world around it. As empty as our marshes must look to an outsider without the benefit of local history, who cannot know that this particular slimy channel has a name, or that a brief rise from the muck of the marsh grass is called a hammock, or that Mr. So-and-So drowned at this bend, and that it was his fault. In splendid ignorance I drove on through the desert, unentangled, a can of PBR growing tepid in my hand. I did have a scare a third of the way through this serviceless area. A sign appeared, announcing a town. Wheat, it read. A few miles passed before I deduced that this sign was all the town consisted of. Either that or it was offering wheat for sale, which seemed unlikely.

I was imagining what life would be as a loyal son of Wheat, California, when it happened. The engine gave a couple bewildered, disbelieving coughs, then stalled. I threw the gearshift lever into Neutral and coasted as silence overtook the car. I rolled on without power for another half mile, then steered the car to the side of the road, into a sand bank. I looked at the odometer. Exactly fifty miles from the warning sign. Well done! The exact middle of nowhere.

I closed the car door quietly and stepped into the emptiness of the desert. The emptiness, of course, turned out to be choked with things, mainly broken beer bottles and cans tortured into odd shapes. All around, the afternoon desert sparkled with broken glass;

apparently, the desert doubled as a shooting range. A scratching sound came from behind me and I whirled around, thinking scorpion or rattlesnake, though no animals were moving in this heat. A yellowed newspaper impaled on a spiny bush was being worried by the wind. I bent down and read the date on the paper. The *Los Angeles Times*, nearly a year old to the day.

I wandered out of the shooting range and onto a salt flat where all plant life ceased. Back to the sun, I crouched, waiting for the world to make its next move. In a world like mine, you never have to wait long.

From the road, I heard the New Yorker's door slammed heavily. Evangeline took a few stumbling steps down the asphalt, clutching a can of PBR, the heat waves bending her body as she came swimming across the sand in my general direction. She looked wholly out of place, as any human being would in these surroundings. She raised both arms to the sky.

"What in the hell is this?"

Finding no answer, she retreated in the direction of the automobile, a place of safety for her, a known object. Or, better, an instrument of escape which, alas, dear Mother, it no longer was.

Leaning against the car, she shouted again.

"Timmy! Timmy Justice!"

I stood up from the salt flat and waved cheerfully.

"Over here, Mother."

"Lord, have mercy, you scared me! Is this your idea of a rest stop? Couldn't you at least have found us some trees?"

"They don't have any trees out here."

She started to step over the sandbank that separated the road from the desert, then thought better of it.

"Would you come here? I don't want to go out there, it's probably full of snakes."

"I don't think so, ma'am. Any snake with half a brain is in his hole. It's too hot for them. We're the only thing moving out here."

"If it's too hot for snakes, then why are we here?"

"Because," I told her, trying to keep the pride from my voice, "because we have run out of gas."

Evangeline took a couple of steps backward and sagged against the car fender, as if I had punched her in the stomach.

"I can't take this. I can't take this any more," she mumbled to herself.

"At least we're in California." I pointed to the expanse of stones and rock and sand and burned brush stretching forever on all sides. "That's California. What do you say? We've reached the promised land!"

"Promised land? How could you have run out of gas? Don't you know how to drive?"

She retreated into the car, seeking shade, though I'm sure it was hotter under the New Yorker's roof than outside. Mind you, at least there was refreshment in there. At my feet, from its impalement on the thorn bush, the newspaper scraped the hard sand. I am a compulsive reader, and to my delight, I happened upon the sports pages and a Los Angeles Dodgers victory, but the way the paper was torn I could not tell who they had defeated, or if any former Indians players took part in the game.

I was so absorbed in the examination of that ancient paper skin and the unfinished story it told that I did not identify the sound gathering out on the road. Then it was upon us, a giant yellow truck with all manner of attachments on the back, for well-digging probably. It sped past us in a great cloud of sand and uprooted mesquite.

I put the paper back on the thorny bush and walked across the field of broken bottles to the car.

"You didn't do anything!" Evangeline said, outraged, from inside the car. "You were supposed to flag him down and get us rescued."

"Nobody did anything," I pointed out.

I reached into the cooler on the floor in back and fished a can of beer from the lukewarm water. My mother hovered over the cooler in a proprietary posture. She was sipping from a plastic mug she had picked up at a truck stop in Arizona. I drink to make other people more interesting, read the mug.

"You didn't flag down that truck because you want to impede our progress," she accused me.

"Don't get me wrong, I want to get this over with, too. But I find it restful here in a funny kind of way."

"Of course, I forgot — you were lost in your thoughts! One of your reflections," she spat, as if it were the worst curse going. "Sounds to me like an excuse for wiggling out of every human situation."

"You could have flagged down that truck. You probably would have had better luck than me in stopping him," I pointed out. "You could have done a lot of things you didn't do, instead of standing around and watching."

With that final reproach, I went around to the back end of the car, where there was a meager line of shadow, which lengthened as the sun slanted west. In the desert, my natural impudence seemed to flower like a cactus after a rainstorm. In this landscape, there wasn't anywhere I could hide it. Concealment did not appear to be of this place, as it was on the Isle of Hope. Perhaps that's why nobody lives out here.

The road went back to being a bare, quiet and endless thing, an extension of the Mojave itself. That well-digging truck might have been our one chance for the day. At one point in the waiting, I drifted up to the side of the car to look in on Evangeline. She turned her head away. I smirked. Hers was not very efficacious punishment.

As often happened at times like these, I recalled Father Dooley. *Efficacious* was one of his favorite words, and at the Academy, a student would receive a subtle nod of grace for being able to sort that word out from *efficient* and *effective*. I remember being surprised in moral instruction class one day when Father Damian Dooley's lecture began with a cure for the hiccups. The afflicted was meant to hold his breath and swallow three times in quick succession; apparently, it always worked. From hiccups, Father Dooley moved quickly on to the subject of faith. Faith, we were informed, was like the cure for the hiccups. It was efficacious. It worked when nothing else did. The other props and measures and strategies of everyday life were not efficacious; only his was.

"Nonsense," I said out loud on this waning afternoon in the middle of the Mojave Desert. What is this business about working, anyway? As far as I could see, nothing worked. Not this car, not the cure for the hiccups, not God, not even reflection. And were something efficacious ever devised, it would not remain so for long. For there is something in the soul that must burn up the solutions that are found, making every one temporary, like a drinking man on the wagon. Such a man has not stopped drinking; he's only waiting to start again.

Several eternities later, a gut-shot pickup truck came weaving down the middle of the road with a desert rat at the wheel. We all but lay down on the asphalt to stop the driver, who nearly ran over us, then stared in disbelief as we came into his view.

He stuck his head out the window. "Shit, didn't see you folks at all — oh, excuse me, lady. Left my goddamned glasses back at Forty-Nine."

He spat discreetly out his pickup window, which didn't look to have any glass in it anyway.

"You folks having a little trouble? Or just admiring the view?"

He cackled at his joke as we climbed in. He must not have been accustomed to carrying people; there was no seat on the passenger side. But before I could get out and jump in back, he was forcing the shift lever into gear and pulling away. Evangeline and I had to hunker down on the corroded metal floor like a pair of stowaways. Dubiously, she looked down at the asphalt road surface flying by below.

"Sims," he said, sticking out his hand. "Simple Sims. Glad to be able to help you. Hope you don't mind riding with someone who can't see shit — excuse me, lady. You must be about the only people left using that road any more."

Then he hunched over his steering wheel and squinted through the pockmarked windshield. Even for a driver who had forgotten his glasses, the road offered few surprises; it could have been laid out with a yardstick. Once or twice I caught him staring at us, a healthy curiosity on his burned, grizzled features, trying to satisfy himself as to just what kind of couple we were. With her hair like a haystack, stiff with windblown sand, and white salt-and-soda scum edging her lips, Evangeline looked anything but maternal. The desert had evened us out.

Night fell as abruptly as if someone had pulled down a window shade. Simple Sims flicked on his headlights, illuminating the sand devils chasing each other back and forth across the road like haints. After a time, we came over a little rise and a line of straggly lights strung out ahead of us. Sims nudged me in the ribs.

"Forty-Nine," he said, chewing on the inside of his cheeks. "You find what you need there, gas station and all. They got them a watering hole there, too. But I don't know as the gas station folks'll be wanting to go back out there with a can of gas this time of the evening. A lot of them won't go out there after dark, on account of the snakes."

He drove on awhile, chewing his cheeks. "Snakes don't bother me. The worst part's in the saying of the name. Just put you on a pair of boots. Anyway, there's no hurry — your car ain't going nowhere out there. Worse thing that'll happen, a kit fox'll have her litter on your backseat."

We coasted out of the high desert and reached the lights of the town, in a great commotion of dragging mufflers and backfiring. Simple Sims pointed out the places I would need, the gas station and the watering hole, then dropped us off at the town's only motel. Wouldn't you know it? It was called the Oasis of Eden. Evangeline looked at it critically. But it was the Oasis, or nothing.

"I can't go on. This time, I really can't go on," she declared once we had paid for the room at the Oasis, and she had had time to contemplate the plasticized bedspread with its cigarette-burn holes.

I was unmoved. She spoke the same words at the end of each day's accumulation of miles. Like every other evening, I went out on foot in search of a beer-vending gas station to help her, and by extension me, pass the time until the next sunrise.

When I returned to the Oasis of Eden, the errand done, the inevitable awaited me. My mother with her simple needs arrayed about her, ashtray and smokes and silly expense pad, and the mug that claimed that drinking makes other people more interesting. In this careful placement of banal objects, I saw how conservative the drinking person must be. If you happen to be one, you must display extreme caution. You must have enough of the correct fluids of the correct color at the correct time. You do not want to be caught short, and have to expend outrageous sums of money and pride you do not have to keep your supply intact. You do not want to have to send a taxi over to the next county on a Sunday at midnight just because you were too self-deluded to pick up that extra bottle at a Christian hour on Saturday.

Not that my mother was a common, simple, foolish drunk. Far from it. I will defend her against that charge, and I am not otherwise inclined to be her defender. She simply belonged to the culture of speaking, and with it, its twin, the culture of drinking. A person did not need to absorb great amounts to belong to it.

I went into the washroom to loosen the tops on the Pabst bottles. On this trip, I had learned many things. One of them was that there are bottle openers under motel sinks, just as sure as there are Bibles in the bedside tables. I returned to watch Evangeline fill her mug and consider it with satisfied eyes. Then she set it aside, untouched, as though she was fulfilled. That woman was a phenomenon: she did not have to drink, to drink.

She cleared her throat and licked her lips. I could hear her words rattling around in her lungs with the Viceroy smoke even before she spoke them. At that very moment, I turned and walked out the door into the bone-dry air of Forty-Nine Palms. It was either that, or matricide.

RAT PALMS

Where did I go? To the Winners' Circle, of course. Where else?

I recognized Simple Sims at the bar. Underneath his scrawny beard, he was chewing away on his cheeks between swallows of beer.

"Where's the little lady?" he asked me.

"You mean my mother?"

"That so?" he said incredulously. "No offense intended, son."

"And none taken. I left her in the room. She just about talked my ear off."

"That might happen in this place, too. You're fresh meat to the folks here. They'll take one look at you and figure you haven't heard all their boring old jokes yet, and that you'd better hear them just as quick as they can tell them." Simple Sims flagged down the bartender. "Give this boy a beer, though I believe he deserves a medal. He's driving his mother right across the damned country."

The bartender came over with the beer. "Just passing through, is that it?"

"Yes, sir."

"Well, keep on driving. Ain't nothing here to speak of." He watched me take a drink, an obviously inexperienced drinker. "Where did you say you're from now?"

"State of Georgia. Savannah. Near it, actually."

"I knew it! I knew by the way you said 'sir.' Nobody says sir around here unless they're talking to the sheriff and they got booze on their breath. This your first time to California?"

I said that it was.

"California ain't nothing but the South in thin disguise, though nobody wants to hear that. All those Southerners like to think they've turned into something else, just 'cause they've pushed their old wrecks across the state line. Turned into what, I don't know. Into Californians? No such a thing. They all come blowing through this desert with their cars overheating, and stop in here, thirsty as hell, and just as eager as hell to get their hearts broken in that godforsaken town they're in such a god-awful hurry to get to. I tell them all to go on home and they get mad at me. I tell them there ain't nothing on the other side of the San Bernardino Mountains. Of course, they don't believe me. And just in case they feel like staying, I tell them there ain't nothing here in Forty-Nine, neither. They believe me on that score — all they got to do is look out the window!"

"That man's wrong," said one of the patrons to me, a bleached-out guy in his twenties. Judging from the looks of him, the place should have been called the losers' circle. "Ain't nothing wrong with this place. Lots of people can't stand the desert. They don't understand it. I love it here. If I want to go home and kick my dog, ain't nobody gonna come around and tell me I can't. Desert's the only place I can live, and I live good. I go to a swap meet, trade some of those rocks that I can find anytime I want to, trade them for money to some of those crazy rock hounds, then I buy me some C-rats, you know, C-rations, Army food. In the morning, I wake up and put one of them cans of C-rats out on a rock in the sun, and in fifteen minutes I'm sitting down to some hot bacon and eggs. Where else you gonna do that?"

I had to admit I didn't know of any other such place.

After the bleached-out gentleman had delivered himself of his recipe for desert living and faded back to his table, the bartender said, "Pure California. That's what happens to them. Their brains get cooked, just like a can of C-rats. Are you going to Los Angeles? Probably are. There wouldn't be any Los Angeles if it weren't for all those Oakies and Southern boys hitting the road."

"Maybe something's chasing them."

"I have considered that. A rusty razor or a shotgun-toting mama."

"What about you?" I pointed out. "You're still here."

"Indeed I am. Ever know of a man to follow his own advice?"

The bartender gave a big, generous laugh, whisked away my beer glass and returned it full.

"Oklahoma," he toasted me.

"The Isle of Hope." I raised mine.

"Don't know as I've ever heard of that state. State of Hope."

"The map'll tell you we're part of Georgia. But actually, we seceded a long time ago. Only, wasn't nobody ever the wiser."

"The best way to get out. You just don't tell them you're leaving. If you're lucky they won't even notice."

At that moment of beery inspiration, the American continent appeared to me as some kind of an unfair pinball machine, with every Southerner shooting through its slots and bumpers and gates, only to tilt west off the end of the country, and down the hole. Next player, please. Step up and if you win, you can achieve the great American dream of going home and kicking your dog, without anyone coming around to tell you you can't do it. Your dog certainly won't tell you, not until the day he rips out your throat.

With the bartender off catering to other thirsts, Mr. C-rats swung by again to elaborate on his version of the desert and offer to take me to a swap meet tomorrow. More of the curious members of the Winners' Circle happened by to see what sort of strange creature had washed up on their dry shore. A toadfish, I wanted to tell them, but did not, because the only fish they had around here were the breaded, stick-shaped variety found in people's deep freezes. I discovered in myself a proficiency in tavern talk. Small wonder. I had attended that academy, and been schooled by a stellar master. A pair of girls came by to investigate me. They commented on my accent, which I did not know I had until that very moment, then complimented me on it, as if it were a virtue I had strived to maintain. *Goddamned Yankees*, I silently swore, then realized there was no sense cursing the North. This wasn't the North, this was nowhere, as the bartender had said, and he should know — he stood at the exact center of it in his bar. In a place that is nowhere, a voice that says *somewhere* always astonishes and inspires nervous laughter.

Then, may the haints of Hurt's Landing forgive me, but I began to spin and play out that old Lazaretto syrup and apply my best shit-eating grin and Benedictine manners to those girls, both dolled up as they were in their Western shirts with round, milky, pearl buttons and big horse teeth in their faces. I did more than that: I positively retailed my past, just as surely as cursed old Jefferson Marster retailed spirits. The effect of my poor stories was not altogether different from that of spirits: the girls felt temporarily happy because they could forget themselves in them, and they called for more. Maybe it is true what Evangeline says about drink making you belong to other people, but at that moment I did not care whom I belonged to, as long as it wasn't to myself.

But be that as it may, I all but sold my birthright for a few watery glasses of beer and some cowgirl smiles. Then again, I briefly reflected, my birthright did not seem to be worth too much these days. I told those girls, Laura and Darlene by name, stories of the Lazaretto as if they had befallen somebody else, and even named the places, with the girls giggling predictably at the mention of Runaway Negro Creek. But though I named Hurt's Landing, I did not name the hurt. I had a little decency left, both for them and myself. Though I named the waters, I did not say what swam beneath. Though I said *Callibogee*, I did not say what kind of love I had witnessed there. To be a personable teller of stories for this audience, I stuck to the surface.

Before long, we found ourselves outside with a waning half-moon standing straight above us, and the night quiet once the Winners' Circle door shut behind us. I walked out onto the highway that hummed like an overstrung wire to the east and the west, from the Lazaretto Road to the Pacific. "Crazy Timmy," Laura was saying to me, tugging on my arm, and though the word *crazy* is a harsh one in my world, her voice was sweet and consenting. She showed me the center stripe on the highway, and how I was standing on it. The sheriff did not approve of such behavior, she told me, and I told her they had sheriffs where I came from, too. And suddenly, almost involuntarily, I was telling Laura of the time I had been afraid of the sheriff on Butler Avenue on Tybee, driving my father in alcoholic repose in the backseat. Before I could get to the relatively happy ending of the story, Laura had danced me awkwardly onto the shoulder of the highway and we were in each other's arms. *Quick*, she urged me, *before anyone sees*, and we kissed.

"Take me home?"

"Where's home?"

She pointed toward the mountainside above us glowing dully in the moonlight.

"The edge of town."

We crossed fields of rock and scrub, divided by broken fencing. She showed me a trailer that sat on a little rise, with dry gravel washes on both sides.

"That's my place. Flash Flood Estates."

She stared transfixed at the trailer, a couple hundred feet ahead of us, at the neon tube in the kitchen window, which was her waiting-up light. I could almost hear it buzzing away in the night. I felt the repulsion it awoke in her, and I knew there was someone or something there she did not want to return to.

"Don't stare at that light, Laura," I said into her hair. The cigarette and shampoo smell was sweet to me. "It'll blind you."

We climbed up the wash in a band of shadow, sheltered from the moonlight and the trailer's windows by a rock ridge. The wash led up to a narrow ledge, wide enough to stand on but no more. She turned and gazed down on the straggling chain of lights along the highway, then kicked a single rock off the ledge and into the wash that poured into Forty-Nine Palms. She watched that rock pick up speed and take smaller ones with it.

"It'll take more than that," I told her.

"Don't I know it!"

Then she turned and took the steep trail ahead of us in two or three determined strides that showed me a fine expanse of rump. The trail led onto a wide plateau, and a landscape the likes of which I had never even imagined. The ground was studded with spiky, twisted trees reaching upward in a multitude of arms. I touched a trunk. It was made of crisscrossed straps of bark as dry and tough as the trunks of our scrubby, low rat palms back on the Isle.

Laura kicked at the ground and sent a cloud of sand flying.

"Here's your desert," she told me. "You like emptiness? I hate it."

"You don't believe Mr. C-rations, that the desert's the only place to be free?"

"Free? Free to be completely fucking crazy in, if that's your idea of being free."

I pulled her closer, and we walked toward a scattering of shacks with hollow windows and doors.

"Homesteaders' cabins," Laura told me. "It used to be you could have a few acres for free, as long as you improved the land once you got it. Some of the people at the bar are leftovers from those days. Improving the land meant building a two-room house on it. That's what everybody did, then they moved right off it. They had to, there was no water. Never was any. There's some pretty small rooms in some of those cabins. But the people got to keep the land."

"For what it's worth."

"Everybody likes to say they own a little land."

We stopped at the threshold of a cabin. I took her hand.

"Are you a real Southern gentleman?"

"I'm a Georgia peach," I promised.

"A freestone peach?"

"More like free-fall."

Laura put one foot on the raised cabin floor.

"You're sensitive," she told me.

I didn't quite know what it was I was sensitive to, but there was no sense in asking her. Then she tested my sensitivity by stomping like hell on the wooden floor.

"Scaring away the snakes."

We sat in the cabin doorway and she dug into the pocket of her cowboy shirt. In the moonlight, she displayed a thin, hand-rolled cigarette, which did not look like any other ones I had seen.

RAT PALMS

"Do you want to smoke?"

I wasn't sure.

"Marijuana," she specified. "People don't call it that any more. It's grass. Pot. Weed. You know?"

"I'm not really accustomed..."

"I know." She leaned over and gave me a friendly kiss. "That's what makes you so sweet."

"Oh, I know about getting high," I hastened to defend myself. "But I've never seen it done on this weed."

"It's different. And better. No hangovers."

We smoked her grass, pot, weed — whatever it was called. It smelled and tasted like rope, and my lungs rebelled. Smoking it involved a rapid, almost furtive ceremony, as if someone could possibly be watching out here in the middle of the desert in the middle of the night. The ceremony did not appeal to me. There was no room for talk, and the stuff burned my tongue. But I soon saw that this grass smoking was not much different than the hooch drinking I had been made to study. Both were licenses to do like the Headless Horseman and throw away your head.

And act crazy, as Laura was doing now. She whirled out of the cabin into the empty moonlit field of scrub and the twisted, God-seeking palms she called Joshua trees. I was glad for the excuse of not belonging to myself, though the harsh grass smoke I had managed to inhale had hardly been enough to transform my gloomy, persevering soul. Not so with Laura, bless the girl. She went dancing across the scrub, a little self-consciously maybe, with her arms raised moonward. Then she began unsnapping the pearl buttons on her shirt. I was transfixed by the sight, by the possibility, and I had to give myself a shake. You let the McQuithy woman get away. Are you going to lose this cowgirl, too?

Like a veritable supplicant, I crawled across rocks as sharp as oyster shells and started working on her jeans as she danced, her breasts moving infinitely high above me. It is difficult to dance with a pair of pants halfway down to your knees, so she shed them. "Free, free," she was chanting to herself, as if saying the word would make it so. I knew nothing of freedom, except that I would never possess it, not even at moments like these. If only I could shed my unwelcome conscience as easily as my clothes!

Laura came wheeling toward me, her body dull silver with moonlight and sweat sheen, exhausted, her dance having accomplished its mission. I caught her and slid her onto the floor of the homesteader's shack.

"I can't afford any splinters, now. You've got to be the gentleman."

I did not have to be asked twice. I lay down on the wood, smooth with generations of wind and sand. Before I knew it she had lowered herself upon me and I was there. I felt a wave of heat around my poor little Lazarus man. The heat of rightness. I didn't quite know what to do next.

"I am not exactly accustomed."

"Just look me in the eye."

I did as I was told and discovered how, abruptly, she had become beautiful. So suddenly and astonishingly beautiful that anything you might have been able to call imperfection in her — horse teeth, cowgirl manner or idle talk of freedom — melted away into forgiveness that was fine and complete. I began to understand why half the world was willing to kill for this thing.

But apparently, admiring and reflecting is not all there is to the act. Laura began to move and buck atop me, and speak things. Now, I know nothing of love, but I did know she was not saying those things to me, and that it did not matter. I held her by the hips to keep her from flying off me, for she seemed so far from me, despite the intimacy. She started in banging my chest with her fists and I felt a little bad about these washboard ribs all but sticking through my skin, but I shouldn't have; her eyes were closed.

Maybe it was the position we were in, but I experienced a sharp, unpleasant memory of my daddy on Callibogee Island, and my natural curiosity and competition made me want to know about how love was made. Though I had no knowledge about what Bud Bandy called poontang, I simply followed the way the thing was constructed. Sex was its own guide, I realized to my relief. I put both hands around her, there where we were joined, and that was the right thing, because she worked harder on me, and for a moment her face went slack and relaxed, and her eyes opened and stared. I looked where she was looking, and saw the spiky shadows of the Joshua trees, and their sharp fronds like so many knives thrown at the moon. She loomed up over me as though she wanted to pull away, but I wouldn't let her go. I brought her down upon me and she cried out, and I knew a moment of conscience and regret, though they were both wasted under a moon like this one. There is where the soul resides, I thought, and you would be a fool to retreat. Then she wrapped her hand around my little Lazarus as if I were the bride and her fingers the ring, and pretty soon I felt my entire poor toadfish life course out of me through my cock and into her.

Like the Headless Horseman, I had thrown myself away. That is the point, it came to me as I drifted, this dispersal, like a newspaper in the desert. To do that, it takes much more than ordinary love.

When I next looked up, the moon had swung around to illuminate the inside of the cabin. Below my bare ass, rodents scratched. I sat up in a hurry.

"It's okay," Laura told me. "Kangaroo rats. Desert's a busy place at night."

She was standing in the doorway, dressed.

"I didn't want to leave you out here all night, but I have to go. You know, Flash Flood Estates. I've got to work tomorrow. I'm in real estate, answering the phone for some crook who's trying to sell off pieces of the desert. Water not included."

"Why don't people just homestead? It worked for us."

Laura smiled. "Those days are gone, except for Mr. C-rats. But he's another story."

I dressed awkwardly under her gaze. Under the floorboards, the rats crouched in defensive silence, waiting for us to leave. From under the floor on the Isle of Hope to on top of it in Forty-Nine Palms. I guess that's what you call coming up in the world.

"How long was I asleep?"

"Thirty minutes, maybe. Not much." Laura smiled again, indulgently. "It's okay, you earned it."

We climbed down from the plateau. Like the highway, this place imposed its code, which was to keep quiet. When we came down into the dry wash, she stopped. The trailer stood dark on its promontory.

"They didn't leave a candle burning for you."

"They know I know my way in the dark."

"Who's 'they' for you?"

She gave me a look reserved for trespassers. I knew that look.

"Nobody. My papa."

I nodded in the direction of the hills, where we'd been. "What would he do if he knew?"

"He'd be jealous. Real, real jealous."

Then she scurried up the slope, kicking out sand and stones behind her, to the trailer she called Flash Flood Estates.

I opened the door to our room at the Oasis of Eden Motel, praying that I might receive the benediction of my mother's sleep. I had all but walked out on her in mid-sentence, the cruelest cut I could have administered. But the lights that burned in that room were a warning not to expect such a favor from the world.

Evangeline was sitting in the armchair, perfectly upright. Her head was cast back on the brown-gray fabric and her eyes were closed. The air in the room was as foul as the air in the Winners' Circle.

As ridiculous as a husband in a television comedy, I tiptoed in with my shoes in my hand. I had to cross in front of Evangeline's outpost to reach the bathroom. As I did, she spoke.

RAT PALMS

"Been out exploring the wild West, boy?"

Goddamned carnival gypsy! Knows all, sees all, even when she's asleep. Or feigning sleep, should I say, for minds like hers are never truly at rest, not when there is such a wealth of wrongs and little injustices to be cataloged and counted up.

"Yes, Mother. I was out."

"Let me guess. The Winners' Circle."

"They asked after you there," I tried to cajole her.

She sniffed the air. "You ought to wash your hair or something."

I took that as permission to continue unimpeded to the bathroom. But that was not the case.

"I envy you," she said. "Your facility with the outside world."

"You should go out more."

"Out?" she queried, as if I had introduced some foreign concept to her, like refrigerators to the Eskimos. "I am not accustomed to going out. I only know my world, not all the other ones they have out there. Besides, the world comes to me, or it used to, in any case. Anyway, what would I do out there?" She gestured toward the drawn blinds. "Go surfing?"

"I don't know as there's much surfing in the desert. But I hear there's a ghost town around here, and that they're having Ghost Town Days."

"No, thank you. We've only just left a ghost town, don't you understand? I don't need another one. That's the point of this trip, boy."

I slipped into the washroom before she could rein me back with another set piece of witty repartee. In the streaky mirror, I considered my reflection. I had lost the grace and sleep I knew on the floor of that homesteader's shack. That's the trouble with the self-forgetting that love brings: it ends too quickly. Afterward, you're back in the hall of mirrors again.

In the toilet bowl, a drowned cigarette floated, oddly reminiscent of a leech with its soggy, overstuffed body. This time, I pissed on it till it broke up, and declined to flush the toilet. Call that progress if you will. All fulfillment had left me by the time I went back into the room.

"I know you think I'm snooping on you," Evangeline said as I tried to figure out which bed would be mine for the night, since both were vaguely and inconclusively undone. "But, you know, you're not that easy to talk to. And I'm only looking for a little chance to talk. I know I'm not very good at it . . ."

"I wouldn't say that. You always were a model for me. It's just that I don't have that much to say."

"What about that report of yours that you so desperately want to write? Surely you could share some of your reflections, as you call them."

"My orders were to write the report. Not speak it. Besides, the content is confidential."

Disappointed, Evangeline slumped back in her chair. I decided to claim the bed closest to the door, lay down and began listening to the noisome buzzing of draft beer in my head. I would have given my right ball to be back lying ass naked on the floor of that homesteader's shack, listening to the kangaroo rats going about their simple, humble business. But that was not to be.

"I'm going to sleep," I announced in this room blazing with electric light.

"Don't make any idle threats."

Another busy night began on the graveyard shift. I briefly made good on my threat to sleep, then awoke to the words, "I'm not going on any further." The overhead lights glared. Malevolently, Evangeline was watching over me.

"You won't have to," I told her wearily, as I might to a child who never listens. "It'll probably take all day to get a can of gas and find someone to take me out to the car. If I can roust somebody out first thing in the morning, we can get on the road by afternoon. We can't be but two hundred miles from Los Angeles. You can be at those mystery cousins you have for dinner."

"I told you I wasn't going any further. You never take me seriously," she muttered. "Anyway, I don't even know if I have any family in Los Angeles any more."

I got up and shut off the ceiling light. Exhaustion and the Winners' Circle drinks pushed me over into sleep again. I conjured up the empty doors and windows of the homesteaders' cabins, a place taken over by nocturnal scavengers, and the words *The House of Love* glowed in my dream, red and angry as a roadside neon sign. Then I awoke to a bang and my own shouting and that faithful, tormenting dream of intruders, and the door opened and my mother peered in, amused. "Don't be shouting at me, son, I'm just making a little trip to the ice machine." I got up to pee out the last of the beer. In the bathroom, in odd proximity to her beauty products, I spotted a member of the swizzle-stick army, Mr. I. W. Harper. I filled half a bathroom drinking glass with the stuff and topped up the glass with tap water. I held my nose and closed my eyes and jumped in. *Geromino!*

"You don't drink, boy."

The all-seeing carnival gypsy was standing in the doorway, freshly filled ice bucket in hand, a mixture of admonishment and vindication in her eyes.

"No. I don't. This glass just jumped into my hand."

"I was watching you there. That looked like a pretty practiced drinker's move. Twirl that top and fill her up. Go to the tap, without the nicety of ice."

"Simply observation and careful study." I took a cube from the bucket. "There. A lump of nicety. If you think it makes any difference."

"Welcome to the family misery, boy."

"No, thank you. I'll do it my own way."

I eased by her and went to stand in the Oasis parking lot. The half-moon had disappeared several eternities ago over the San Bernardino Mountains. I had to marvel at the kind of world that would put a lonely, unprepared child toadfish like me in a motel room in the desert in the wee small hours, arguing about whether ice makes any essential, moral difference in a glass of bourbon. Even cut with tap water, the fumes rising out of the glass suddenly sickened me, and I threw the contents of the drink onto the asphalt parking lot. While I was at it, I let the glass go, too.

For Your Protection.

15

My bacon and eggs didn't look too good to me the next morning. I probably didn't look too good to them, either. Upon waking, I had been greeted with the smell of Evangeline's warm, half-consumed toddy on the night table that separated our beds, and this had not put me in good spirits. I recalled that my protector Simple Sims had volunteered to drive me out to Mile 50 of the Wheat road with a full gas can to rescue the New Yorker. I was pushing around the pale-yellow egg yolk with a little square of toasted white bread when he flagged me down at the restaurant.

Crouching down on the bare metal floor of his truck, watching the road flashing by through the holes in it, I learned the name of the real estate office where Laura worked. And also, that she was married to the very man — a crook, she had described him the night before — who sold the little squares of dry desert to a new generation of homesteaders. Disappointing, but not surprising news. Between Forty-Nine Palms and Hurt's Landing, the world's recreation was pretty much the same.

The car stood where I had left it yesterday, with no kit fox litter in the backseat. But Evangeline and I had been so eager to jump into Sims's corroded pickup the day before that we'd forgotten all about closing the windows. The inside of the car was full of sand and bits of mesquite bush. Sand had gotten into the turn signal lever and kept it from working right. But that hardly mattered any more. It was all straight ahead from here on in.

Back at the Oasis of Eden, Evangeline was making good on her threat. Her rear end was cemented securely into the armchair. A game show was on TV. She had spread the contents of her suitcase over every conceivable surface in the room.

"I told you I wasn't going any further."

"So I see. You planning on spending the rest of your life in Forty-Nine Psalms?"

"Palms," she corrected me.

"Of course. But don't you understand that you have to keep going? This is your idea. California is your idea."

"This is California." She swept her hand over the room. "You said so yourself."

"No. Los Angeles is California. That's where we're going. That's where you want to go, that's where everyone wants to go. It's the end of the line."

There was a knock at the door. The maid walked in, saw us, then retreated in a shower of apologetic Spanish. Though not before her eyes slid from Evangeline to me, and her mouth bestowed an indulgent smile.

The rest of the day and the one that followed it are best left undescribed and, if remembered, best quickly forgotten. Though forgetting is not my strong suit; I think you've understood that by now. I went by the Phillips station that had lent me the five-gallon gas can and traded it in for a six-pack of PBR, then headed up the stony track that led onto the plateau of Joshua trees. Now, I'm not pretending that fucking another man's wife, horse-toothed or not, real estate or not, will make you a man in return. But doing it did hand me the keys to the world in an unexpected way. *The* world? Let's say *a* world. A world of idleness and waiting for a woman to bestow her gift on me. Talk about belonging to someone else! Well, why not, Evangeline, why not belong to someone who lets you stop belonging to your own sad self?

On the plateau, I attempted to sit and drink beer under a Joshua tree, but the species provided no shade. Buzzards turned overhead, hope in their hard little hearts. At one point I heard garbled voices, and figured the combination of warm PBR and sun had gotten the better of me. Then a pair of enormous, beet-red, bareheaded hikers double-timed past me, pointing in all directions and reading out loud from their guidebook. After they had evaporated, I thought it best to look for shade, and found it in a cave hollowed out by the wind. Lulled by the piss-warm gas-station beer, I tried sleeping. When you awake, I consoled myself, the Winners' Circle will be open. And, with a little luck, perfidious Laura will be there. I will try to coax a bit more desert real estate out of her.

This became a routine of sorts, and an escape from the Oasis of Eden. After the careful moral measurements of the Isle of Hope, to pass entire afternoons in the shade cast by a bare rock or the back end of our quickly decaying New Yorker, or to wake naked with Laura in the full blast of the sun's heat, the backseat wringing with sweat, was a positive luxury. After spending a long season on the Lazaretto knowing only my own unknowing, Laura was sweet antidote. Our love was by needs itinerant. Once in the New Yorker parked on a hard sheet of glittering soda that had probably been a lake in the days of the saber-toothed tigers. Another time in the very office of the Joshua Wells real estate company, where I accidentally, I think, knocked an expensive-looking typewriter onto the floor with a ferocious and impulsive leg kick.

"My sweet blank slate," she called me after that exercise.

Then made me simulate vandalism to justify the broken typewriter, complete with forced entry and soaking the file cabinets down with bourbon. I watched admiringly as, naked, my sperm running down both her thighs, she telephoned the sheriff to report the crime.

The next morning I awoke in a different but identical homesteader's cabin with lightning flashing behind my eyes. Blank slate indeed! It was crisscrossed and scored with a killing hangover. Besides, I was near to dying of thirst. At that precise moment I realized the vanity of this business of trying to murder your conscience, as if you could do so, and not have the body start stinking on you immediately. This is what happens when you throw your head away, said the Headless Horseman of Sleepless Hollow: it hurts when you get it back. From exceedingly close by, a lizard was staring at me with a frank, appraising gaze. I looked out the gaping door of the cabin and asked myself, What is a house, if not a figure for the soul? With a heart full of self-disgust, I marched off across the stony field in search of the car. It was nowhere in sight. To make matters worse, there were not even any roads. I walked for hours, it seemed, trusting that my steps would be guided by a few unbroken strings of memory. And it was so. After a time I came to a butte from which I could survey Forty-Nine Palms. Far below, in the sunlight, the car roof shone. The car was parked in an original fashion, but at least I hadn't lost it.

It was a laborious climb down the dry washes into the town. At the end of it, in the glaring sun, I saw Laura strolling along the service road that paralleled the highway, with forced casualness. We stopped in front of one another. She turned and considered the car, all askew, as if it were an explanation.

"You forgot to wake me up before you left," I told her plaintively. "I could have frozen up there, or gotten rabies from a kangaroo rat bite."

"You look like Mr. C-rats. It sure happened fast with you."

"He must live inside each one of us."

She took that in. Then announced, "You have to leave this town. If you don't do it, today, someone'll kill you."

"That jealous, huh?"

She walked away. I didn't even get my kiss of peace.

RAT PALMS

I opened the door to the Justice family compound at the Oasis of Eden. First to meet my gaze was a stack of white Styrofoam food containers from a Mexican take-out restaurant and an empty six-pack with the cans still hanging on the strap. That technique of beer-drinking gave me pause for reflection. Mr. Harper had also fallen in the combat. He lay with his top knocked off next to an untouched food tray on what had been my bed.

"Hello, son." Evangeline made a vague gesture in the direction of that bed. "I ordered dinner for you but you didn't come back to eat it. It must be cold by now. Several days cold. What time is it?"

"Apparently, it's time to go."

I considered her, and the room around her she had fashioned to fit her image. I considered myself, too, so lately a derelict. Seeing this room, this portrait, would have been enough to motivate me out of this town, even without Laura's threats. If nothing else, I realized, this is what separates us: Evangeline, Daddy and me. Pride. Plain, ordinary pride that revolts and says, *I will not become this thing. I will go so far down, but no further. Then I must come up.*

I started picking up her things, beginning in the bathroom. Beauty products, a nightgown, the infernal mug with its lying message, her expense pad, her traveling scarf, a *TV Guide*, matchbooks from every stop we'd made, the motel ashtray, swizzle sticks with naked mermaids and golf clubs on them. The whole sad collection. She watched me pack up the room with only moderate interest, as if someone else had been residing there. When I finished zipping up her bag and mine with it, she stood and allowed herself to be led, sparing me what could have been the most disagreeable part of the clean-up. I escorted her, as gentlemanly as death himself, arm-in-arm to the waiting automobile. A minute later we had turned onto the highway and were heading into the late-afternoon sun toward Los Angeles.

I don't know what I was expecting. A stone gate like the one at Wormslow, with Abandon Hope carved into it? The arrival at some vantage point from which Los Angeles could be seen to seethe and pulse below like an immature vision of hell, the city all spread out like some hairy-holed whore? Nothing of the sort, dear traveling companions. First, I never even knew exactly when I got to Los Angeles. After staring into the sunset for an hour or two through my inefficacious truck-stop sunglasses, I noticed town after town reeling by us along the freeway, but saw no place called Los Angeles.

Beside me, my mother was stunned, contrite, self-concerned and drinking. I was all those things, too, and unwashed.

I saw more that night before I reached my destination than any toadfish could tell. The place was prodigal. We passed a movie house advertising *The War of the Worlds* on the marquee. For some reason, owing to exquisite fatigue and wisps of precocious alcohol poisoning, no doubt, I found this irresistibly funny. "What's the matter, don't you know how to hold your liquor?" my mother grumbled, because, I must add out of fairness, I had leeched away a couple Christian Brothers brandy miniatures along the way. In this state of high awareness I began to truly listen to the words in the kind of talk that surrounds a bottle, no matter the proportion, the way moths surround a porch light. I saw how comical the proposition was: that we actually could hold our liquor, as if in fond embrace, whereas everyone knew it was the other way around. In the midst of this perverse hilarity a man burst from a side street onto the wide boulevard I was traveling on. He was wrapped in dirty flowing robes, a kind of derelict Arab, and he came rushing into the middle of the street, screaming theatrically, pushing a shopping cart in which a skeletal puppy dog rode. When he saw me coming at him he stopped dead in his tracks and waited, a beckoning, hopeful, eager smile on his face. I did not give him the satisfaction. I swerved, clipped the cart and scattered the puppy, but missed the man.

Yet another question of lucidity and will. One more haint on the road. I drove on with a shattered headlight.

I passed the most astonishing array of commerces selling things I did not know anyone needed. Fingernails and eyelashes. Seat covers that looked as though they had been sewn from recently slaughtered lambs. A storefront that read Ethical Drugs. A hospital for dogs and cats. A taco stand that would also wash your car, fill it with gas and shine your shoes while you ate. And all along the streets, the gaunt yet comical palm trees stunted by streetlights as orange as the Cheddar cheese in a truck-stop sandwich.

Then there it was at the end of the boulevard, a great expanse of darkness. The Pacific Ocean. Last stop, everybody out! I turned to report this discovery to my mother; her head was cocked to one side and her eyes were shut tight. If you stay up all night, I suppose, sleep will catch up to you sooner or later.

I rolled to a stop in a parking lot. A pier pointed into the ocean, as our dock had once pointed into the Lazaretto, except here, the waves swelled and crashed under the planks. I stumbled along the uneven boards of the pier like the drunks I had studied. Here, at last, was the end. Deliverance. Incarnated by a pier lined with fried-fish cafés, a bumper car ride that was closed for the night, a shack with a palm outlined in neon tubing where I read, Doreena, Psychotic Adviser. I blinked my eyes hard. Doreena, Psychic Adviser, the sign read now.

On the pier, the air was cool and restorative, and the night fishermen dropping their lines into the surf made it seem as though life might even be possible here. Do Not Eat White Croakers, a notice announced not far from the fishermen. I changed my mind about the pier. What kind of fishing drop could this be if you could not eat your own catch?

Along the railing were little blue telescopes at regular intervals. See America, they ordered, and for a quarter you could see America for twenty power more than with your natural eyes. I figured I had seen all the America I could stand, but what the hell, I put a quarter in. I swung the telescope around and aimed it inland until I picked up the New Yorker parked under the scrawny palms. Nothing was moving inside that car. *Bang!* I went, and it disappeared just as my quarter's worth of seeing America did.

But when I took my eye away from the telescope, the car was still there, sitting askew across two parking spaces, pointing at the Pacific. I was in dire need of sleep, even if the car was as welcoming a refuge as a tomb. On my way to it, I considered the bumper cars parked behind their wire fencing. They would have made an original bed for the night, if only that ferocious German shepherd didn't work there. I got behind the wheel; it was getting to be a natural posture. In the dome light, I saw that Evangeline had applied her earplugs and black-out mask again in the interim. I rummaged through the combination trash bag and toddy repository till I found a couple forlorn miniatures. I put them out of their misery, then jacked the seat lever back and fell into a forced sleep.

Did you hear that? It said, *Thump, thump.*

Now it's back. Now it's saying, *Scratch, scratch.*

Shut up, I ordered Thump and Scratch. Can't you see I'm trying to sleep? Don't you think I've earned it?

But Thump and Scratch would not let me be.

The wind whistled through the crack in the window. In the ignition, the keys sang together.

I opened my eyes and saw the heads of the palm trees, bending low in a sudden squall. The sky was predawn black and the floodlights lit holes in the mist. Something was dropping out of a tree, turning over and over as it fell. A miniature body. It hit the parking lot and went still.

That's when I felt a hostile animal presence. I looked straight out through the windshield. Clinging to the wipers was a yellow-eyed rat.

Even through the glass, I could smell its bad breath.

That's when I heard Thump. A rat hit the hood and went still. A line of red-brown blood trickled down the front of the car.

I had left my island and come all the way across the country, and

RAT PALMS

now it was raining rats on me. I turned the ignition key one click forward and threw on the windshield wipers. Get out of my sight, Rat. But Rat clung to the rubber blade with all four claws. It rode back and forth across the glass, its back feet scratching furiously at the windshield, raising an intolerable sound.

I put the wipers on high. Take that, Rat. But Rat rode it out, teeth and claws sunk into the wiper blade. It was like a roller coaster for rats. You could tell Rat was trying to figure out what to do in a situation like this. It was his first time he was faced with such a thing.

That makes two of us, Rat. Should we talk?

I bailed out of the car. You can keep it, Rat, the papers are in the glove compartment. Hope you like roller coasters, Rat. But bailing out proved to be a mistake. The palm heads were bowing low in the wind and the rats dropping from the trees like manna from hell. On a grassy spot under one palm, three surprised rodents sat in a heap, sniffing at the air, looking out of place in a parking lot. Which way home, rats?

Finally, I got the bright idea to get out from under the trees. Like a man under fire, I ran crouching across the parking lot. The oceanfront street was lined with benches that had nothing but black, empty sky above them. I used one of them as my temporary refuge.

I was startled awake by another mammal experience. A large red floppy dog was licking my face and slobbering all over my neck with its cooked-ham tongue. I have never cared for cooked ham.

I jumped up and shooed the mutt. It flew back a few paces, its front paws out and its head down, ready for some game. "It's the middle of the night in the promised land, a night fit for rats, not men. You want to play?" I asked the dog. The dog said he did. I went through the motions of unscrewing my head and throwing it as far as I could down the street so the dog could retrieve it. But it would not come off. The dog saw this. He was mystified.

"Hey, man, you all right?"

A girl was standing a few paces away, looking on.

"Yes . . . I was just playing with your dog. He woke me up."

"She. You shouldn't sleep on park benches. It isn't safe."

"Well, I didn't intend to. I was in my car, over there, and everything was okay. Then all of a sudden something funny happened."

"Yeah?"

"Yeah. It started raining rats. From out of the trees. I had to get out of there."

"I can imagine you did."

Both of us looked across the little strip of grass to the parking lot, which was an unnaturally bright, Cheddar-cheese color in the floodlights. The New Yorker sat there under the trees. Its wipers were moving in slow motion across the windshield on the little bit of juice left in the battery.

"It was raining rats," the girl repeated.

"I'm afraid so. It doesn't sound very likely. Some kind of wind blew up and the palm trees started shaking. They were dropping out of the palms."

The girl's eyes moved slowly from the parking lot to my face. Then she patted her thigh. "Come here, Rainbow," she said, and the dog flew to her side. I had never heard of a dog being called Rainbow.

"What are you doing out here?" The girl pointed toward the car. "You live in that?"

"No, no . . . I guess I must have fallen asleep . . . I don't know, I wanted to see the sunrise, you know, over the ocean."

"In that case, you're on the wrong coast." The girl slapped her thigh again. "Let's get out of here, Rainbow."

Then she and her dog strode briskly down the street. I had to admit she was right. This was the wrong coast for watching the sunrise from.

III
THE ORDER OF THE SHINY BLACK SUIT

16

A few days later I was lying back in a train, rolling across the dark Carolinas, listening to the soft fall of the dice in a gentlemen's crap game on the other side of the partition in the sleeper car. It had taken me God's own eternity to get across this big impassive continent by rail, but that's the way I wanted to do it. I wanted to travel the way Daddy Zeke had, and see his country. That's why I was going back to Savannah. To retrieve Daddy Zeke.

How did I get the money to travel in so leisurely a fashion? After both girl and dog had retreated from the madman's image I must have been showing there on the oceanfront boulevard, I walked across the parking lot toward the car. I was in search of rats, dead or wounded. I saw none. The one that had taken the roller-coaster ride on the wipers must have jumped off, dizzy as all get-out. Nothing unusual there. But what about the one that had crashed dead onto the hood? It had disappeared, too. As had the ones that had struck the concrete parking lot and broken their little rat backs.

Normally, dead rats don't get up and walk again like Lazarus. And rats aren't exactly known for carting away their dead to offer them decent burial. Rats are, well, *rats*. It occurred to me, in my rodent-searching position on all fours by the car's front bumper, in that deserted parking lot in that deserted hour, that perhaps there had never been any rats in the first place. I couldn't decide which was worse: that the thing had really happened, or not.

Inside the car, Evangeline was sleeping like an innocent. Her lips were parted, and little puffs of whiskey-tainted wind passed through her mouth at every breath. I cut the wiper switch and the ignition. Then reached into the backseat and found her purse.

I should have known. There was the roll of hundred-dollar bills from Distinct Intent. I counted them carefully. Twenty-nine remained. I took fourteen for myself, left her the bigger half. I was committing an act of justice of a kind, and I had no regrets. Evangeline would get along; she had people here. She'd said so herself. And it was my money, too. It was my due. I looked at it as a disability payment. A dismemberment benefit. An insurance policy of a kind. I grabbed my bag, whose principal source of weight was one granite baseball, locked the door carefully and went out looking for a taxi to take me to the train station. Even in California, I reasoned, they still must have trains.

I spent a good part of the eastward trip sleeping. When some helpful soul suggested I was wasting the beautiful scenery, I laughed in her face. I knew what I was missing. Finally, in Baltimore, somewhat restored, I picked up the Panama Limited, and now I was rolling home.

On this, my mission, that crap game on the other side of the partition and those gentlemen's voices became an odd source of comfort to me. Though the voices were muffled, I knew every word that was spoken, and every sentiment unspoken, as they traveled across the dark landscape with me. A pair of dice coming to rest on a felt board has a particular sound, as do the expressions of dismay or gratitude that are bound to follow. This was familiar ground. And though I knew the evening could end with handshakes all around, or with a pistol shot, I felt such sweet longing for that world. And this, despite the fact that it was closed forever to me. Despite how it had hurt me, despite knowing that it did not exist any more, or worse, that it was as virulent and full of evil intent as a corpse left to rot in the woods.

At one point in the evening the bourbon must have run short, because my half-sleep was interrupted by concerned voices and much cajoling of the black porter, who presumably owned the key to some secret cache of toddy. Then, in their pleas, apparently fruitless until then, there came a short silence that a bank note of considerable proportion always creates. That silence was followed by charmed deference in the porter's voice. And the next time I lent my ear, the game was back in progress, with the telltale splash of bourbon into plastic cups, and the universal sound of a brown paper bag being crumpled shut.

Later on, after the game or my interest in it had played itself out, I stepped out of my compartment and walked down the aisle of the car. As if walking to the front of the train would get me into Savannah faster, where I did not know what I would do when I got there, or whom I could turn to who might help me with what I wanted to do. Where, more likely than not, I'd just have to wait for a sign.

I slid open the door at the end of the car. In the little space between this one and the next stood a man, holding desperately on to a black case and shivering uncontrollably, as if suffering from pellagra. The train swayed over rough track, and he wrestled with the snaps to open the case. It could have held a flute, but it was wider than a flute case. I went to squeeze past him, and smelled on him the kind of smell a man acquires after having slept in his clothes a few days. Pretty much the way I smelled after crossing the continent twice, I imagined.

I had just about made it past him when the train took a curve and he lurched heavily against me.

"You want to help me out with this thing?" he asked.

He had a caved-in, pinched face, and an uneven beard that half covered his pasty, grits-eating skin. Something from out of the piney woods.

He caught me eyeing the necklace of metal fragments he had on around his neck.

"You ain't never seen a man wear a necklace before, have you?" he challenged me.

"Not unless it's got a cross hanging on it," I admitted. "Or something else against the evil eye."

"This does work against the evil eye, as a matter of fact." He grabbed the necklace. "This here thing is made out of shrapnel they dug out of my side in Vietnam. It repels the bad spirits. Keeps away the rest of the shrapnel floating around out there."

"I do appreciate a superstitious man," I told him.

He cocked his head and looked at me. "Do you even *know* where Vietnam is?"

"Sort of," I lied, and when I felt he could sense that it was a lie I added, "We're not much for newspaper reading where I come from."

"I bet you ain't."

He handed me the case, and I braced myself against the back of the door. He got his hands to calm down and flipped open the latch. He opened it a cautious few inches. There was no flute in there; instead, I saw an instrument of a different nature. An automatic pistol with a couple of spare clips, and all along the top, a row of marijuana cigarettes more expertly rolled than Laura's, all held in place with red velvet snaps.

"That's quite a case," I complimented him.

"Hey, that's a sumbitch thing to say! I like you!" He gave a hoot of laughter. "The name's Lynn."

We shook hands. This Lynn had a mad, howling laugh like a monkey. Maybe he got it in one of those jungles they were supposed to have over in Vietnam. It just seemed natural that he would pick on me to expose his madness. As soon as any madman saw my innocent, toadfish face, he just had to corrupt it with all the tools at his disposal, and with all due dispatch.

"This here is my survival pack," he confided in me. "Got to have both kinds of weaponry when you're riding the rails, getting to know the old U. S. of A. again."

"I imagine so. If you smoke that stuff, and you don't like the things you see, you always got that gun to shoot them with."

"You righter than you know, boy!" He slapped me on the shoulder and my teeth rattled. There was some power in that scrawny body of his. "'Cause this is some ominous weed."

"I have had a little experience," I let on.

He shook his head. "Don't matter how much experience you got in the general. There's no getting used to this in the particular."

The noise was deafening between the cars and we kept getting thrown from side to side, and into each other, which made for a haphazard sort of intimacy. But what we lacked in comfort we made up in privacy. Lynn licked the cigarette and put it in his mouth.

"I'm warning you, this ain't no civilian weed. We're gonna lose the war on account of this stuff."

"Does that bother you?"

Lynn shrugged. "That war? Their war? Shit, no!"

I tried to draw the smoke in deep and let it feel at home in my lungs, employing the Evangeline Marster method of smoking. But I couldn't hold it for long.

"I see what you mean. What do you put in this stuff, napalm?"

He squinted up his eyes at me at the mention of the word. "You told me you ain't much for newspaper reading. Well, that don't matter. Them little yellow gooks we're fighting grow it that way so we'll stop caring whether there's a war on or not. Then when we've stopped caring, they come in and cut our grapes right off."

Lynn gave his mad monkey howl of laughter.

"You figure there's a moral in there somewhere?" I asked him.

"Sure is! Keep your legs crossed when you're fucking stoned."

I laughed. As I laughed I realized there was nothing funny about Lynn's joke, and that made me laugh harder.

"Oh, shit, you ain't one of them hyena highs, are you?"

"I couldn't say. All I know is Christian Brothers brandy."

Lynn shrugged. The cigarette had burned down to his yellowed fingertips, but he seemed unaware of the fact. "It's all the same. Takes your mind off your troubles, whatever it is. Puts a whole ocean between you and the things you have to do to get by."

He dropped the butt on the floor. For a moment I watched it burn out on the sheet metal, studded with worm patterns and shifting and sliding up over itself on the turns. It took no particular effort to imagine that metal plate opening and my body falling through, into noise and shredding.

"Shit, this *is* some grass." I listened to my voice and realized I was talking to keep down the panic. Just like Evangeline. "Now I know what they mean about the Marines making a man out of you."

"Ha! They make a fucking machine out of you. Half animal, half machine, and dressed to kill. That's their idea of a man. Then they set you free in the zoo we call the world."

I listened to his words in the smoky enclosure, words full of terror but strangely distant. Made almost comfortable by the grass.

"This weed of yours is a war in itself."

Lynn nodded. "Part of the survival pack. Choose your weapon. I credit this grass with keeping my ass in one piece. Like I say, it's ominous. When I smoke it, I can feel the attack gathering against my position, even before it happens. Creative paranoia. Over there, the attack will *gather* on you, like a storm, like the wind. That's because those little gook people over there are made of earth. You can't fight the earth and win. You can only hold on and hope. To do that, you've got to keep your ass in a permanent state of alert."

"Where's the next attack coming from? I mean now, now that you're home."

"That's the problem when you're campaigning on the home front." Lynn shook his head. Sadness and defeat came into his voice. "Everyone looks the same — they all look like your own people. But they're not. A lot of them hate you because you've been over there, because you remind them there's a war going on. It's even worse here than over in Nam, and you could never even tell over there."

Lynn pulled another of his cigarettes from the case and toyed with it.

"Maybe you'd better stick to bourbon," I told him. "Keeps everybody backslapping happy. Keeps the wheels of talk turning. No terror. At least, that's what I've seen."

Lynn shook his head. "Doesn't make any difference. It's just a choice of weapons."

I raised an imaginary glass to the man. "To each his refuge!"

We stood and let ourselves be buffeted in that roar between the cars for a time, then Lynn admitted, "When you're involved in the kind of war I am, you just can't secure a perimeter. You just can't tell where it's going to come from. It's in the middle of the night, it's inside you, it's everywhere. You can't be everywhere at once. I know, I tried, and it wore me out."

"Sounds like a civil war. There's no other kind." I waved off his offer of smoke. "That's why I'm going back home. I'm going to mop up."

I discovered that the smoking man didn't like smoking alone any more than the drinking man enjoyed solitary indulgence. If I wasn't in on his smoke, I was out of his world. He slid open the door and went out of our noisy little cell toward the front of the train. My car was toward the back. Poor Lynn. He did not seem to appreciate the old Marster lesson from the Isle of Hope. That if you must have pain, at least embrace it. If you must fight a war, at least have the decency to lose it. And in a gentlemanly manner, if possible.

I wheeled down the aisle and aimed my body through the doors of my sleeper and into my narrow bunk. Mr. C-rats. Lynn. That's what this country is made of. Men of war. Well, add my name to the list! Okay, my war is gentler so far, its weapons more intimate. But only because I'm younger, and newer at it. With those reflections, I let that train drive me down South, properly anesthetized for the occasion, lulled and furred and slaughtered by a continent's worth of sour mash and Lynn's Tet Offensive marijuana. Ominous, indeed. If I'd had his survival pack close at hand, a dozen times during my agitated sleep I would have taken out that automatic and shot this train car full of holes. When those dreams gather around you like gnats, sometimes you've got to make a loud noise to scare them away.

I flicked open my eyes the next morning as the Panama Limited was making its lumbering approach into Savannah's Union Station. The conductor rapped on the glass with his ticket punch and shouted, "'Vannah, Georgia," as if I did not recognize the river docks and the great turning basin beyond it. I gave the granite baseball a good-luck squeeze and zipped up my overnight bag.

A minute later I was standing under the great cupola of Union Station, where Old Paul Gant had sung his song. In his stead, the PA system was echoing away, announcing my train's arrival and all the places it had been. This time around, that tinny voice did not have to compete with any human beings. In the time I'd been gone, old Paul Gant must have transformed into a haint. Either that, or they had locked him up in the state home for singing in tongues.

I stood there and looked up at the gray-green girders where Gant's song once had roosted. Suddenly, I was returned to that afternoon as I waited for my father to step off the train from up North. And, with it, to that state of unknowing and expectation, to a time before this trip, when I was little Timmy Toadfish, his hand grasped too tightly by his mama as she strived to communicate all the fear she harbored. How much I'd learned about her fears since then, and how many more of my own I'd added on top, and how hard I'd worked to learn to live with the whole teetering edifice.

I saw into the horror of that time of waiting. How akin it was to the state of childhood, when you must suffer other people's madnesses, and all you can do about it is wait, wait, wait. Thank God for the American continent — and Laura — for putting all that behind me.

So don't be surprised if I got out of that station as quick as I could. Fuck memory lane. Sometimes you don't need a destination to want to move fast.

I walked through the early summer heat along West Broad, my grip in my hand, a dull, weary ghost in a haze, a proper state, I suppose, for an unannounced homecoming. The ignorance of an Isle of Hope upbringing must have masked it from me, but I had never noticed upon what hard times West Broad Street had fallen. I turned onto Broughton. The first block had more boarded-up stores than active ones. An empty lot was covered in charred timber and blackened brick, the result of an insurance fire, or a civil disorder, or both simultaneously. Maybe the street had always been in this state, but it was something a Marster boy would not have been given to see.

Things did not get much better for Broughton as I neared the corner of Bull, the intersection of my daddy's misfortune. Seeing so many boarded-up storefronts, I had to wonder where Evangeline had done all that shopping of hers, those times when she rushed down the Lazaretto Road in the car, ostensively to Broughton Street. Poor Evangeline, I had not spared her much reflection since walking away from her the morning after the rain of rats. A cruel but necessary move. If you need me, I addressed her on the street of her alibis, you'll know where to find me.

At the corner of Bull Street, I stopped. I stared down at the pavement. The place where my father had made a spectacle of himself. There was nothing out of the ordinary about the spot. No chalk mark on the asphalt.

Then there came a sign, as they say down in Sandfly Crossing. It came in the shape of an aged black sedan gliding up to the curb next to me, and in the whir of power windows.

"Say there, son," a man's voice called out.

I was almost too afraid and too moved by superstition to turn around. What little lesson had the hometown prepared for me now? It could have been Father Damian Dooley at the wheel, with an exhausted God sitting next to him in the death seat. Or old Jefferson

Marster, beet-red and dressed in his funereal Sunday best. Or Calvin Fleetwood, wringing his hands over his cowardice, a tub of leeches riding in the backseat. Or my own Daddy Zeke AWOL from the asylum, wearing a scavenged Indians uniform like madman's robes. It was the voice, you see. They all shared that whiskey-cured, gravelly, sporting man's voice.

I turned to look.

Mercifully, it was not any of those people. Though I knew the mold, at first I did not recognize the man, with his big, bulbous, booze-blown nose, the swelled-up fingers pinched by a sapphire ring and the loose flesh hanging off his massive jaw.

"Sir," I said.

He looked at me, insulted that I did not recognize him. "Would you be needing a lift?" he inquired.

I didn't need a lift because I wasn't going anywhere. But I got into that big black boat of a car precisely because I had nowhere to go. And because it was a sign.

"Where can I be taking you?" the man asked once I had settled in on the front seat, with my bag in back. "Are you going on some kind of a trip?"

"Coming home," I told him. "Panama Limited."

He nodded.

"Train is a fine way to see the country. Meet some fine people on it. Play a little cards, maybe, talk to some folks. You been gone long?"

"It feels like years, sir."

"And you didn't have anybody to pick you up at the station? Now, that's a shame."

"Sometimes you like to get off a train and go for a little stroll first. Get your feet wet before you get all wrapped up with your people again."

"You may be right. That's not something I would know much about. I always had someone to meet me at the station."

RAT PALMS

The man nodded his heavy head as we drove along Broughton at an excruciatingly slow pace, as if he was not wholly sure what was out there on the other side of the windshield. I know that man, and he knows me, too, I thought, even if I can't place him. He is a bad man; he holds some power over me because of my father, because of something shameful that I can't quite put my finger on. Something that he knows and I don't.

"You give me plenty of warning when you want to get out. My reactions aren't what they used to be."

"You can't be that old, sir."

"Oh, I'm older than your father, I'm willing to bet."

"You're a betting man?" I asked him.

He would have squirmed if he hadn't been so tightly packed in behind the wheel.

"I was in my time. But the sporting man is not what he used to be. He doesn't know the game. All he cares is winning or losing. Yes, this used to be some town for shaking the dice, believe you me. Now there ain't nothing but a few shreds of the old life."

I looked out the car window at forsaken old Broughton Street. "I believe you."

Then I had another sign. This time, it was a tavern sign. I saw Pinky Marster's establishment down a cross street, a block off Broughton, where it had always been.

"If you don't mind turning here, sir, to the right."

He swung that big old boat down McKennedy. When we came to the next street I asked him to stop.

"This home?"

"No." I pointed to Pinky's. "But when I saw that establishment, a sudden thirst came upon me."

"My, son, but you do talk well. You don't hear many young people who speak like that nowadays. With a tongue like that, any educated man from this town would know you come from a fine Savannah family."

"Fine, indeed." I nodded toward Pinky Marster's. "As you know, that establishment is in the family."

He nodded, slowly, as if his neck muscles could hardly bear the weight of his head.

"You're Zeke Justice's boy."

"That's right."

"I'm acquainted with the family. The next time you see him, and I assume that will be soon, you tell him Joe Jackson sends his regards. Now don't you forget, son."

"I couldn't forget."

"Joe Jackson," he repeated.

I reached back for my grip and got out of the car. Then I stopped.

"Why in hell are you telling me your name's Joe Jackson, Mr. Peep?"

Then I slammed the door as hard as I could, as if I could wreck that old hearse with the sheer force of my hatred.

Inside Pinky's, a pair of leathery, lizardlike men looked up when I slid onto a bar stool. Neither, mercifully, was Jefferson Marster, proprietor. There was a customer whose eyes swam like fish behind his Coke-bottle glasses, and who looked vaguely familiar, as so many people did in this town. The bald bartender was rubbing the bullet crease across his forehead, which he had acquired in a holdup attempt the year before. I was acquainted with that holdup. It had been the cause of no end of family trouble when my father had dared defend the Negro kids who had done it for a sack of quarters, saying at the supper table, "You feed me shit for years, and I'll spew in your face, too."

The one with the glasses stared at me in unmasked surprise, as if I had been an alligator walking on two legs, uttering human speech.

"Goddammit, but I thought you and her was gone!" Then he clapped his hand over his mouth. "Excuse me, we ain't even been introduced and I'm talking this way to you. I know you don't know me, even though we've met. And if you don't, I don't blame you. Fucking sugar disease ruined my eyes, and half the rest of me, too. I don't look like myself any more. I'm Ray Marster, your uncle on your mother's side. Your mother is my sister."

"Uncle Ray." I went to shake his hand.

"Don't you Uncle Ray me, you don't even know me. Come here anyway, you disgrace, and give your uncle a big greasy hug."

I stepped across that barroom floor and hugged the old man tight. Too tight, I knew, but he let me do it. I could have rested forever in that womb of leathery skin and hair tonic and cured bourbon smell. The smell of reconciliation with the Isle; it was nothing short of that. I would have stayed there forever, except there was no staying forever anywhere any more. When I pulled away from him I had tears in my eyes, and I knew that was permitted in the company of these men.

"Maybe we didn't know each other before, but we do now," I told him. "Looks as though we're part of the same tragedy."

"Shit damn, if you ain't got your daddy's tongue in your mouth!"

"I'm afraid I do. And with my own, that makes two. With all that meat in there, sometimes it gets hard to talk."

"You've said a mouthful, boy! Now stop rubbing that hole in your head, Shank," he told the bartender, "and give this young man what he wants."

"What I want," I told my uncle as a shot of bourbon in a pony glass appeared before me, "is to sort out all these tongues in my head. I thought I'd start out by trying to find the owner of one of them. He's in a place for those who have lost their lucidity, I hear."

"You must have heard that from my little Evangeline, by the sounds of it. That's something she'd say. But I thought . . ."

"That she went to California. The place where people go when they've overstayed their welcome elsewhere," I quoted her, and Ray Marster winced at the words. "We went there, all right. But I came back. She didn't."

Ray Marster laughed sadly. "She *would* say something like that about California. Always making things sound better by dressing them up in words. Maybe that's why her and your daddy had so much trouble getting on. They both liked to talk so much they forgot to listen — but then again, it's not for me to say."

I picked up my little toddy and gave it a quick sniff. Warm and brown, like marsh water, except a little deeper. And just as good for you as drinking marsh water, too.

"Your daddy used to smell on his whiskey before he drank it," the meddling bartender put in. "Used to get his nose right down in it. Otherwise, he said he didn't get the true flavor."

Shit, I said to myself, and drained the pony glass. I've got my father's tongue in my head, and his glass in my hand. Don't I have anything that belongs to me?

Yes, you do, I answered myself. As long as you get the hell out of this place.

A truck rumbled down McKennedy Street, and the window glass shivered as though it wanted to jump right out of its lead.

"You're back to see your daddy," Ray Marster said after the truck rolled by.

"Yeah. But I didn't phone ahead. I just showed up."

"Sometimes it's better to do it that way . . . I suppose I won't be surprising you if I tell you the man's name has become a curse around here, in some circles anyway, though I never did understand why. More harm was done to him than he did to others, only it didn't always look that way. Like with that beaning down at the ball field . . . Anyway, people have already started to forget. It happens fast. Well, they haven't exactly forgotten — it wouldn't be right to say that. Some new shame has caught a hold of their interest, that's all.

"But not me. I never held anything against the man. Even if I do worry about my little Evangeline."

We sat in the silence of Pinky's, in this place designed to keep the outside world out. The soft light coming through the windows off McKennedy Street was like streams of understanding and forgiveness to my heart. It is too late to undo what is done, that dusty, sienna light said. So let us at least seek balm in talk of reconciliation, for the only way to understand the world is after the fact.

It was easy to picture Daddy Zeke within these confines. I could imagine why a man who believed himself misunderstood would take refuge in a place like this, with light like this. But what could he have done or said here, I wondered, to have made Jefferson Marster march across the field at Grayson Stadium and lecture him in front of all and sundry? Just *talk*? Philosophize?

I turned to Ray Marster. "Why do you figure Evangeline was in such a hurry to quit this place anyway?"

"Oh, that's not for me to say," he drawled, which was his prelude for him saying his piece. "You know, old Jefferson filled her ears with so much Marster shit, all about the cost of honor and the importance of how others see you. She ended up believing it, though why, I'll never know, because the two of them got on like a mess of crabs in a sack, and the old man never really did believe in his own words anyway. The two of them were just too much alike. Like a couple of kids double daring each other to cross an imaginary line on the goddamn sidewalk. But she was her daddy's girl there for a while, or at least she wanted to be. If you ask me, for her to cut and run that way, she must have decided to use the old man's ways for her own reasons. And those, we'll never know."

"Even if we asked her?"

He laughed uneasily. "You ask her if you want to. Go ahead. If anyone has the right to, you do. You're the one —"

"Who got hit the hardest," I finished his sentence for him. "I don't know if that's true. There's my daddy, too."

Ray Marster pulled off his glasses, but I knew he could still see me, even through unfocused eyes destined to blindness from the sugar disease. We eased into silence. Another whiskey appeared unbidden before me. This time I was careful not to sniff at it before putting it away.

"You don't mind me asking," I said, "but where were you when all this was going on? I can't picture you there at all. Couldn't you have done anything?"

"I ask myself that same question every night for Zeke, and for my little Evangeline. Now I'll have to ask it for you, too. Shit damn! I could give you some damn fool answer about how at the time I was up in Statesboro, looking after some store that sold — I don't even remember what it sold — haberdashery, I believe. And about how you just don't invite yourself into a family without being asked first, and start handing out the advice. About how I believed in the old way of doing things, which means looking the other way, even though I could see what was going to happen a mile away. And sure enough, it did, while I stood around with my hands in my pockets. That's what makes a lifetime of regrets, boy."

Upon the word *regrets*, Shank the bartender eased his belly over in my direction and made to fill my pony glass. I waved him off.

"No such thing as an innocent victim, not in this family, at least," Ray said. "Innocence would be too easy for us, now, wouldn't it? Sometimes I think your daddy just got lazy, and decided he didn't want to look after himself any more. Maybe he really can't, who knows, because from what I understand of his affliction, it doesn't sound like the easy way out of anything. One thing's for certain, he doesn't have many people left in this town to help out, and for one reason or another, he never felt the inclination to go back to his people up North. I might as well tell you: he's down at the Chatham County Home now, though they've taken to calling it the Vets' Hospital."

"He was a veteran?"

"You see, after that beanball business, when he started acting sick, he kept going on about how he was a vet. Nobody believed him, of course, because part of his ravings were about the Civil War, and everybody naturally thought that's what he was talking about. But I thought to check, and wouldn't you know it? He was right. A damn good thing, too, because now he's got the government looking after him."

RAT PALMS

"The Chatham County Home," I repeated.

"Best call it the VA Hospital. *Home* don't mean what it used to. I reckon if he's not there, they'll have some idea of where he's gone to."

I accepted the bartender's largesse, then drained the contents of my glass, which provided thin comfort against what was on the other side of Pinky's screen door. But I had to leave sooner or later, and this was the time. I couldn't spend the rest of my life in this terrarium.

I shook Ray Marster's hand.

"You're a good man. I don't want you worrying about how you should have stepped in and set it right on the Isle of Hope. I tried myself, in my own way. All I did was bring more misery upon myself."

Ray pulled at his glasses and shrugged. "A man's got a right to feel regret for what he wants to. That's my choice. But listen, son, next time you see my little Evangeline, be it in California or wherever, you give her my best."

"I will."

"And if you two ever get into one of your talking moods, and I can just imagine the two of you and a little hooch around the dining room table and it just breaks my heart to picture it, you ask her something her brother Ray wants to know. You ask her how she could have come to hate her father the way she did, then turn around and believe every damn fool thing he told her."

"I'll do that," I promised. "But we'll have to be right down to the bottom of the bottle before I get around to asking that one. I could ask. But that don't guarantee an answer."

"Don't I know it! Shit, old man Jefferson was one of those kind of people who don't want a certain thing for themselves, they can't use it, and they wouldn't know what to do with it if they had it. You can call that thing life, if you want to. But somehow they feel they've got to spoil it for everybody else, especially those who's closest to them. Like a bunch of damn priests and preachers, they are."

We shook on the matter again. My feet felt as heavy as lead. It must have been those Marster roots growing up out of the oaken floor into my soles. I had to take my imaginary broom and sweep my ass out of there before I got stuck to the spot.

17

McKennedy Street lay cool and harmonious and singing with crickets and sharp with the eager beginnings of a bourbon buzz. I walked down to the next square where a gazebo stood. Under its little round roof a girls' choir was practicing. Catty-corner from it some carpenters were fixing up the austere old house where Mary Flannery O'Connor once lived. In the park, the music mistress was conducting the choir in sharp, repetitive thrusts, managing to work up quite a sweat from the looks of her blouse, massacring the music with her insistence. But the girls' voices triumphed over her. *Each with his bonnie lass, a-dancing on the grass*, they sang. On their faces I saw the strain to love that music. Call it nostalgia, willing blindness as sure as Evangeline's blackout mask, but I felt the scene had such rightness. Even as I knew each of those girls' families hid more than its share of wrongness, as mine did.

I walked a few streets west to Drayton Street. The girls' joyful refrain to gallant love faded. It was odd, to know every leaf on every tree in every square in Savannah, yet feel so desperately out of place. Beneath the graceful, spreading live oaks, I heard the whisper of the terror of Pascal's infinity, here in the place where I had first learned it, where Damian Dooley had tried to teach us that efficacious illusion was antidote enough to such terror. The naïveté of the man!

These neighborhoods were Savannah's pride, her historical district. I was well acquainted with the lives lived behind the frilly curtains of the district. I knew how history was manipulated there into being something quaint, to be put on for a dress-up party, like a horrid hag dolled up in a gown. Everywhere I stepped, on every cobblestone sidewalk, Marster roots and Marster despondency sprang from the ground. *That* was history.

To fend it off, I did what I had often seen done. At a toddy shop, I secured a half-pint, then stepped into the street and flagged a cab.

"The Chatham County Home," I told the driver.

"That's mighty far," he mumbled out of a toothless mouth. "Other side of the county."

"How big can Chatham County be?"

"Well, they say Georgia got more counties than any state in the Union. I guess that means they all got to be kind of small, to fit in and all."

"That's what I figured. I'm good for it if you are."

He turned over his meter and took off toward the old Home. Excuse me, the Veterans' Hospital. Like Ray Marster had said, *home* doesn't mean what it used to.

I had not known that Broughton Street had become a boarded-up, burned-down strip of pavement, all but unshoppable for a proper white lady, so how could I have figured that the countryside south of town was being devoured by shopping plazas, whose single advantage was the availability of free parking? I should have known: one event followed the other, in logical corollary. The farmland past the edge of town, on the Richmond Hill road, had been cut up into divisions for houses in a style I had seen driving into Los Angeles. Strange, now, to see them in my own country. Though it did make sense. If Broughton Street had turned into charred lumber and scorched bricks, money had to go somewhere to get spent. So it left town and went to the shopping plaza. Just as, at the beginning of the century, it had fled overcrowded Savannah for the imagined safety of the Isle of Hope.

Or maybe that wasn't quite the right relation. Maybe, in its perverse and petty little mind, money decided first to go to the shopping plaza, and only afterward did Broughton Street die.

In the middle of these new tracts of houses sat the old Chatham County Home on its rise of green lawn. Its original architects had placed it purposefully far from town so its inhabitants and their misfortunes could be more easily forgotten. But the city had caught up with it. The infirm, the innocent and the foolish now found themselves surrounded by civilization again. I wondered if they liked it; I suspected they did not. I wondered if they ever strolled over to the shopping plaza for a Sno-Cone and a matinee show.

We swung up the driveway, past the new Veterans' Administration sign. The Home was three stories of red brick, a central pavilion with wings on either side, all with identical rows of curtainless windows.

"You want me to wait on you?" the driver asked at the front door. I had told him to keep the change from a twenty.

"I don't think so. There's no telling how long this is going to take."

He looked up at the building. You could tell he was glad he wasn't inside.

"I just may hang around here awhile. It isn't too many cabs come out this way."

At the front desk, I inquired after the whereabouts of one Mr. Zeke Justice from a woman wearing a bushy black hairdo.

"Outpatient or in?"

"I don't know. He might be both."

"Date of admitting?"

I named the day I had returned from Bonaventure Island to find the house packed up.

"You might have it down as the day before," I told her.

"You're not sure of the admittance date? What's the motive of your visit?"

"Family motive. I'm his son."

She looked at me hard, then paged through her big book of unfortunates. There was the name, typed in black on white.

"Take the elevator to the nursing station," she ordered me, and gave me the floor and ward designation, "and identify yourself to the head nurse."

"Hope I can get out of here easier than I'm getting in."

"That depends on how you behave. This is an institution, you know. Anyway, you ain't a vet, don't look like it to me."

"Depends which war."

Then I flashed her a syrupy, Lazaretto smile and headed for the elevator. When she had turned back to her book, I cut left and slipped up the stairs. Fuck the institution. Daddy Zeke was mine, he belonged to me. I wasn't going to apply for him. I didn't want his case explained away by a stern yet kindly nurse whose job it was to domesticate the savage mind with talk. I had done plenty of explaining already, I knew how that worked. I didn't need any more. Maybe he would be horrible to see, I didn't care. It had been horrible once, I'd survived, and I'd been a lot less equipped to defend myself than I was now.

I came up the stairs to the top floor. A glass door separated me from the hallway. That sly, sneaky boy observer resurfaced in me. Little Lazarus would find Big Lazarus, unimpeded and unexplained. I listened as the efficient clip-clip of nurses' feet went by, then stepped into the hallway. It didn't take me long to figure out the way to go. Hospitals are made for getting around in quickly. Dayroom, read a sign that pointed left. Wards B, C, D were in the other direction. A bunch of wards with letters meant nothing to me, but Dayroom did. It was another word for bedlam.

I moved quickly down the hallway, trying to look as though I had some respectable business in the Home or, failing that, like a patient playing at visitor. The dayroom wasn't far. I looked through the double door with a glass panel reinforced with chicken wire, then pushed open the door and walked in.

You never imagine you might not be able to recognize your own father, any more than you might entertain the notion of seeing an unfamiliar face in the mirror one morning. But for a second or two I wasn't sure if I'd be able to spot him, and the thought terrified me. I couldn't count on him to be wearing his Savannah Indians uniform, here in this room of pajama-clad veterans, some shabby and stumbling and lost inside their gowns, others unnaturally alert and jittery, as if expecting ambush.

I cast my eyes left and right, skipping over the faces of the orderlies. I was in the start of a panic myself, wondering how much even a few weeks of madness, or semi-madness, could change the way a man looked.

But when my eyes came to rest upon his face I knew immediately. Automatically. It was Daddy Zeke, Daddy, Zeke Justice, Elzéar Lajustice. And my heart filled with love at the ease of recognition.

I crossed the room to that tall, undone, slumped, gray, handsome man.

"Hey, Daddy, you look all right."

He raised his eyes to me. Not that surprised.

"Son. Toadfish. Timmy. Finally, you're here."

I sat down in front of him and slid my bag under the low table, on which were set all kinds of primitive instruments for improving the mind's powers of concentration. Card games, checkers, construction paper, chewed-down ends of colored pencils.

"How long has it been?" Then he motioned around the dayroom. "I'm kind of ashamed."

He waited a minute.

"They tell me I don't have much control over it."

"I know. When you told me about control, out behind the house that day I wanted to catch you, I got real mad at you. I'm sorry."

He looked puzzled, tried remembering, then gave up.

"I don't quite recall. But it's okay, anyway. Forget and forgive."

He considered the room again, as if he wasn't too sure what he was doing here with such a sorry collection of human curses.

"You want me to get you out of here?"

"No, no." He made a vague gesture. "I'm no prisoner. Sometimes I'm home" — he tapped his head — "and sometimes I'm not. Nobody's fault, so they say. If it just weren't so white in here."

"You mean clean? Bright?"

"No, white. *White.*"

I reached down and eased open my bag, keeping an eye on the intent, mean faces of the orderlies. I got my fingers around that comforting smooth feel of a sneaky little half-pint.

"I brought you something that's a little less white."

My father dropped his hand under the table and I made him touch the neck of the half-pint. When he did, his face fell. I didn't know what he was expecting; maybe he didn't know, either. Maybe I didn't understand what he meant by *white*.

"Gee, son, that's real nice of you to think of me. Only I don't drink any more. I . . . I don't like it. I don't like what it does to me."

"Doesn't it work with the medicine they've got you taking?"

"No, no. I mean I don't like it. Imagine that, me, turning down a drink." He laughed weakly, then lifted up the bottle in plain sight and laboriously examined the label. "Good stuff, too. Too bad."

I made him hide the bottle under the table again. "Go ahead, try," I told him. I took out a Dixie cup from my bag. "Look, I brought a cup, special for the occasion."

"No," he insisted. "I don't like what it does. I can't do it any more. It gives me a headache."

"Come on, just once."

"No. I can't any more."

"It'll help get you out of yourself."

"But I *am* out of myself. That's why I'm here. Don't you see that? Anyway, it gives me impulses."

"We all have those," I tried to joke.

"I used to have them, too. But these aren't the real impulses of a man. You can't do anything with these. They tear the top of my head off, I start barking things, nobody wants me around. That's why I'm here."

"You talk French," I told him.

He glared at me, offended. "How could I? I don't know French any more. I've forgotten every word of it, and let me tell you, it wasn't easy."

There was no sense arguing. He did know French. He couldn't forget it; he could only deny that he knew. Trying to forget it must have drained him, as the effort to beat the Marsters had. He'd failed at both battles. This is where it got him. The Chatham County Home.

I leaned down and touched his hand. It was inert, like a dead man's hand. The bottle was still in it. It took no effort to ease the half-pint from his grasp.

"I'll just take this back, and we'll say it's the thought that counts."

"If you don't mind, son, just leave it here. I'll give it to one of the fellows. There's a lot of home brew around here, but no one hardly ever sees any of that good store-bought stuff. They'll be happy for it. I'll trade it for something I need."

"What do you need?" I seized on the hope. "Is there anything I can bring you?"

He reflected a moment, shook his head. "No . . . No. I don't really need anything. You can leave the bottle in the little hidey-hole I made in my shitter."

We shared a laugh over him outsmarting the orderlies, and a man's need for a private place for himself.

"You're just like normal," I insisted. "Are you sure you should be in here?"

"Just wait till I have one of my impulses. I only hope it doesn't happen when you're around. I get ashamed in other people's eyes. Imagine, me, ashamed in their eyes! Though hoping it won't happen is the best way to make it happen, or so they tell me. Impulses. Seizures. Incontinent nostalgia in the speech centers. That's what they call it. They've got a damn code word for everything, just like the goddamned Catholics. That's how they stay in business, these people. They say I'm speaking frog. But there's no way I could do that, any more than you could."

That placed a stillness over us, and we inhabited it for a time. Then the double doors flew back and two nurses came in, pushing a trolley full of paper cups, and in each cup was a festive bouquet of pills. The women were joking among themselves, about the patients, I imagined, about how Mr. So-and-So couldn't even recognize the stink of his own shit, about my own father, maybe. I knew when the pill ladies swung around to us, my unauthorized visit would be over.

"In town, on the way in, something funny happened," I told my father. "An old guy stopped and offered me a lift. He looked familiar to me, but at first I couldn't place him. He seemed to know me, too. He knew the family, anyway. Before I got out of the car, he made me promise that the next time I saw you, I'd tell you that Joe Jackson sends his regards."

"Joe Jackson?" he shouted. "Joe Jackson the baseball player? Joe Jackson is dead! How could you have seen Joe Jackson?"

My father sat transfixed, staring at something that was not in the dayroom of the Chatham County Home. At the ghost of Joe Jackson, perhaps, who they said used to live not far from here, out by Waycross. The man who had thrown the World Series in the days of the Chicago Black Sox.

"I know it wasn't Joe Jackson," I told my father. "That's what I'm saying to you. It was Mr. Peep from Bo-Peep's. Why the hell did he say he was Joe Jackson?"

Then my father had an impulse of sorts. At least, that's what I would call it, though I know nothing of incontinent nostalgia and the private medical words used to describe what the rest of us would call madness and pain. His impulse was to tell all, in hopes of being forgiven, as if the great brackish vase of concealment had split.

"Set up! Set up! Set up!" he shouted, and I glanced nervously at the orderlies. "I was set up, I'm telling you, set up! All that time I was laying down my money on the games at Peep's, he was ratting on me to the league. He'd take my money, smile, pocket his percentage, then turn around and squeal on me. Every last penny. He kept track. Told them everything. Though he never forgot to take his cut. I don't know why he didn't like me. I hated his guts but so what, everybody hates the bookie. When you decide to be a bookie, you know everyone's going to hate you, it comes with the territory. He told the league I bet against myself. I never bet against myself, I never bet against my own arm. A man can't afford to bet against his arm when that's all he's got. There's no percentage in it."

He paused, took a gulp of air and started in again.

"He kept me out of the Bigs. There was never anything wrong with my curveball. It wasn't great, but it was as good as a lot of other pitchers'. When I got called up he went to the majors and told them everything. A few days later they're hitting my curve, supposedly, and down I go. I've always been a sporting man, I admit it. I'm not the only one. But they took advantage of me. Joe Jackson, shit! Joe Jackson, Joe Jackson, fuck Joe Jackson! They took advantage of my weakness!"

A couple of burly orderlies in smeared uniforms came drifting over in our direction, looking for trouble. They didn't seem to care that I was on an unauthorized visit. Just don't rile up the patient, asshole, their eyes said.

"By the time I got it figured out," my father lamented, "I was in no shape to do anything about it, or have anybody else do it for me. Shit, by then everybody had stopped caring. I was out of the picture."

The pill ladies were swinging around in our direction. One of them spotted me. I had to work fast. My father was collapsing into himself, and I was afraid of what would come next. The kind of pain for which there are no medical words.

"I'll get him for you, Daddy," I whispered. I don't even know if he heard me. "I'll get him, I promise, I really will. It'll be my mission."

That was my goodbye. I skipped out, a step ahead of the pill ladies with their paper cups full of cheerful-looking uppers and downers, antidepressants and anticonvulsives.

I hit the hallway and made for the stairs. Then stopped. I went to the nursing station, and using my best thank-you-ma'am Lazaretto ways, I pried loose the number of my father's room from a naive and charming young lady from these parts.

His room was a miniward. Four beds. Three empty, one full. The guy in the occupied bed was not open for business. He was on an IV and his eyes were taped shut. I went into the john to look for Daddy Zeke's hidey-hole. I tried to slip my fingers behind the toilet, but it was plumb against the wall. No room for a cache there. I opened the water tank lid. Sure enough, he had built himself a little platform above the toilet's workings out of some crisscrossed hangers. There were some gentlemen's magazines in there, and the baseball annual, and on that paper shelf I gently deposited the half-pint. It held.

Trade it for something you need, Daddy. If you ever figure out what that something is.

But I didn't get through the doors of the Chatham County Home for another half hour. After my charitable visitation to my father's hidey-hole in the head, I was apprehended in the hallway by the two pill ladies. "What kind of business do you have, haunting these halls?" one of them demanded. I wondered what sort of punishment she could possibly mete out. Sequestering me with Daddy Zeke, perhaps, and letting us ruminate over every hurt on Hurt's Landing until the both of us were plumb crazy, or perfectly reconciled to the world. Or both.

But the second of the pill ladies took one look into my frightened face and said, "Aren't you Mr. Justice's son?"

"By the grace of God, ma'am, yes."

Then Mrs. Dupree and Mrs. Leclair, so their name tags read, took me into a holding room decorated with *Road and Track* magazines and overflowing ashtrays, and a picture of Lyndon Baines Johnson on the wall. There, in that chamber designed for the counseling of difficult cases, they told me some things I already knew, other things I had always known and never admitted to, and still others that either did not matter now, or that I had not wished to find out. Mrs. Dupree and Mrs. Leclair, bless their Frenchy names, believed in that tired proposition according to which if you talk about something bad, somehow, magically, by itself, it will transform itself into something good.

They told me how my father had been picked up raving on the corner of Bull and Broughton, speaking a language no one could understand. There were those who claimed he was speaking in tongues, but Mrs. Leclair said, No, I knew he was from the North, and excuse me for saying this, but speaking in tongues is hardly what you'd call a Northern custom. Besides, as far as I could tell, he did not have a religious bone in his body. He was brought here, and on and on he raved until one day, by some stroke of luck, someone walked through the ward, heard your father and said, Mrs. Leclair, do you know you've got a Frenchman locked up in here? How do you treat him if you can't understand a word he says?

"That was my very first day on the floor," she said in her Yankee accent. "Before I got so dreadfully and so quickly used to all these sad cases. I brought someone in from the state college who knew a little French. Unfortunately, it was not that simple. Your father was speaking French, all right, but he refused to believe he was. He would not respond to French, because he did not want to be speaking it, because it was out of his control to be doing so."

Then Mrs. Leclair and Mrs. Dupree told me things I had guessed from my father's unraveling speech that afternoon, which had turned out to be my last afternoon on the Isle of Hope, before I hit the

Lazaretto in the *Elzéar* and he the pavement of Broughton Street. He had suffered an injury while serving his country in Korea, not in combat, it turned out, but from an explosion in an ammunition dump long after the fighting had ceased. An injury that the beanball had reawakened. From that trauma on the field at Grayson Stadium, he regained some things that had once been automatic, but which he had long since discarded, like the shameful old immigrant language, and lost other things that had been automatic and which he wanted to keep. Like the ability to throw a baseball to an exact location, sixty feet and six inches away.

Mrs. Leclair said to me, "I am alone in this opinion, which doesn't bother me a bit. But I believe Mr. Justice could get along quite well on his own, outside our institution, at least to a certain extent. But I understand your father used to be someone special in Savannah. A lot of people wouldn't cotton to the idea of a man of his stature and popularity wandering around the town, occasionally barking out something in a tongue no one understands. It might be a little off-putting, I admit, but he is not dangerous. And the poor man can hardly be blamed for everything that befell him."

Then Mrs. Dupree held a Baptist finger in the air, and corrected Mrs. Leclair by reminding both of us, as if we needed it, that alcohol consumption had most certainly played a part in Mr. Justice's neurological misfortune.

The nurses escorted me to the elevator. I was too exhausted to take the stairs down. As long as I identified myself first, they told me, I was free to visit any time I wished to. I told them there was not much chance of that happening.

Outside, the cabdriver was still waiting, asleep at the wheel as his dispatcher appealed for help.

I tapped him on the shoulder through the open window. He sprung awake.

"That wasn't too long, buddy."

"Not for you."

Union Station and out of here, I felt like telling him. But my mission was not complete. Little Toadfish was going to go swimming in some mighty deep and murky waters.

"The John Wesley Hotel," I told the driver.

I knew my history. The Benedictines had not instructed in vain. John Wesley was a tight-assed preacher who landed in this loose land of ours many years ago. His sole saving grace was that he loved music. To be exact, he came ashore on the mosquito-ridden tidal flats along Cockspur Island, out by where Fort Pulaski now stands. The time it takes to read the plaque commemorating his landing, put there by some of his latter-day followers, and your face will be so bit up by mosquitoes you won't recognize yourself in the mirror. I know. When I was still among the Benedictines, one day Father Damian Dooley took us out to that swampy island to marvel and scoff at the fool reformer. When the man and his retainers slopped ashore, through muck and silt and marsh and swamp, amid the haints and hoodoos, they must have decided then and there that what the colony needed was some sphincter-tightening religion to cool everybody's blood down. They must have been spoiling for a challenge.

Funny, then, that poor old dead John Wesley had lent his Methodist name to a hotel and office block in downtown Savannah that housed a glorified bookie joint called Bo-Peep's. Bo-Peep's was run by Mr. Peep, whose real name was Mr. Wolf. I can say this much about Wesley's fate: the land has a way of rising up and claiming a man's bones for its own purposes.

When the cab pulled up in front of the John Wesley, I was a shade disappointed. Or disappointed in the shades, perhaps. Crossing the country twice in the very recent past might have had something to do with it, but I saw the hotel was not as grand as it had been when I'd hup-hupped past it, a soldier for the Lord with the Benedictines. Now when I looked up, I saw its row after row of disconsolate, gaping windows, and shade pulls dangling in the still, hot air, and the hanging window shades that some men probably did not bother to draw for the night. Bo-Peep's lounge and betting establishment was around the side. I knew the heavy door well. But the fat man with the puffy fingers and the great, fatigued head had his rooms upstairs.

And when old Mr. Peep turned on his water tap to splash his greasy, large-pored face, Little Lazarus was going to come twisting out with a shit-eating grin, the likes of which no man has ever lived to describe.

I took a room and paid for it up front, cash on the counter. Once I'd signed my form, I asked the front desk girl, "Would you try Mr. Wolf's room for me?"

A few rings later she set down her receiver.

"He doesn't seem to be answering, sir."

I laid on all my toadfish charm and said, "I'll try him later, there's no hurry. He's an old friend of the family. So I don't have to disturb you every time, would you be at liberty to disclose his room number to me?"

"Why, yes. He's in the corner suite on the fifth floor. Room five hundred, but everyone just calls it the corner suite. He's been there forever."

"Yes, I'm aware of that."

As I rode up the elevator, which was operated by a facsimile of Freeman Prince wearing glinting gold-framed glasses and a sea captain's cap, I reflected on how I was giving myself away to everyone in sight — if ever some radical misfortune should befall Mr. Peep. Though I had written an invented name on the registration form and paid cash, and though it was true, as my father had said, that no one likes the bookie, still, I knew I stuck out in this town. No one with the local Lazaretto accent takes a rented room in a big, gloomy mausoleum like the John Wesley. A man who is supposedly home at last does not normally seek lodgings at a hotel.

But conventional matters of detection did not worry me. I didn't know what it would be, but whatever was going to happen between Mr. Peep and me would be greater than simple, petty crime.

I told the elevator gentleman to wait for me. I dropped my bag in my room, then rode back down with him.

"That's one short stay, mister."

"I intend to get reacquainted with the town. Is Mr. Gammon's store still in operation?"

"Some things never change, and when it comes to Mr. Gammon's, I'd have to say that's a good thing. Only they don't deliver no more."

"Really?"

"No, sir, they don't. That poor little delivery boy would come riding down the street on his bicycle, and here comes some bad man jumping out from behind a bush and sticking a spike in his spokes. That boy would fall off his bicycle, and the bad man steal all of Mr. Gammon's bottles. They had to stop that delivery thing."

"A sad story."

"Yes, sir," he agreed as he opened the elevator door onto the lobby. "But at least that way you get you some exercise."

It always seems to be football season among some fans in Savannah, even in midsummer. How could I have forgotten the Bulldogs? Johnnie Gammon had not forgotten. On the floor of his store, just to the right of the entrance, he had built an entire model football field out of miniature liquor bottles. The gins were playing the bourbons in an epic struggle between the forces of light and dark. From what I could gather from the formations, the gins had the ball at midfield. They were driving for the goalposts, which were devised from two forty-ounce bottles of Scotch. The bourbons were about to put on the blitz, as they often did. On the other side of the sideline markers, which were made of swizzle sticks laid end to end, the gin crowd, represented by hundreds of miniatures in orderly rows on thin planks, was being led by its cheerleaders.

These people sure do like to prettify their alcohol!

"Who's winning?" I asked the counterman.

"Some people pulling for the gins, other people pulling for the bourbons. But it don't matter, because they all going to get drunk up when the game is over."

I nodded and went to inspect the sipping whiskies. If Daddy Zeke would not drink, I would have to do it for him. Perhaps I'd even drink myself into the solution about what to do with Mr. Peep. Johnnie Gammon had absolutely everything on his shelves. His specialty was the discreet pints and half-pints so favored by the clientele. A thoughtful, wise and understanding man, this Mr. Gammon. I chose three pints of the names that had been favorites around the Isle of Hope. One for me. One for Mr. Peep. And one for Daddy, in case he changed his mind and decided to get better.

I put my purchases on the counter.

"I see you pulling for the bourbon side," the counterman remarked.

"Yes, sir. I see how the gins got the ball, and they're doing pretty good, so I decided to be for the underdog."

"That's mighty fine. But watch out for the bourbons. They'll intercept you when you least expect it."

Ain't that the truth, I thought as I crossed through the streets and squares toward the John Wesley Hotel. Then along Oglethorpe with its palms and memories of marching for the Lord and the Benedictines. Under those trees I could feel the presence of Father Dooley, and at that moment I would have gladly turned to him for wise counsel. But for readmittance to his Academy, he had warned, I would first have to complete my report, which I had not done. My delinquency was still unrepented for.

It's almost ready, I promised him.

My room at the Wesley was shaped like an ice cube, with the ceilings as high as the room was wide. Most disorienting. I went through the preparations for what could be a long siege. I set out my boxes of cocktail crackers from Johnnie Gammon's, a stock of ice from the machine down the hall, and I filled a pitcher with water so I would not have to journey to the bathroom for mix, and risk shattering the glass on the metal spiggot or porcelain sink.

Drink in hand, I went to the window to watch over Oglethorpe Street. From above, the commemorative palms looked flat and crushed. Like rats on a hood, I reminded myself. I thought of Evangeline waking up deserted on the oceanfront, I thought of the madness of people like Lynn crisscrossing the country, I thought of the uselessness of blaming Mr. Bo-Peep for anything that had happened. I sipped off the top of the bourbon and water, and heard my mother's voice: *you don't drink*. In her mouth it was half hopeful declaration, half accusation. But I do, I addressed her and the other absent family members and members of the little island society that made me. I do, to discover what to do, or to not care if I don't.

I finished the diluted sweetness of the bourbon and water, then left the empty glass on the sill. To visit Mr. Peep I would need lucidity, with that sense of rightness and righteousness, and not be teetering on the edge of turning maudlin and self-important about the whole errand. Otherwise, Peep would feel it the way a wolf senses sheep for the taking nearby, and take me in with his sporting man's instincts. In the car, he had confided in me that his reactions weren't what they used to be. When a man tells you that, that's when he's at his most dangerous.

I gave one last little tug on the pint. One for the hall. A visit demands some sort of token, so I took the pint with the most expensive-looking label and rewrapped it in Gammon paper, then moved out into the corridor.

At the end of the hallway, I took the fire stairs one flight up to the fifth floor. Early evening, and the Wesley was as quiet as a morgue on a Sunday morning. Not much call for room service yet, and if there still was a businessmen's clientele here, it had not come back from its meetings yet. I opened the door to the fifth floor. The hall was empty. I wondered whether Peep and I were the only ones in this place, left alone in a deserted hotel to act out our destinies. To the right, a private corridor led to the corner suite. I knocked.

Knocked again, then turned the knob. No wonder Peep hadn't answered. The door opened onto an antechamber, with a coat rack and an umbrella stand. A single forlorn topcoat hung from the rack, with a gray felt hat atop it.

I closed the outer door behind me. If the first door was open, why not the second? Why bother to knock? He himself claimed to be a friend of the family. I pushed open the door, and discovered Mr. Bo-Peep hanging most awkwardly from the chandelier hook, a rope around his neck and a desk chair on its side beneath him.

Goddammit, I thought. He's already had a visitor. His own fucking conscience got him before I could.

I slumped down in a big leather chair in front of him. It let out a sigh of comic lamentation like a whoopee cushion. I unwrapped my gift for him and broke the seal. To you, you old cheat, I toasted the corpse, and the only worthwhile thing you've ever done. Then put a reasonable dent in the bottle. Fuck it. All that shit I was going to make him tell me — well, now, I'll just have to make it up by myself.

After another reasonable dent, I got up and circled around hanging Peep. The sheer bulk of the man, all that bloated, swollen, edemic flesh. Amazing he stayed up there. His body was stupid and clumsy and laughable, but his face was horrible. That's where death nested. Mouth open in a scream that would never be heard, eyes popping and staring, his florid color draining away, the stains on his clothes, the private, sick smells.

Then I had a vision of Peep crashing down from his hook and taking me out with him, in a final act of revenge against the Justices. I ran out of that corner suite without closing the door.

All that evening and night, the weight of Mr. Bo-Peep hung above me from one floor up. I retrieved the glass I had neglected on the windowsill, and freshened it up with the bottle I forgot was still in my right hand. I drank once more to Mr. Peep, and declared the first part of my mission complete.

But it was not a restful night. Peep's death had not provided much satisfaction. After all, nothing had really been his fault. His only sins had been pettiness and vengefulness and small-time cheating, which were no special distinction in this town. I was unhappy that he was dead. Even though I had wanted him dead. I wanted him dead, all right, but only after a long talk. Dead on my terms.

I woke up once during the early hours of the night, with all the lights in the room ablaze, my head in my arms and my arms on the desk. *Joe Jackson*, Peep's words echoed in my memory. And with them, the slam of his car door which had taken on an ominous finality in my dream. That slam, I realized, had woken me up. I rose and went to the window and my empty glass. I gave it a smell. It smelled of the motel room in Forty-Nine Palms. To chase away the staleness that lurks at the bottom of a drinking glass, you have to fill it up again.

Peep is not the issue, I told myself as I gazed upon the dark, flat masses that were the palms on Oglethorpe Street. And if he is, he is only part of it. The issue is the spoiling of life. Of my life. It is a family affair.

The next day, I awoke into the queasy mid-morning light, stretched out on top of the bedspread with its white caterpillers of lint. Awoke to hear a giant crash from one floor up.

Dead weight, coming down.

Now, it's time to go get Daddy Zeke.

18

My mission began with the hidey-hole in Daddy Zeke's head down at the Chatham County Home. I gathered up the gentlemen's magazines and the baseball annual and the curative pint of classy-brand bourbon that, who knows, might prove itself useful, if not for him then for me.

Hole in the head, indeed! How could anyone accuse me of vainglory in words, when the world conspired to give the word *head* so many unusually useful applications?

Actually, my mission began before the raid on the head. I started by reconnoitering, then penetrating, our former home on the Lazaretto Road, without the benefit of a key. Can breaking into one's own house be a crime? A similar crime, I thought, boosting myself up to an unlocked window, to overstaying one's welcome in one's own home territory.

Inside, I found deathly silence inhabiting the house. Every step I took set off echoes of infinite loneliness. Except for the original, unmovable Marster pieces, the place was empty. Welcome to the Lazaretto Museum, said Timmy Toadfish, tour guide and cat burglar intent on making off with the past. I am your guide for this tour, and if I speak unnaturally loudly, it is only to disperse the legions of evil spirits that inhabit the echoes of my footfalls. For remember, this and all museums are, in truth, cemeteries. Mind you, this is no Telfair, though the chairs — I slid to the floor and sat, ass on oak plank — are just about as comfortable. Welcome to Lazaretto Estates, where those who have walked walk again. This is where Daddy Zeke and I will live. This is where he will get better. Or worse.

How shall we live here? Effortlessly. Gifts of the freshest shrimp will be brought to our door, already headed. And summer trout, and butter beans, and scuppernongs, and cauldrons of she-crab soup. We will live as children do in a fairy tale: on love and grace and crumbs.

I stated my claim to our former and future home by emptying the contents of my overnight bag in a corner of my father's study. Then telephoned Mumbles the Cabbie to drive me across the county to the Home.

"This time, wait for me, and don't fall asleep," I told him when we reached the turnaround in front of the forbidding building. We were developing a kind of relationship, fueled by the winnings from Distinct Intent. Poor Mr. Mumbles, he couldn't believe his luck.

As I said, the magazines and the annual and the hooch went into my bag. There were no witnesses to my act of repossession. The fellow with the IV and the taped eyelids was gone, replaced by a crisply made bed. I had an inspiration and threw open the bureau drawers. Strangers' garb in every one. Except for the last one, lower right: a freshly pressed Indians uniform, intact.

That, too, went into my bag.

When I heard the pill ladies' trolley bustle by in the hallway outside I froze, then retreated to the shitter. Mrs. Dupree and Mrs. Leclair had invited me to visit any time, but this was not a visit they would appreciate. Besides, I was afraid of the friendly, understanding nurses, especially Mrs. Leclair. I was ashamed. They knew all about us.

When the coast was clear I walked with dignified tread down to the dayroom. Don't panic, I lectured myself, or they'll smell it and lock you up in here. Besides, this place exists thanks to taxpayers' money. There must have been someone in your family who once paid taxes. Therefore, this place belongs to you. So walk calmly.

That efficacious illusion got me all the way to the dayroom door and inside. Where the sight of Daddy Zeke scattered all other illusions.

He was standing in the center of the room, pacing in circles, on what could only be a pitcher's mound. Barking out sounds in a language I did not understand. Now, I do not know French, and there is no reason for me to, not on the Isle of Hope, but I knew he was speaking the language. His fellow patients were hooting and hollering, encouraging his madness. It gave them something to watch that was not the television.

For a few terrible seconds I watched my father teetering on his imaginary pitcher's mound, in awful dread of tumbling off, as if it were a high mountain, with the sharp, malevolent rocks of reality awaiting him greedily below. On his face there was the pain and puzzlement inspired by his own madness, as if he honestly could not understand why these sounds from the past, which he had worked so hard to banish from his mouth, had returned to inhabit it again. Why am I so cruelly visited? he seemed to be asking himself. I saw that he did not understand the very meaning of the words he spoke, nor how he was able to speak them, and with that realization I saw the pain and horror of his situation, and how there had never truly been any complacency in his attitude, only helplessness, and what I had taken for complacency was simply the justifiable pride of a man who will not admit that his mind has escaped him.

I saw him in all his predicament. This was the moment of forgiveness I was living for.

I stepped into the center of the room. Onto his playing field.

"Elzéar Lajustice!" I called.

He turned to me, but grudgingly so, because I had addressed him in the old tongue.

Then I pitched the granite baseball to him. A nice easy lob in case he could not recognize the nature of the object.

But it worked. He caught it flawlessly and admired the beautiful, smooth rock. He rubbed it up in his hands, the way any pitcher would. The way he used to do in the days of his minor-league glory at Grayson Stadium.

"For the kindest white man in Savannah," I reminded him.

I thrust the clean Indians uniform into his arms and made him feel the comforting fabric. These are the things that bring us back to life.

"Get the heck out of those pajamas, and put these on. We're getting out of here. We're going to the big game."

I helped him into his uniform. It was like dressing a child. He knew which arm went into which sleeve, and how not to put both legs into the same pant leg, but he wasn't particularly coordinated at doing it. Fucking pills, I cursed, still unwilling to blame him. Around us, half his fellow patients had begun to sulk spitefully, and the other half were shouting abuse. I had spoiled their fun. I told them to turn on the television if they wanted to see real-life drama.

I got him dressed and stepped back to admire my work.

"Now you're a sorry sight!" I laughed. "You're the sorriest father I have ever seen! We've got to get you looking like something else, and quick."

He looked down at himself. At his shuffling, invalid slippers. He laughed along with me, and for a moment I swore things were going to be all right.

I shouldered my overnight bag with his personal effects inside. He wouldn't let me take back the baseball.

"I would keep it, if I could. It's got some luck left in it."

That was fine with me. We would need all the spirits on our side that we could muster. I took him by the hand and led him toward the dayroom door, then glanced through the chicken-wired glass panel and saw the hallway was empty. The half dozen steps from the door to the stairway that led downstairs were the longest ones I have ever taken.

His tread was slow and shabby, and I all but pulled him down the first flight of stairs. We ended up in a heap on the landing.

"You okay?" I asked him.

"I'm light as a feather. I am insubstantial." He stood up and brushed off his uniform. "I don't mind following you — you're my boy. But would you mind telling me where we're going?"

"Back home, for starters," I told him.

He shook his head. "I don't know as I can follow you there. It's not exactly the best place for me. It has been the theater of my misfortune. I'd just as soon stay here."

"If you want to, we'll go somewhere else afterward. Let me get my things there, at least."

Then he clapped his hands over his pants pockets, and his face lit up with the pleasure of recovering a usable memory.

"My winnings! Distinct Intent! I told you they'd cut my pockets. They took everything!"

"They didn't. I have the money."

He didn't seem to hear me. His face went dark.

"That means I'll have to go back to Peep's again. Shit!"

"No," I told him, trying to move him down the stairs. "I have the money, and you're not going back there. Peep is dead."

"Dead? Did you kill him?"

"No. He did it all by himself."

My father let out a yelp of joy. "Well, that son of a bitch! Spited everybody again. Well, I'll be damned! Justice reigns supreme!"

"That's right. Now let's get out of here. I'll remind you that we're standing on the landing of a flight of stairs in the Chatham County Home, which is no place to be, especially if you intend to get out of it."

I hustled him down to the main floor. We marched right by the main desk where the black lady with the bushy hair sat with her big book of names and cases.

"Hey, you!" she called out indignantly. "You haven't been released.

You can't just walk out of here without the proper paperwork being done! We're responsible for you!"

I pulled up short in front of her desk, jerking Daddy Zeke along with me. I didn't know what to tell her. Then it came to me. I opened my mouth and commenced to let out the scariest, bottom-feedingest, haint-conjuringest Lazaretto howl that has ever been given to anyone, human or toadfish, to hear. And just in case she didn't know where that came from, I testified to the source.

"Little Richard! Bobby Blue Bland! Screaming Jay Hawkins! James Brown! Ivory Joe Hunter!"

Then I turned to the front door, and with wholly exaggerated dignity, me and Daddy Zeke strolled to freedom. The two of us. Little Lazarus and Big. Toadfish and his favorite minor-league star.

Mr. Mumbles was awake and waiting in his cab.

"Isle of Hope, first," I told him.

He pulled away. We hadn't gone but a mile toward town when my father shouted, "Callibogee!"

I nearly jumped out of my seat. "What about it?"

"We ought to go to Callibogee. I got another one hundred dollars waiting on me there. Rainy-day money. It's amazing the stuff I'm remembering now."

"I've got money, I told you. Part of your winnings."

He shook his hand. "Man's got to have his own cash. It's a law of nature."

I didn't like Callibogee any more than he liked the house on Hurt's Landing. "Callibogee's where you got hurt. I don't know if it's such a good idea."

"I promise I won't cross over no more dead things." He grinned. "Let me have it, Timmy, just this one time."

"Shit, how am I supposed to say no to that?"

"Some people have."

"I ain't some people, and you know it."

I looked to the front, and caught Mr. Mumbles staring at us in the rearview mirror. Our eyes met. He looked away.

"You thinking of going to Callibogee?" he asked. "Ain't nothing there but snakes and niggers."

"Oh, but they is some good niggers," my father said, mocking the cabdriver's talk. Then he tapped his head. "It's the onliest place to get a spell taken off, if you got one cast upon you."

"White people don't believe that shit," the driver said, and turned back to his duty.

In front of the house on the Lazaretto Road, my father watched with keen interest as I peeled off the bills for Mr. Mumbles.

"We don't have to go to Callibogee for a hundred-dollar bill," I told Daddy Zeke. "We got ourselves a few left on this island."

"Callibogee's a safe place for me. At least, it has been in the past. It can be again, if I don't misuse it."

We stepped out of the cab, my father with his granite baseball, I with my all-but-empty overnight bag. We stood on the asphalt road in the little warm breeze off the river, in the green shade of the live oaks. Hard to imagine that so much trouble could have inhabited such a place of peace. There were no cars on the road once Mr. Mumbles drove off, and no traffic on the river. Which was just as well, considering the big, sad, handsome, shabby excuse for a man in an Indians uniform who was standing there, stunned, beside me. The place was utterly quiet, suspiciously quiet, I should have thought at the time. There was a kind of a stillness in the air, as there'd been the morning my father had returned from Grayson Stadium and the two of us set off to Callibogee. We went up the little walk and suddenly I saw the house as he might see it: sinister, the lair of the enemy, where nothing curative could possibly occur. I moved him up onto the porch and he went along unwillingly. I understood his reticence, but there was no place else to go for now. The key to the boathouse was inside. So were the contents of my bag. And we could not very well stand out here on the Lazaretto Road, waiting for directions.

I had left the front door unlocked this morning, and we walked inside, into the empty dwelling place. My father tossed the granite ball up in the air, caught it, his eyes scanning the emptiness around us. I knew then that this homecoming was a mistake. If the house stands for the soul, this abandoned building was the worst possible medicine.

"They really tore it down," he said. "Why'd they do that, you figure?"

"I don't really know . . . Evangeline just kind of packed up everything. She was scared, I guess."

"Scared? Scared of me?"

He walked into what had been the dining room and I followed, afraid to leave him alone, afraid to be with him, too, and with no sense of what to do with him, now that I had him home. Knowing only that I had to do something, and fast. In the middle of the dining room the table still stood, but the chairs were gone. He leaned against it heavily.

"She was scared of me. Why? What did I do? It wasn't my fault. Okay, I hit her once, I shouldn't have. But a lot of men do that. And it was only just once . . ."

I moved up next to him and touched the shoulder of his freshly laundered uniform. A clownish, mocking accessory.

"I think you're right," I told him. "I think we should go to Callibogee. Wait right here. I'll run upstairs and get my bag."

I grabbed the boathouse key off its hook in the pantry, then took the stairs two at a time and went into my father's study. I rescued the few souvenirs of my trip west, wondering what we would do on Callibogee. We were trading one asylum for another, but if my father thought that the low, sandy, haint-invested island, with no bridge to the mainland, could be a kinder, more forgiving asylum, then it was my duty to take him there. For a man who could not help but talk in tongues, Callibogee was a better place to be.

As for myself, Timmy Justice, I belonged in no place. Not on

Callibogee, nor on the Lazaretto Road, nor at the Chatham County Home — not yet. The place where I belonged I had not seen yet.

I was pulling the zipper shut on my bag when I heard the front door open. I rushed out of the den to the head of the stairs.

"Mother!" I called.

But those footsteps on the porch and the proprietary way the front door flung open could never have belonged to Evangeline. From the top of the stairs I saw Jefferson Marster lurch into the front room. He looked years older than the last time I saw him, or maybe he had been into strong drink. But it was more than sour mash. The decay was visible on the man, like hoarfrost on a windowpane in winter, and he was carrying a shotgun.

The dead will steal life from the living. The earth has become a place of the dead. This island, all the islands, cemetery islands like Bonaventure. Any living being who frequents them will pay for it, in body and in soul. Like the crazy McQuithy woman. Like us. If only I had left Daddy Zeke in his kindly asylum with those two nice understanding pill ladies, none of this would be. Why couldn't I have left him in safety? Jefferson Marster and Mr. Bo-Peep are one and the same, both soul destroyers, keepers of the lost order. I saw the shotgun in the old Marster's hands, but I still wouldn't let myself believe he intended to use it. He'll wave that old thing around to make us listen to him, and then speechify for a while. Because when you're old and useless and have nothing but bitterness driving you, no one wants to listen to you. You have to take extraordinary measures to command attention.

I was wrong, like in so many things.

He brought the shotgun up level and advanced upon my father. My daddy watched him come, unbelieving and unmoving, and I realized he could not quite place this figure and this figure's gun and what the inevitable outcome would be. It is wrong to do harm to those in puzzlement, for they do not know the meaning of defense. I went to shout those words at the old fossil coming at my father, but nothing issued from my mouth but a sigh of air. By the time my father saw what was coming at him, it was too late.

With all his strength he threw the granite ball at Jefferson Marster's head. He missed. Marster squeezed the trigger. I shouted now but that did no good. My father flew back against the wall of the front room with his chest blown out of his body.

I ran down to the foot of the stairs. Jefferson Marster turned toward me, but I was unafraid. What more could I fear?

"There's nothing left for you to do now but kill yourself," I told him. "Like your friend Mr. Peep did."

For once, someone around here listened to me. Not that it mattered any more. Jefferson Marster tried to aim the shotgun at himself, but his arms were too short and the gun too long, and he couldn't get the angle right. I had plenty of time to stop that awkward old man. I did not take the opportunity.

He squeezed the trigger again. The shot hit him where the bottom of the jaw meets the neck. The blast made me close my eyes. Involuntarily, because I did want to see it happen. When I opened my eyes, the destroyer of life was just about headless.

His blood and my father's ran together on the floor. That was the only injustice in the act.

I walked out onto the porch to get away from the shotgun echoes in the room. Then across the Lazaretto Road in a daze, and out onto the dock. A pair of mourning doves that had been disturbed by the shots came settling back down on the electric wire. In the stillness, in the utter emptiness, more empty than any other kind I had known until then, the Lazaretto flowed. *All this belongs to you*, my mother once had instructed. *Indeed it does*, finally I agreed with her. So let us make inventory. My father has his heart blown out of his chest. The man who did it has his head blown off the wrinkled stalk of his neck. Some inheritance, Mother. How do you propose I invest it?

From the last plank on our dock, I stood and let out the longest howl of pain and misery that any poor toadfish has ever been given to release. The rats were shaken from the trees and the marsh grass opened like the lips of a wound, the Lazaretto parted and the green-black waters rolled back like the mouth of a rotting corpse. Everything hidden was revealed. It was the Judgment Day of the Isle of Hope soul.

The world would call that howling. I call it singing. But whatever it was, when I finished it up and the world had again assumed its heavy, impassive, indifferent form, I addressed myself to Father Damian Dooley. There, you asshole doubter, you, I have completed your report. This is it. I have qualified for readmission into your Academy. But forgive me if I decline your kind offer. I have surpassed your Academy long ago, and I do not believe there is an academy anywhere in the coastal empire that could be useful to me, or that I could serve without hypocrisy. So I'll see you on the other side of the river, Father.

Once those messages had been passed, I still had the problem of what to do with myself. Where to go, simply stated. It was then that I became aware of the boathouse key fastened to my finger by way of its metal ring. Why not? I thought. I'll go to Callibogee, or take the Intracoastal Waterway all the way up to the Holy Perpetual, in Canada, or some place more local, like Bonaventure Island, where I may lie down with the crazy McQuithy lady. So I set out upon the waters in my little bateau called the *Elzéar*, all unprepared for this world, but so richly versed in the ways of the dead.